THE CLASSICS OF WESTERN SPIRITUALITY

George A. Maloney, S.J.—Director, John XXIII Ecumenical Center, Fordham University, Bronx, N.Y.

Bernard McGinn—Professor of Historical Theology and History of Christianity, University of Chicago Divinity School, Chicago, Ill.

John Meyendorff—Professor of Church History, Fordham University, Bronx, N.Y., and Professor of Patristics and Church History, St. Vladimir's Seminary, Tuckahoe, N.Y.

Seyyed Hossein Nasr—Professor of Islamics, Department of Religion, Temple University, Philadelphia, Pa., and Visiting Professor, Harvard University, Cambridge, Mass.

Heiko A. Oberman—Director, Institute fuer Spaetmittelalter und Reformation, Universitaet Tuebingen, West Germany.

Alfonso Ortiz—Professor of Anthropology, University of New Mexico, Albuquerque, N. Mex.; Fellow, The Center for Advanced Study, Stanford, Calif.

Raimundo Panikkar—Professor, Department of Religious Studies, University of California at Santa Barbara, Calif.

Jaroslav Pelikan—Sterling Professor of History and Religious Studies, Yale University, New Haven, Conn.

Fazlar Rahman—Professor of Islamic Thought, Department of Near Eastern Languages and Civilization, University of Chicago, Chicago, Ill.

Annemarie B. Schimmel—Professor of Hindu Muslim Culture, Harvard University, Cambridge, Mass.

Sandra M. Schneiders—Assistant Professor of New Testament Studies and Spirituality, Jesuit School of Theology, Berkeley, Calif.

Huston Smith—Thomas J. Watson Professor of Religion, Adjunct Professor of Philosophy, Syracuse University, Syracuse, N.Y.

John R. Sommerfeldt—Professor of History, University of Dallas, Irving, Texas.

David Steindl-Rast—Monk of Mount Savior Monastery, Pine City, N.Y.

William C. Sturtevant—General Editor, Handbook of North American Indians, Smithsonian Institution, Washington, D.C.

David Tracy—Professor of Theology, University of Chicago Divinity School, Chicago, Ill.

Victor Turner—William B. Kenan Professor in Anthropology, The Center for Advanced Study, University of Virginia, Charlottesville, Va.

Kallistos Ware—Fellow of Pembroke College, Oxford; Spalding Lecturer in Eastern Orthodox Studies, Oxford University, England.

Ibn 'Abbād of Ronda

LETTERS ON THE SŪFĪ PATH

TRANSLATION AND INTRODUCTION BY

JOHN RENARD, S.J.

PREFACE BY

ANNEMARIE B. SCHIMMEL

PAULIST PRESS
NEW YORK • MAHWAH • TORONTO

Cover Art:
Poet in Garden. Early 17th century. Painting on paper. Goloubew Collection, Purchased, Francis Bartlett Donation of 1912 and Picture Fund. Courtesy, Museum of Fine Arts, Boston.

Library of Congress
Catalog Card Number: 85-63313

ISBN: 0-8091-2730-X (paper)
0-8091-0365-6 (cloth)

Published by Paulist Press
997 Macarthur Boulevard
Mahwah, New Jersey 07430

Printed and bound in the
United States of America

Contents

Translator of this Volume

JOHN RENARD, S.J., born in 1944, entered the Society of Jesus in 1962 and was ordained a Roman Catholic priest of that order in 1973. He received his B.A. (in Philosophy and Classical Languages) and M.A. (in Biblical Literature) at St. Louis University. In 1978, he received a Ph.D. in Islamic Studies at Harvard University, in the Department of Near Eastern Languages and Civilizations. Since 1978, he has been Associate Professor of Theological Studies at St. Louis University. Other academic interests include teaching in the areas of spirituality and religion and art.

Author of the Preface

ANNEMARIE BRIGITTE SCHIMMEL, born in Erfurt, Germany, in 1922, earned doctorate degrees at both Berlin University and Marburg University. She has held professorships in Islamic Studies at Marburg University, Bonn University, and, since 1967, at Harvard University. She is a member of several scholarly societies, among them the Middle East Studies Association, the Association for the Study of Religion, the British Oriental Society, and the German-Iranian Association. A contributor of articles to professional journals, she is also the author of a number of books, including *Mystical Dimensions of Islam*.

Preface

Sufism has many faces. Many modern Westerners connect it with, if anything, "Sufi Dance" as it is taught in American cities. They do not know that mystical concerts and whirling dance are basically meant to provide the Sufi with some relaxation after his unceasing, hard spiritual exercises and have come to form an integral part of Sufi ritual only in one order, the Mevleviyya. Other Westerners, who have read scholarly books on Sufism, mainly those from the nineteenth century, may claim that this trend is nothing but unabashed pantheism—for the first European scholar to devote a book to Sufism, F. D. A. Tholuck, felt compelled to call his study *Sufismus sive theosophia Persarum pantheistica* [Sufism, or the pantheistic theosophy of the Persians]. The German theologian Tholuck, like many others before and after him, had access only to comparatively late utterances of Sufi poets, mainly from the Persian tradition, and it is indeed easy to find in the ecstatic songs of mystical poets (not only in Islam!) the feeling of all-embracing unity, condensed in the recurrent expression *hama ūst* [Everything is He]. This expression was generally used to sum up the complicated and highly refined theosophical system of Ibn ʿArabi (d. 1240), which became the source of inspiration for generations of Sufis, particularly in the rapidly expanding Sufi brotherhoods. Persian poets, again, were very outspoken in their ecstatic claims, and it is easy to take their words at face value and then see in them expressions of a religious attitude that is a far cry from the solid basis of Islamic orthodoxy: a religiosity in which all differences between the faithful devotee and the debauched infidel, between Kaaba and idol temple, between the pious shaykh and the idol worshiper, seem to be obliterated; rather, the latter might even be preferable to the ostentatious ascetic and form-worshiping Muslim. One understands not only why uninitiated European readers were shocked (and sometimes delighted) by such utterances but also why Muslim modernists found this kind of mystical poetry "more dangerous than the hordes of Attila and Chengiz Khan" (thus Muhammad Iqbal).

The lover of Persian and Persianate poetry would also constantly be faced with expressions of longing for suffering and yearning for death. This is quite a normal feeling for anyone who knows that "death is a bridge which leads the lover to the Beloved," as the early Sufis discovered, and it made the Sufis willing to enjoy the trials and tribulations that were showered on them. But in poetry, this feeling is expressed in increasingly cruel images, and as much as one admires the power of this imagery in which roses, blood, fire, and wine are ingeniously related, or enjoys the constantly recurring allusions to the fate of the martyr-mystic al-Ḥallāj (d. 922) and his death on the gallows, which become for him the "bridal bed," yet, with all admiration for the artistic side of these poems, it is generally difficult for a Western reader and for a modern Muslim to fully appreciate this kind of Sufism.

Some readers may also think in connection with Sufism of the dervishes who perform weird feats such as piercing their limbs with knives and needles and emerging unhurt, or taking out their eyes—performances that have nothing to do with the essence of Sufism but represent an interesting case for the psychologist. But few people would think in connection with the word Sufism of the sober trends that exist but do not show themselves as do the just mentioned external—both attractive and appalling—expressions of the Sufi tradition. Yet it is these sober trends that are at the basis of Sufism. The early Sufi fathers in Baghdad and elsewhere in the Middle East and Iran developed their ideals out of a strictly law-bound attitude and if they differed from the majority of the faithful it was not because of their laxity or latitudinarianism but rather because they took on themselves supererogatory works of piety such as additional fasting and nightly vigils. Into this stern ascetic attitude the central issue of unconditioned love of God was introduced—as far as we know—by the Basrian woman Rābi'a in the mid-eighth century.

The outstanding member of this sober school was no doubt Muḥāsibi of Baghdad, whose surname points to his constant *muḥāsaba* [reckoning], that is, introspection in order to eradicate even the smallest signs of activity of the lower soul, *nafs*, which struggle has been called the "greater Holy War." This current was lucidly expressed in the work of Abū Ṭālib al-Makkī in the tenth century, whose *Qūt al-qulūb* [The Nourishment of the Hearts], remained a favorite with all sober Sufis and was largely used by Abū Ḥāmid al-Ghazzālī (d. 1111), the master of moderate Sufism. However, later Sufis in North Africa found even Ghazzālī's writings almost too daring in his dealings with spiritual and mystical revelations.

Three major schools of "sober" Sufism exist to our day. The Suhrawardiyya developed in the late twelfth century in Iraq and soon spread to the borders of Bengal, and the introduction to the mystical Path by its second master, Abū Ḥafs 'Omar as-Suhrawardī, the *'Awārif al-ma'ārif*, remained the spiritual staple in most of the Sufi fraternities. The Naqshbandiyya, originating in Central Asia, where it reached its first climax in the late fifteenth century, is well known everywhere not only for the refined practices of meditation (silent *dhikr*, breath control) but also for their commitment to "political" activities in the widest sense of the word.

The third sober order appeared in the time between these two, that is, in the thirteenth century. It is the Shadhiliyya, growing in Egypt, then especially elaborated in the Muslim West, and still active and successful. The Shadhiliyya and the brotherhood derived from it have attracted a number of highly sophisticated Europeans as well, apparently possessing an appeal to modern man that many of the other orders cannot boast.

Perhaps the letters of Ibn 'Abbād of Ronda furnish us with a tentative answer to why this is so. Ibn 'Abbād, who studied Mālikite law and theology in Fez and became the favorite disciple of Ibn 'Ashir, the saint of Salé in Morocco, was prevailed upon to write a commentary on the short pithy sayings, *ḥikam*, of the Shadhili master in Egypt, Ibn 'Aṭā Allāh al-Iskandarī (d. 1309)—sayings so beautifully worded that it has been remarked that if it were permitted to recite in prayer any text outside the Koran it would be these aphorisms. One can ponder them for a long time, partly attracted by the author's talent to condense the deepest realities in a few simple-sounding words, partly for their sheer beauty in the Arabic language. It was Ibn ʿAbbād's commentary on these sayings that made him famous, and on the basis of the Shadhiliyya teachings he slowly grew into a mystical leader—not a leader who wanted absolute obedience or forced his disciples to imitate his every word and step, but rather a director of souls who, with great care and tenderness, tried to guide the disciple the way that was meant for him. Later this unambitious man was the main preacher in the famous Karawiyyin mosque in Fez, where he was called by the Merinid ruler and where he spent his last sixteen years until his death in 1390. As a preacher, he faithfully fulfilled his duties, convincing his listeners not by force of argument but rather by his subtle way of guiding them toward what seemed to him the center of man's life, namely sincerity, certitude, and gratitude.

Ibn ʿAbbād, "wrapped in the cloak of modesty," as one of his biographers wrote, did not leave a large output of works. There is no poem, and one looks in vain for ecstatic utterances, for descriptions of the different states and stations of the Sufis, for ravishing hymns about the Beloved whose eternal beauty is overwhelming and for whom one wants to suffer and to die—nothing of these central themes of Sufi poetry can be detected in Ibn ʿAbbād's letters. Nor can the favorite topics of Sufi theoreticians be found in his writings—no discussion of the different worlds through which the soul has to pass, no complicated deliberations about the One Whose Existence Is Necessary, about absolute and contingent being, about the archetypal figure of the Prophet Muḥammad: As far as Ibn ʿAbbād is from the lyricism of Persian mystical songs, as far is he from the philosophically inclined Sufis of the Maghrib like Ibn Masarrā and especially Ibn ʿArabī, who seem so typical for a more intellectual trend in Maghribī mysticism.

Ibn ʿAbbād appears before the modern reader as someone who was always composed and calm. He never claimed to have even attained *dhauq* [the immediate "tasting" of spiritual bliss], but was content with what he learned, as he writes modestly, by studying the books of the early masters. His whole thought is centered on the purification of man's soul in order to fulfill the obligations of absolute monotheism. He is convinced that exaggerated attempts are good for nothing: even someone who leads an impeccable ascetic life for the sake of asceticism is still in the claws of self-love, the worst quality. For there is only the One on whom man can rely; only One who is responsible for everything created, and that is God, the Creator, Sustainer, and Judge. To serve Him in sincerity is man's duty and privilege. Man can neither rely on himself nor on other creatures—his only source of help is God, and he has to understand and realize that whatever comes from God is good and has to be accepted gratefully. Even to try to fight the *nafs* by human means is futile—only God can rescue man from its ruses if man gives himself completely into His hands.

The Sufis of yore had spoken about the contrasting mystical states of *qabḍ* and *basṭ* [contraction and expansion], and some of them, like Junayd (d. 910), the leading master of Baghdad, had expressed the view that *qabḍ* was preferable to *basṭ* because in the state of utter despondency man feels that there is nothing but God to trust, whereas in the state of happiness he forgets all too easily that his joy is not the work of mortals but is solely due to the Lord's kindness. The emphasis on the state of *qabḍ* and its importance for the spiritual life has led M. Asin Palacios to see a relation between the early Shadhilis, especially Ibn ʿAbbād, and the teachings of St. John of the Cross: He found in both the concept of the Dark Night of the Soul. There is no doubt that the similarities are great; it is, however, difficult (as Père Nwiya has shown) to find out on which way the concept of the Dark Night might have traveled from Ibn ʿAbbād to St. John.

For Ibn ʿAbbād, there is one central concern for man's progress on his path toward God: that is, to grow in gratitude and in certitude. Certitude, the unquestioning trust in God's wisdom, is the highest state the wayfarer can hope for, and he who has reached it will not need any revelations of hidden mysteries: His is the clear vision. But certitude is connected with gratitude. The early Sufis had defined, in dozens of sayings, the complementary stage of *ṣabr* [patience] and *shukr* [gratitude] and had discussed the relative value of each of them. But for Ibn ʿAbbād, gratitude is the heart of the matter. In his letters he admonishes his disciples and friends to be grateful for everything that happens: When God leads a man through afflictions, it means that He wants this person to turn again to Him Whom he had forgotten in the midst of worldly planning and scheming. He knows that there are three forms of gratitude: in the heart, on the tongue by praising the Lord, and, most importantly, by actions: to prove one's gratitude by fulfilling God's law and to show active love for the neighbor as well. Ibn ʿAbbād would wholeheartedly have agreed with the old Sufi formulation that the final stage of gratitude is "gratitude for being able to render thanks."

It is this concept of gratitude that makes Ibn ʿAbbād's writings so important for today. In a time when fear and horror are growing, when hopelessness seems to prevail in large segments of the population, and when it is almost fashionable, in certain circles, to see everything in a negative light, Ibn 'Abbād can teach his readers that there is always a reason and a way to thank God for something—and the more this constant gratitude grows the more it becomes a habitus of the soul, and man does no longer worry unnecessarily: He feels safe "like a child in God's lap," as the master of Ronda says with a beautiful image that can be easily adopted by Christians as well.

We do not find any references to ecstatic experiences in Ibn 'Abbād's work—and that may endear him to those who find mysticism not very attractive for a modern, sober mind. He has not been surrounded by miracle stories and legends, as have so many other Sufis—and that again may make him acceptable to many readers who tend to shy away from all too exaggerated claims to miracles in any religious tradition. We rather find in Ibn 'Abbād a quiet friend in whom we can trust, a man who does not dazzle us with flashes of glorious ideas or confuse us with theosophical pretentiousness; a friend who does not press his ideas on us but rather waits until we come and listen to him and thus slowly understand his deep responsibility for the spiritual wellbeing of his readers.

While Ibn 'Aṭa Allah's aphorisms are available to the anglophone reader in Victor Danner's translation, Ibn 'Abbād's work has not until now been translated into English, only French studies about him being available. That is why the translation of parts of his letters by Father J. Renard is most welcome to the reader, who will perceive, through this translation, the figure of a man who appears made of pale gold—gold that has been cast in the crucible time and again but knows that the master of the crucible means well, for has he not every reason to thank Him who purifies him with loving care? Few are this man's works, and they need to be patiently read; but the reward is great for those who look for a Sufi teacher whose attitude can be shared by modern man and is relevant in our day.

Foreword

Just over half a century ago, the Spanish Islamicist Miguel Asin Palacios (1871–1944) began what he could scarcely have known would be a slowly but steadily broadening circle of interest in the writings of a fourteenth-century Spanish-born Muslim religious figure named Ibn ʿAbbād of Ronda (1332–1390). Prior to Asin Palacios's 1933 study that saw in Ibn ʿAbbād a "Spanish-Muslim forerunner of John of the Cross," the Ṣūfī was unknown among non-Muslims. One need not agree with the conclusions of that work (recently translated as *Saint John of the Cross and Islam*, by E. H. Douglas and H. W. Yoder, and published by Vantage Books) to find in Ibn ʿAbbād a man worthy of further study. Very few people before Asin Palacios had succeeded in appreciating how significant are the connections between Islamic and Christian spiritualities, while remaining unquestionably loyal to the Christian tradition. Asin arrived at many important and valid reflections on those interrelationships precisely through his acquaintance with Ibn ʿAbbād.

Asin Palacios's close friend Louis Massignon (1883–1962) was likewise fascinated by the affinities between the two faith traditions, as discerned in their mystics. Massignon, too, regarded Ibn ʿAbbād as an important personality in the history of Islamic spirituality, and he managed to communicate that interest to a student of his, Paul Nwiya, S.J., now widely renowned as a scholar in the field of Islamic mysticism. It is thanks largely to Father Nwiya's dedicated scholarship that the life and works of Ibn ʿAbbād have become quite accessible to students of Islamic religious history over the past three decades.

Paul Nwiya (1925–1980), a native of Iraq, labored for twenty-five years on Ibn ʿAbbād and on the latter's spiritual predecessor, Ibn ʿAṭāʾ Allāh, publishing two editions of the Letters offered in the present volume, as well as an excellent comprehensive study of Ibn ʿAbbād and an edition of Ibn ʿAṭāʾ Allāh's *Hikam* with translation and commentary. Nwiya had hoped also to publish an edition of the "Large Collection of Letters" of Ibn ʿAbbād. It was Paul Nwiya who thus aroused my interest in the Ṣūfī from Ronda. This volume owes a great deal to the Jesuit from Iraq.

The Classics of Western Spirituality series has to date made available in English translation, from both Arabic and Persian, four volumes from the Islamic tradition representing the writings of five major religious figures. What can yet another hope to add to the perhaps already surprise presence of Muslims in the ranks of Christian and Jewish spiritual luminaries? Is the series to become merely a collection of primary sources for the study of comparative religion? Or are the publishers making an important and rather bold statement, at least indirectly, about what must evolve as a new understanding of "Western" spirituality?

Any volume of the series will offer the reader a challenge, for one must stretch just to begin taking the measure of a true spiritual classic. But those who venture into the world of the Muslim authors available there are in for a double challenge. That is to enter the world and mind of an author not merely from a distant time and place, but of an unfamiliar religious tradition. Of the Islamic authors in the series, Ibn ʿAbbād is in some ways the most accessible intellectually and emotionally. As a spokesman for a religious tradition related in so many ways to Judaism and Christianity, he puts before the reader numerous themes and concerns of a rather everyday and ordinary nature that will sound a familiar chord with non-Muslims as well as Muslims. In another way, also, Ibn ʿAbbād can claim to be not only a classic, but a Western classic in a way few other vintage Muslim spiritual writers can. He lived and wrote at the very occidental brink of the medieval Islamic world. Even so, Ibn 'Abbād will require considerable introduction. He is as Western geographically as John of the Cross, and his imagery sometimes recalls that of John and other Christian and Jewish authors; but that more familiar vocabulary is still nestled in a way of thinking uniquely formed by its Islamic roots and context.

A word about where Ibn 'Abbād stands in relation to the other Muslim writers in this series may be helpful at this point. He is, first of all, nearly an exact contemporary of Sharafuddin Maneri (Sharaf ad-Dīn Manīrī), author of *The Hundred Letters;* but Maneri wrote in Persian, in a more formal and somewhat less "personal" style, and at the opposite end geographically of the Muslim world of the fourteenth century. As examples of epistolary spiritual direction, the two complement each other very well. Ibn 'Abbād was the spiritual successor to, and chief commentator and interpreter of, Ibn 'Aṭā' Allāh, author of the *Book of Wisdom*, to which Ibn 'Abbād alludes very frequently. Ibn 'Aṭā' was in turn profoundly influenced by, and a staunch defender of, the thought of Ibn al-'Arabī, whose *Bezels of Wisdom* is also in a Classics volume. Greater still was the latter's influence on Ibn 'Aṭā' Allāh's younger contemporary who lived almost as far to the east as Maneri, Fakhr ad-Dīn 'Irāqī, author of the *Divine Flashes*. All those mentioned thus far had some connection with a formally constituted Ṣūfī religious order, but the most ancient author in the Classics, Anṣārī, predated the earliest formal orders, lived in the east (Afghanistan), and, like Maneri, wrote in Persian. Unlike 'Irāqī, Anṣārī, and Ibn 'Aṭā', Ibn 'Abbād wrote no poetry. And unlike Ibn al-'Arabī, he was not the author of an elaborate system of thought, nor was his manner of expression strikingly esoteric.

What is most important about Ibn 'Abbād in this context is that he forms a link between two areas of interest in Islamic spirituality: the formal and esoteric on the one hand (for he was a member of a religious order and well educated in the classic sources of spirituality) and the more "popular" aspect of Islamic life (for whose benefit he seeks to interpret and make accessible the mystical vision of people like Ibn 'Aṭā' Allāh). As an interpreter of the mystical tradition, Ibn 'Abbād is a key figure in propounding an understanding of Sufism as virtually synonymous with a vibrant spiritual life, available to all who put their trust in God. He represents an important melding of the spirituality of a major religious order with a kind of emerging lay spirituality.

The present volume includes a translation from Arabic of the text of sixteen of Ibn 'Abbād's letters, the whole of the "Small Collection," notes that attempt to identify as many of the historical and literary references as the limited research resources at my disposal allowed, and an Introduction. A list of abbreviations of titles most frequently cited in the notes is provided, as is a selected bibliography. All references to the text of the Qur'ān appear in parentheses within the text of the translation. The numbers that appear in the margins of the text of the Letters refer to the page numbers of the primary manuscript used by Nwiya in both editions of the Letters; the numbers thus provide a reference to either RS^1 or RS^2.

I wish to acknowledge gratefully Dr. Ilse Lichtenstaedter of Cambridge, Massachusetts, without whose encouragement and support this project would never have been completed; and Professor Annemarie Schimmel of Harvard University, who initially reaffirmed for me the merits of translating Ibn 'Abbād. Special thanks also to Dr. Schimmel for graciously providing a Preface.

Note: The order in which the letters are presented here is that of the original document; but I believe they may be read with greater profit in the following order: Letters 15 and 16; 10 through 14; 7 through 9; 2 through 6; and, finally, Letter 1.

Introduction

It is never easy to enter without prejudice into the world of another human being, even when access to that person's mind and heart is facilitated by actual presence, direct communication, and a growing appreciation of the people, places, and events that have shaped that person's experience. To meet another across the considerable distances created by differences in time, place, language, culture, and religion is still more challenging, even if less risky. Reading the letters of someone whose experience of life is radically different from one's own can never substitute for encountering a living proponent of another point of view; but a classic of religious literature can nevertheless call the reader to set aside stereotypes and grow beyond accustomed frames of reference. Such a work can achieve that by touching the reader's essential humanity and appealing to common needs and aspirations even as it leads the reader into a world that seems quite new and strange.

Fortunately, the door that leads to the study of a spiritual classic from another age and religious tradition swings both ways. In order to read with appreciation the Letters of Spiritual Direction of Ibn 'Abbād, we need to address a variety of questions about the life and times of the author. What kind of a culture would produce a spiritual director whose letters are collected and kept for centuries? If I were to walk down the street behind Ibn ʿAbbād some Friday morning as he made his way to the principal mosque in fourteenth-century Fez, what kinds of conversations would I hear him engage in and with what sort of folk would he stop to chat? What were the important human issues of his day and to what honored fonts of wisdom did Ibn ʿAbbād turn for guidance as he composed his Friday sermon or responded to the searching inquiries of the addressees of the Letters translated here? This Introduction will attempt to deal with such questions as these; but because a classic is never merely a thing of the past, it also poses vital questions for its reader here and now: questions about power and weakness, riches and indigence, joy and desperation, certitude and aimlessness, faith and self-centeredness.

How the reader and the classic can meet each other half way, the reader stepping back into the fourteenth century and Ibn ʿAbbād finding a path into the twentieth, is the subject of the Introduction. Its three parts will explore, first, the central themes and concepts in Ibn ʿAbbād's spirituality; second, the sources, formative influences, and context of that spirituality; and finally, Ibn ʿAbbād's life and writings.

It need scarcely be mentioned that readers of the Classics of Western Spirituality come to the works with some prior interest in "spirituality." Interest in spirituality does not, however, always bring with it the kind of focus, definition, and serviceable methodology that can help one derive the maximum benefit from the study of a spiritual classic. Given that, and given that this volume presents a work not only of *Islamic* spirituality, but of one of a variety of Islamic *spiritualities*, some clarification of terminology and method will be helpful. Briefly, then, I suggest, first, a working definition of "a spirituality"; second, a description of several key formal aspects of a spirituality; and third, four functional aspects.

A spirituality can be understood as "the expression of a dialectical personal growth from the inauthentic to the authentic."[1] Distinguishing the worthy goals from the unworthy by means of "organizing forms" or images that become its hallmark, a spirituality articulates a progress through various levels or stages of development, which are traversed as the individual person makes his or her life choices. From a formal point of view, every major religious tradition may be said to have its characteristic system of organizing images (e.g., Exodus-Covenant-Land; Creation-Prophetic/Apocalyptic expectation-New Creation; Meaningless life on "this shore"—Dharma as Raft—Other Shore). A variety of spiritualities may then develop within a larger tradition and be characterized by a focus on some particular variation on the overall system (e.g., Life as Desert Experience, as Ascent of Mountain, as freedom from slavery, as Pilgrimage, etc.).

One spirituality may be more active than another, more community-oriented; another might emphasize individual growth, be less inclined to formal liturgical expression, and so forth. Each spirituality will have its preference for particular images to express its perspectives on God, creation, history, the self. Ibn 'Abbād, for example, is especially partial to images of God as Master of the Universe, whose creation is full of benefits—even severe trials are positive, whose creatures are His servants poor and altogether needy, and who must struggle to fix their gaze on God alone as history becomes more chaotic the further removed each generation is from the time of Muḥammad.

From a more functional point of view, a spirituality might be said to operate in four ways. It indicates, first of all, the point or points in the lives of individuals and communities where they confront Mystery, the Holy, the Transcendent. Frequently, as in Ibn 'Abbād's case, a spirituality will find positive value in experiences and circumstances that at first seem hopeless or simply banal. A second function is the construction of supports "to protect and nourish this experience of Mystery . . . and thus contribute to the likelihood that the Mystery will appear to us again. Whatever form these follow-up activities take, they constitute the intrinsic 'devotions' of the spirituality." Closely related to this is the role of spirituality in focusing attention so as to render the individual ready and primed to meet the Transcendent yet another time. Ibn 'Abbād speaks often of such methods of prayer as recitation of litanies of the Divine Names, and contemplative chanting of scripture (the Qur'ān). M. Neuman observes that "from a phenomenological perspective, every style of prayer—meditation or contemplation or ritual movement—reflects a particular way of organizing and stimulating consciousness to prepare for Mystery." Finally, every spirituality elaborates a method for growth and conversion, along with a standard by which growth can be tested, at least in a general way.[2] As we shall see in greater detail later, the Ṣūfī spiritualities within Islam developed a number of quite complex typologies capable of making very fine distinctions between levels (stations and states) in spiritual growth.

In the following pages these few methodological considerations will, I hope, provide structure enough for readers encountering an Islamic author for the first time, without seeming to veteran students of spirituality to force their approach to Ibn ʻAbbād into an unhappily Procrustean bed.

1. Themes in Ibn ʻAbbād's Spirituality

Bearing in mind the proposed working definition of a spirituality, we turn first to an overview of the organizing forms and images within which Ibn ʻAbbād articulates what he understands to be the nonnegotiables of human existence—the facts of life in the most fundamental sense of the term. Next, the framework of the four functional elements will provide a way of summarizing what Ibn ʻAbbād proposes as the most effective ways of responding to those "facts." Finally, a look at our author's notion of Ultimate or Mystic Truth will shed some light on the nature of the goal in store for the seeker of God. Since the imagery of the spiritual journey is so prominent in Ibn ʻAbbād's writings, as well as in an enormous range of Islamic religious literature, I have chosen it here to serve as the organizing form of the first segment of this Introduction.

a. Revealed Law [*Sharīʻah*] as Main Road

If there is a notion in the Islamic tradition that may be said to be all-encompassing and evocative of Islam's religious thrust as a unified whole, it is surely that of the divinely Revealed Law. God has set His people in the direction of return to their Creator. In the Islamic mystical tradition, *sharīʻah* has often been seen as part of a triple image: It is the main road off of which branches the more arduous Path [*ṭarīqah*] leading to the Truth [*ḥaqīqah*].[3] Here are some of the key images with which Ibn ʻAbbād illustrates his views of God, creation, history and tradition, and the self. He writes not as a theoretician or systematic theologian, but rather from the perspective of a spiritual director using the best "pastoral psychology" available to him.

God. God's absolute unity is the beginning and end of the spiritual life for Muslims. Particularly in the mystical tradition, the seeker's lifelong task is that of purifying the realization and acknowledgment of that unity and uniqueness. Every word of spiritual counsel Ibn ʻAbbād has to offer ultimately resolves itself into some form of affirmation of this central concept of *tawḥīd*. Especially in Letter 9 of this translation, the spiritual director makes it clear to his addressee that his every shortcoming is a result of the weakness of his conviction of God's unity, and of his belief that one does not go to God except by God's agency. It is the loss of the "contemplative vision" of the true nature of the deity [*al-mushāhadāt at-tawḥīdiyyah*] that gives rise to all manner of preoccupation with self—believing that one is capable of anything alone, that one exists independently, and so forth. Only in total acquiescence in God's good pleasure, renunciation of one's own will, and surrender to what the Master sets before the servant is *tawḥīd* made perfect.

Ibn 'Abbād does not discourse at length and in the abstract about the essence of the divinity. He is more concerned with the actual and potential consequences in an individual's life of a spirituality with a point of departure and a goal so utterly and simply focused. And the aspect of God's unity that relates most immediately to concrete human experience is transcendence. Oddly put, to be sure, but not intended to be merely enigmatic. What Ibn 'Abbād wants his directee to understand, feel, and sense about God most keenly is that to be in God's presence is never to be quite fully comfortable and secure. He has a word that epitomizes this state of affairs, and it expresses a concept that is in a fascinating way even closer to the heart of Islamic spirituality than that of *tawḥīd* (closer not in a "dogmatic" way, but in terms of its implications for a living spirituality). That word is *makr*, and it has been variously translated as ruse, wiles, machination, and strategem. I have used the last of these most frequently here.

What is so intriguing about the notion of divine strategem is that it describes how God can be utterly transcendent and yet actively engage human beings. The unity of God is a magnificent and beautiful idea, and Muslims reaffirm their adherence to it many times a day in the brief creed that begins "There is no god but God." But by itself the notion of *tawḥīd* possesses no affective charge. It is a potent and effective concept for focusing and organizing one's world view and epitomizing a religious and psychological orientation; but "oneness" is too elusive, too bland. Its very austerity is quite telling and authentically expressive of an important facet of the spirit of Islam. Note, however, the enormous difference in your own emotional temperature when you try to conceive of God as One, and when you find that you must fairly force yourself to allow that perhaps God is a schemer whose word cannot be taken at face value.

It is a splendidly scandalous idea. Small wonder, then, that Ibn 'Abbād was moved to devote the greatest part of Letter 1 to calming the fears of a correspondent who had read about the divine strategem in a tenth-century spiritual classic. As Ibn 'Abbād points out, the more usual and spontaneous response is to "think badly" of God. That is precisely why the notion of *makr* is so important: One cannot but respond to it, if only in shock. It has far more than mere shock value, however. It is a stark reminder of how difficult it is to place no preconditions on God, who appears here under the image of a sovereign who offers no guarantee of safety and security but who nevertheless demands absolute confidence of His subjects. To move from the inauthentic to the authentic in this instance is to let go one's preconditions and, in utter confidence, "think well" of God.

For those far advanced in the spiritual life, the simple acknowledgment "God is One and therefore *I* am not God" may be the whole of the experience of thinking well of God. For most, however, knowing only God's inscrutability and relying only on God's unpredictability are not enough. A little of the Holy as *Mysterium Tremendum* goes a long way. Fortunately, God is also ineffably attractive, fascinating, and approachable. Innumerable are God's beautiful qualities—more than enough to balance the majesty; and countless are the blessings bestowed. Reflection on and recollection of these make thinking well of God a living possibility. The Islamic tradition of the Ninety-Nine Beautiful Names of God is of great importance to an appreciation of Ibn 'Abbād's spirituality. When we come shortly to the second functional element, the devotional, a translation of a portion of Ibn 'Abbād's own "Meditation" (a sort of Litany) on the names will be offered. For now it will suffice to note that the Ninety-Nine Names are a treasury of highly evocative images that suggest both transcendence and immanence, and sum up how the One accommodates the human tendency to experience multiplicity.

Thinking well of God manifests itself in a more specific and identifiable kind of thought and behavior, as does thinking badly of God. First there is gratitude [*shukr*]. It is the sum and scope of the way to God, and, as Nwiya notes, it plays the same role in Ibn 'Abbād's spirituality that charity plays in the Christian life. Gratitude is "the station [i.e., spiritual level] that subsumes all other stations." Ibn 'Abbād speaks of three types of gratitude: of the heart, acknowledging God as the sole source of grace; of the tongue, singing God's praises and announcing His beneficence; and of all the senses, doing good works. As Nwiya explains in summary: To be grateful is to know the most basic truth about God and oneself, that God is all and that a human being is nothing. It is impossible to recognize and appreciate the magnitude of God's largesse without a keen sense of God's grandeur and the pettiness of the self.[4]

Diametrically opposed to *shukr* is *shirk*, which means literally "associating anyone or anything with God, setting up a partner with God." It encompasses far more than the more blatant forms of idolatry and denial of God's unity. *Shirk* is most insidious in its "hidden" forms. Ibn 'Abbād applies all his gifts as a spiritual director to helping his directees ferret out their subtle propensities toward *shirk*. Such tendencies manifest themselves in every form of attachment to or fear of anything that is not God, every manner of setting up and worshiping the godlings of false security, misplaced hope, and flight from what can ultimately pose no threat. Ibn 'Abbād characterizes all such variations on the theme of Godlessness as self-centeredness, pretense, and presumptuousness [*da'wā*]. We shall come later to a more detailed investigation of the method of spiritual discernment he uses to distinguish *shukr* from *shirk*.

One more image of God needs to be mentioned as central to Ibn 'Abbād's spirituality. The following text from the Qur'ān is its source:

> God is the Light of the heavens and the earth. The likeness of his light is as a niche in which there is a lamp. The lamp is within a glass which is like a shining star enkindled from a blessed olive tree, neither of east nor west, whose oil would glow almost of itself even if no fire touched it. Light upon Light! And God guides to His Light whom He will. [24:35]

Without the Light (one of the Ninety-Nine Names), the journey of life is fraught with dangers and no traveler's vision can penetrate the haze of self-centeredness. The image of God as Light that suffuses all the universe is one that unites the divine transcendence and immanence. Ibn 'Abbād, sometimes following the lead of Ibn 'Aṭā' Allāh, often talks of God's intimate presence to the individual as a light in the heart. History itself is frequently described in terms of the preponderance of light or darkness in a given age or generation of people. All of creation is replete with "signs" of God's presence, but they cannot be discerned without the Light. Throughout the next three sections of this Introduction the imagery of light, sign, and journey will begin to come together more clearly and emerge as perhaps the three most suggestive reminders of how Ibn 'Abbād interprets and teaches the traditional Islamic wisdom about personal growth from the inauthentic to the authentic.

Creation. Far more interested in humanity than in nature as a whole, Ibn ʿAbbād is nonetheless highly sensitive to God's creation, the world of time and space, as a theater of His "signs." From effects one can learn of the Cause. Ibn ʿAbbād's view of this world has been formed by the Qur'ān's frequent summons to discover God's traces everywhere:

> Behold, in the heavens and the earth are signs for those who believe. And in your creation, and all the wild creatures He has scattered over the earth, are signs for a people of firm faith. And the alternation of night and day, and the sustenance that God sends down from the sky, quickening thereby the earth after her death, and the ordering of the winds—these are signs for a people who understand. [45:3–5]

He believes that if it is on this earth one must journey, it is here also that God will show the way; and that "those who reject Our signs are deaf and dumb and in profound darkness. God allows to go astray whom He will, and He places on the Straight Way whom He will" [Qur'ān 6:39].

Ibn ʿAbbād surely did not look forward to staying on this earth forever, nor would he have liked to do so. The words "this world and the next" appear frequently and formulaically in his letters, and "the next" has a decided edge. But the Ṣūfī would, I suspect, not have been entirely at a loss to understand Robert Frost's "Earth's the right place for love. I can't imagine where it's likely to go better" ["Birches"]. One has to begin with what one is given, and in that sense, this *is* the best of all possible worlds. This world was made for God's purposes and that is ultimately the way things will work out. In the meantime, it is precisely in and through this time and this space that God speaks to this individual person.

Without intending to suggest in any way that Ibn ʿAbbād's thought "influenced" that of Ignatius of Loyola, I believe that the "Principle and Foundation" of the *Spiritual Exercises* can serve as an accurate recapitulation of Ibn ʿAbbād's attitude toward creation.

> Human beings are created to praise, reverence, and serve God our Lord, and in that way reach salvation. All other things on the face of the earth are created to assist us in attaining the end for which we are created. . . . Therefore, we must become indifferent to all created things, to the degree that we are given

> free choice and are not under any prohibition. Consequently, as far as we are concerned, we ought not prefer health to sickness, riches to poverty, honor to dishonor, a long life to a short life. The same holds for all other things. Our one desire and choice should be what is more conducive to the end for which we are created.[5]

Ibn ʿAbbād likewise counsels a kind of "indifference" in the sense that the individual must always deal with the actual situation first, whatever it may be, and find the hand of God there.

Two clarifications about the practical consequences are in order. First, authentic indifference is closely related to "thinking well of God," and is a very advanced attainment in the classic Islamic typologies of spiritual growth. Ibn ʿAbbād and many of his predecessors use a term that might be translated "satisfaction" or "contentment" with God. It is therefore very different from a garden variety of apathy or nonchalance. On the one hand, the goal of seekers is a point at which they are not inordinately elated at the arrival of ease or the departure of adversity, nor unduly saddened by the opposite of these. On the other, Ibn ʿAbbād consistently advises his addressees not to be too hard on themselves in any case, and, if they are to ask for anything in prayer, let them ask for blessings. He is only too happy to quote sayings of the Prophet Muḥammad to that effect. For example, "God has made things easy; don't try to make them more difficult."

Second, marvels or charismatic gifts, understood as interruptions of physical laws and the natural order of creation, are neither necessary nor intrinsically helpful. The ordinary workings of the created world are wondrous enough to show forth God's signs. Those occurrences that appear to go beyond the ordinary may be a deception; they can have a narcotic effect and cause the seeker to cut short the search prematurely. The Sūfī tradition is full of stories that warn against being too impressed by miracles or what passes for the miraculous. Ibn ʿAbbād cites several examples of the genre. Another charming tale tells of how a famous spiritual master had someone say to him with great ceremony, "So and so says he can go to Mecca in a single night." The shaykh replied, "Satan also goes from East to West in the opening and closing of an eye. Nevertheless he is accursed by God."[6] In any case, warns Ibn ʿAbbād, one can hardly expect God to interrupt the accustomed patterns of nature's behavior if one is not first willing to alter for the better the course of the lower self's tendencies.

INTRODUCTION

History. "The earth has gone dark with the extinguishing of its lights and the setting of its suns and moons," says our author in Letter 8. Had Ibn ʿAbbād lived in our time, he might have written what Hans Urs von Balthasar wrote a few years ago in his book *Prayer*:

> We live in a period spiritually arid; the images of the world that spoke of God have become obscure signs and enigmas, the words of Scripture are mauled by sceptics and rationalists, men's hearts, in this robot age, are crushed and over-ridden, and they no longer believe in contemplation. When people turn to prayer, they start from a feeling of hopelessness and futility; they drag along the ground and despair of ever rising. They are drawn to anything and everything negative, to doubt the existence of God, to withstand him to the face, perhaps hate him for letting the world go on as it does, and because, exalted as he is, he feels no call to intervene; because secure in himself he abandons his children in the dark and anguish of a boundless universe, leaving them no other hope than nothingness, no other consolation than certain death. The temptation to negation and despair is so great, it presses so heavily upon those who still remain sensitive to the question of the meaning of life that they need to use all their strength to go against the stream.[7]

Ibn ʿAbbād describes his own age as a time when injustice, oppression, irreligiousness, and superstition were rampant, and when there was no one to set a good example for the people. His more famous contemporary Ibn Khaldūn, celebrated for his writing of what some regard as the first "philosophy of history," shares Ibn ʿAbbād's assessment, but from a slightly different point of view. Ibn Khaldūn looked at a disintegrating political structure, declining agriculture, weakening economies, and inadequate military defenses. He saw in the dynasty that ruled Fez all of Ibn ʿAbbād's lifetime, the Marīnids, a dynasty that had lost its Islamic legitimacy. Lacking a historic religio-political mandate to hold it together and facing major weaknesses in so many other sectors of society, the Marīnids had nothing left to fall back on. Ibn Khaldūn believed "that he was living at the end of a world. He felt this and described his feelings with such poignant intensity that no Maghribī writer since has been able to free himself from a sense of impending doom."[8]

Taking a more explicitly religious stance than Ibn Khaldūn, Ibn

'Abbād manages to hold on to the hope of renewal somewhat more firmly. He is steadfast in his confidence that God is the Lord of history. What he sees around him does not make him happy, but economic and political forces are not what ultimately determine the destiny of society and the world. Governments may come unglued, princes may be dissolute, soldiers may desert their posts, but so long as there is a grain of faith in someone's heart, all is not lost. Ibn 'Abbād focuses his critique on the religious leaders, the jurists who have become too comfortable in their enclaves, who have forgotten the real needs of ordinary people, and who have taken the inviolability of caste privilege too much for granted. He sounds the alarm for the priority of reform in religion:

> Reform on the temporal level depends on religious reform; reform of the morals of princes depends on this and on reforms of teachers of the Revealed Law. But the jurists will reform only if God removes laziness and torpor from their hearts. Then they would open their eyes to the world they live in, with its disorders and deficiencies. They would sound the depths of the evil there, and would set about the primary concern, namely, that which can renew the morals of the people and those they direct.[9]

In order to understand precisely how Ibn 'Abbād's picture of his own time and his call for renewal relate to his spirituality, it is essential to appreciate something of how he regarded the overall drift of history. The reader may be surprised at the kind of impression of gloom Ibn 'Abbād gives, especially in two of the present letters. In Letter 3 he cites a number of sayings of the Prophet called Traditions of Discord [*aḥādīth al-fitan*], and then concludes it with a rather grim excerpt of a doomsday sermon by the dour ascetic Ḥasan al-Baṣrī. Letter 8 then summarizes a generation-by-generation critique by one aṣ-Ṣaqallī, describing the post-Prophetic generations as in the throes of an almost cosmic spiritual entropy. The views of Ḥasan and Ṣaqallī are shared by many authors and historiographers both before and since their times all over the Islamic world. They are founded on the resigned belief that things will never again be quite what they were in the halcyon days of the Prophet and his Companions (virtually a technical term referring to the first generation of Muslims, with the second known as the Followers). Underlying this opinion is the assumption that " 'the good is the ancestral' and that a specific tradition, viz., that of the Prophet and the early generations of Islam, provided the surest source of knowledge and the best guide for action."[10]

Put together Ibn 'Abbād's sense of urgency for renewal in his own time with the received wisdom about the sources capable of nourishing such a revival, and it is not difficult to appreciate the recommendations he makes most insistently to his directees: meditate on the Qur'ān, and imitate the Example [*sunnah*] of the Prophet and you are assured of living in accord with the Revealed Law. Two texts from the Qur'ān, about itself and about the Prophet's mission, will help to recall the imagery of journey, sign, and light; but now the context has shifted slightly. Now we read the scripture bearing in mind that it was precisely the revelation of the Book to the Messenger that marked the critical turning point in human history. From the Muslim point of view, history may be described as happening in three segments: the time of darkness and paganism before Islam, illumined only by the appearance of a succession of prophets sent to heedless peoples; the pristine days of Islam; and the post-Prophetic age in which renewal calls for continual struggle. Here are the two texts:

> He [God] is the One Who sends manifest signs to His servants, that He might lead you from the depths of darkness into the Light . . . O you who believe! Be mindful of your duty to trust in His messenger, and He will bestow on you a double portion of His mercy: He will provide for you a Light by which you shall walk and He will forgive you . . . [57:9, 28]

> It is not fitting that God should speak to a human being except by inspiration [here using a technical term reserved for a revelation given to a prophet], or from behind a veil, or by sending of a Messenger to reveal, by God's leave, what God wills . . . And thus We have, by Our command, sent an inspiration to you [Muḥammad]. You knew not what the Scripture was, nor what the faith was. But we have made it [Qur'ān] a Light by which We guide such servants of Ours as We will. And truly you [Muḥammad] guide them to the Straight Way, the Way of God, to Whom belongs whatever is in the heavens and whatever is on earth. [52:51–53]

While Ibn Khaldūn was working out the categories and methodology of a more properly philosophical or even social-scientific approach to history, Ibn ʿAbbād considered history purely in terms of its religious and spiritual implications. Tradition would have been a much more useful category for Ibn ʿAbbād than history, though he does not use a term that translates neatly into either of these English words. Even more concretely, he would understand tradition to be that which defines a living community of faith and value. The "authentic" in history, therefore, is that which is conducive to religious and ethical cohesiveness. Ibn ʿAbbād is not interested in simple conformity, however. As we shall see in greater detail later in this Introduction as well as in various letters, he employs some very sophisticated and discerning principles of interpretation as he advises his addressees in their interiorization of the Qur'ān and the Example of the Prophet. These two fundamental sources must be interpreted in the context of what is known of the "forefathers in the faith" [*salaf*] and with reference to the collective wisdom of the classic masters of the spiritual life. But in the final analysis, God deals with the individual as such; and the touchstone of authenticity is not a matter of eating for breakfast what Muḥammad always ate, but of fidelity to God's promptings at this moment.

Perhaps the best way to understand what Ibn ʿAbbād would mean by an authentic view of history in relation to the life of the spirit is to see the authentic as the mid-ground between two extreme positions. On the one hand there is "unquestioning acceptance of authority" [*taqlīd*] on the basis of prestige, numerical strength, or antiquity. On the other stands "innovation" [*bidʿah*], including all manner of factionalism and refusal to seek genuine consensus, as well as the products of the kind of speculative inquiry that is implicitly rooted in intellectual arrogance. As Ibn ʿAbbād indicates clearly and at some length in Letter 3, both are equally treacherous and destructive. Neither tendency truly respects either the lessons of the community's authentic sense of tradition or the integrity of the individual before God. Ibn ʿAbbād would love to envision a thriving, burgeoning community of believers; but, given the vicissitudes of his day and his own conviction of the individual's value, he accepts the saying of one of the ancients: "If on some mountaintop there remained but one person of understanding, that person would constitute the assembled community."

Finally, Ibn ʿAbbād never thinks of the need for reform on the macrocosmic level, that of society and community, without also being intensely aware of the need for a corresponding renewal on the part of the individual. In some cases his thinking seems actually to work the other way around: Look at the individual and the condition of the community will come as less of a surprise. One of the two letters partially dedicated to the issues treated above also deals specifically with the need for continual conversion. Letter 8 in fact begins with a thorough discussion of the manifold aspects of the station of repentance, or conversion [*tawbah*], to which we shall return later. The next section will take a closer look at the individual and at the prospects for a new dawn in the heart of each believer.

Self. "Journey toward God though you be lame and broken" (Letter 2) aptly sums up Ibn 'Abbād's advice to the seeker. Do not become so preoccupied with your human weakness that you collapse in self-pity on the roadside, but do not presume that you can soar on your own wings. A kind of hopeful realism in confronting squarely the most basic facts of the human condition, no matter what the actual situation, is what Ibn 'Abbād calls "proper demeanor" [*ḥusn al-adab*]. This does not refer in itself to any specific behavior, but rather to an overall attitude adaptable to every circumstance, that is, every "spiritual state" the seeker experiences at God's hands. Letter 15 is devoted exclusively to a treatment of a variety of possible "moments" [*awqāt*, a technical term that will reappear shortly], and suggests some particular responses appropriate to each. Our "functional aspects" will focus on several.

There are, however, some constants in Ibn 'Abbād's assumptions about, and insights into, the human person. To begin with, it will be well again to recall that the individual, like all of creation, is a theater of God's "signs." In the words of the Qur'ān: "We [God] will show them Our signs on the horizons and in their very selves, until it becomes clear to them that it is the Truth" [41:53]; and "On the earth there are signs for those of firm faith, and in your very selves. Will you not then see?" [51:20–21]. Secondly, God can and does enlighten the human heart with lights innumerable and unquenchable, and He does so virtually on request from the sincere seeker.

But wherein lies sincerity? What is the price? What are these signs and whither do they point? What is the knowledge of self toward which Ibn 'Abbād strives to help his addressees orient themselves? Three key images of the self in the Letters will provide an approach to such questions as these: the indigent self, the struggling self, and the recipient self. We will look at each in turn, attending as necessary to the most important technical terms Ibn 'Abbād employs, and which I have endeavored to translate with some consistency throughout the Letters.

Every person who makes a sincere and ongoing effort at self-knowledge will, according to Ibn ʿAbbād, have to swallow the bitter pill of recognizing that a virtually bottomless need is a fact of life. Acknowledgement of one's poverty is the other side of the coin of proclaiming God's unity and transcendence. Since Ibn ʿAbbād subscribes to the epistemological proverb "Things are known by their opposites," he is firmly convinced that one can know God's fullness only by first knowing one's own emptiness. Finitude was no more fun for a fourteenth-century Moroccan than it is for a twentieth-century Missourian; neither was the experience of it any less essential to living an authentically human life.

For Ibn ʿAbbād, that means "servanthood" [*ʿubūdiyyah*, a term that might also be translated "worshipfulness"]. But since things are known by their opposites, it will help first to characterize what he regards as "inauthentic." Earlier mention has been made of the notion of self-centeredness, presumptuousness, pretentiousness [*daʿwā*]. This is fundamentally a species of idolatry [*shirk*], for it attributes to the individual human being that which is the prerogative of God alone, namely, self-sufficiency. Presumptuousness is often very subtle and occurs under a variety of masks and guises. It includes all kinds of false humility, for feigned self-effacement is merely another way of garnering praise for oneself. Even delight in good deeds and remorse over evil deeds can be a form of self-centeredness, so long as the individual clings to either of those two responses for security. Service of others through public office or charitable acts can also prove to be self-serving. Likewise the fear of death can be a type of self-centeredness, if the fear is motivated by attachment to this world. Making a pretense of praying to God out of pure devotion, as though one had no need of any of God's gifts (i.e., disdaining prayer of petition), is also a form of *daʿwā*, even when the one who prays that way claims to be motivated by simple trust in God.

To assume the attitude of a servant, on the other hand, is to deal realistically with creatureliness. Commenting on Ibn ʿAṭā' Allāh's saying, "No more is demanded of you than the acknowledgement of your compelling need," Ibn ʿAbbād writes:

> The servant's recognition of his need for God that is requested of him consists in not presuming to possess in himself even the smallest bit of power or capacity for anything, and in not believing that he disposes of any created resource on which to lean or depend. Rather, he considers himself like a shipwrecked person on the point of drowning in the sea, or like a

> traveler lost in the middle of the desert. In other words, he sees no possible help other than that of the Lord, and expects to be saved from perishing by no one except Him.[11]

Once a person has begun more or less habitually to interpret his or her experience in terms of the infinite chasm between God's sufficiency and human poverty, the central issue becomes the struggle to keep the attention focused on the Sought rather than on the seeker. That involves moving always toward "thinking well" of God without ever falling into the trap of self-hatred.

In order to live a life of authentic servanthood, one has to struggle continually against a basic human tendency to rebelliousness. Ibn 'Abbād identifies that tendency with an aspect of human nature traditionally called the *nafs*. The term is variously translated as "carnal or fleshly or sensitive soul," though I have opted for the phrase "lower self." *Da'wā* is the result of failure to struggle against the centrifugal tendency that is most often signified by the term *nafs* (even though the latter word does not *always* carry such a negative connotation). Ibn 'Abbād consistently uses the term to refer to the human propensity to resist God's sovereignty. The lower self is the voice that says "*You* can change your lot in life, *you* are in control." In good times it says, "Nice work!" In adversity, it says, "You don't have to put up with this. Surely you are clever enough to get out of this scrape!"

The struggle lies in arriving at a simple trust in God without shrugging off any culpability for "acting out" one's human weaknesses. One needs to learn both how to acquiesce in human limitations by "leaning into" even the most frightening experiences of "anxiety, restlessness, depression and anguish" (Letter 2), and how to be penitent for one's complicity without assessing one's own guilt. It is up to God to praise and to blame.

Just as the most difficult part of human poverty is that in the end one cannot cling even to the poverty as though it were one's own, so the struggling self has finally to surrender to God's mercy. Ibn 'Abbād likes to quote sayings of the Prophet and of famous saints about God's refusal to lift the burden of rebelliousness from His dearest friends. They must continue the struggle against the lower self knowing that they will sometimes lose the fight. If human beings did not sin, they would be easy prey for something much worse—arrogance, presumptuousness. Even more important for Ibn 'Abbād, if God were to protect all His servants from rebelliousness, there would be none left in need of His mercy and forgiveness. St. Paul was speaking Ibn ʿAbbād's language when he wrote, "God has imprisoned all in rebelliousness, that He might show mercy to all" [Rm 11:32].

What remains after all is the self as recipient pure and simple. Ibn ʿAbbād uses several metaphors to suggest the various ways in which human beings receive and interpret the data of experience. The two most important for an understanding of the present Letters are the images of the heart [*qalb*] and the core of one's being [*ṣadr*]. The first is from a root that can mean "turning forward or backward, going around, etc.," and it is the means by which God makes His light known to the seeker. Ibn ʿAbbād quotes the saying of Ibn ʿAṭā', "The light is the army of the heart just as darkness is the army of the lower self." Heart is therefore in a sense competing with the *nafs*. The second term, *ṣadr*, is a kind of barometer of one's overall spiritual well-being. Drawing on long-standing Ṣūfī usage, Ibn ʿAbbād describes the *ṣadr* as undergoing either expansion, dilation [*inshirāḥ*,] or constriction, narrowness [*ḍīq*]. One could translate *inshirāh aṣ-ṣadr* as "consolation," and its opposite as "desolation"; but I have chosen to retain an equivalent of both words in each instance, so as to distinguish these key phrases from two other terms also often translated expansion/consolation [*basṭ*] and contraction/desolation [*qabḍ*]. *Ṣadr* is related to a root with meanings like "origin, source, emanation." My translation "core of one's being," while not as sleek as I would like, has the advantage of preventing confusion between this term and a host of others in Ṣūfī psychology associated with the "heart, breast, innermost self," and so forth.

In short, if the heart is "polished" (like a mirror) and illumined by God's lights, the core of one's being will be expanded. The first indication that something is wrong interiorly will be the sense of restlessness, anxiety, tepidity, or sadness that Ibn ʿAbbād calls a constriction of the core. It points to the lower self's (temporary) victory over the "army of light," and is a virtually infallible clue to the quality of the spiritual experience a person is currently having to deal with. Without the light in the heart, no one is able to discern God's blessings as such. The seeker stumbles along the way, finding only reason for discouragement, and often falling into the trap of self-reliance.

With these two metaphors of the recipient or experiencing self, our arbitrary distinction between formal and functional aspects in Ibn ʿAbbād's spirituality has begun to blur. Ibn ʿAbbād was a practitioner, not a theoretician; he was far more interested in making suggestions first about how to name one's experience for clarity's sake, and then about what to do about "symptoms" that seemed to point to a lack of light in the heart or a feeling of constriction. The formal and conceptual background outlined thus far becomes much more vital as one encounters the material in the Letters. It is meant to supply, along with the more concrete functional elements to which we now turn, a sort of lexicon for a crash course in conversational 'Abbādian.

b. The Path [*Ṭariqāh*] of the Individual Seeker: Four Functional Aspects

In order to appreciate more fully how Ibn 'Abbād's spirituality *works*, it will be helpful to think of it as answering four critical needs of every seeker of God. His spirituality provides: a way of discerning the presence of God; suggestions as to specific activities that can help one acknowledge and respond to that presence; a "spiritual style" comprised of slightly more generalized "methods" of attentiveness to God; and a way of assessing and, to the extent humanly possible, encouraging and promoting growth from the inauthentic to the authentic. We shall briefly discuss each of the four in turn.

The Presence of God. The seeker faces no greater temptation, in Ibn 'Abbād's estimation, than that of harboring the suspicion—even the outright conviction—that there are times, places, and situations too trying, too small, or too miserable for God to work with. It is one of the subtlest forms of "hidden" *shirk*, for the individual can become so fascinated with human weakness, mortality, and alienation as to be riveted on the self's most negative characteristics and thus unable to turn toward the Lord of the Universe. Ibn 'Abbād's consistent approach to the problem can be summed up in the simple directive "Be a son of the moment." (Arabic is not a sexist language, mind you; if he had been writing to a woman, Ibn 'Abbād would have counseled her to be a daughter of the moment.)

God is the utterly Transcendent, artfully eluding all human categories, and yet near enough to dwell in the heart. God is closer to the individual "than the jugular vein" [Qur'ān 50:16]. The problem is not one of finding God, but of allowing oneself to be found; not one of having God "present," but of being present to God. Every single "spiritual state" is a moment in which to attend to God, and the reader will find these Letters dealing with a variety of instants that are part of every human being's experience as uniquely designed for each by God.

There is no such thing as an exhaustive list of these moments, obviously. Nevertheless, spiritualities have a way of becoming schematized, largely for pedagogical purposes and to assist the seeker in modifying particular types of behavior. In his commentary on Ibn ʿAṭāʾ Allāh's *Book of Wisdom*, for example, Ibn ʿAbbād cites the schema of another of his spiritual predecessors, Abū 'l-ʿAbbās al-Mursī (about whom more will be said in the next major section of the Introduction): "There are four 'moments' of the servant of God and no more: happiness, adversity, virtue, and sin. In each one it is encumbent on you, with regard to God, to perform some one of the duties peculiar to your servitude to Him, one that is meritorious in virtue of His sovereignty."[12] Ibn ʿAbbād's personal analysis of the meaning of moments involves a distinction between external duties and internal duties. The former he associates with religious obligations, such as the fast of Ramaḍān, Pilgrimage, ritual daily prayer—and other related matters to be mentioned in the next section. Of these, Ibn ʿAbbād notes that the law allows for some delay in performance, so that an omission can be made up. But once an inner moment has passed, an opportunity has simply been missed, for it is a spiritual state brought about by a unique inspiration from God, to which one can respond only as it occurs.

All of Letter 9 deals with the problems experienced by a man who is discouraged with his actual condition and with his apparent inability to move beyond it to a state he would rather be in. Ibn ʿAbbād most skillfully guides him toward an appreciation of how it is precisely in and through that state that God has chosen to manifest Himself. It is hard to imagine how Ibn ʿAbbād could take the experience of his directee more seriously. He maintains that attitude of focused concern throughout these Letters.

The Moment's "External" Exigencies. Ibn ʿAbbād is also heir to a strong tradition of religious practice, and he takes that seriously as well. As the individual's experience is in some ways mediated by God's signs in creation, in the community's history, and in the self, so the individual's response is mediated and assisted by the devotional tradition, whose ritualized activities in turn can become further moments in which to experience the presence of God, and so forth.

At this point, the application of the criteria of authenticity becomes somewhat more complex. The historic community of Islam has, in its ongoing consensus and interpretation of its sources, consistently required certain activities of all. In addition it has recommended certain other practices, with emphasis varying according to its several "spiritualities." For Ibn 'Abbād, as for all other Muslims, required practices include the ritual prayer five times daily, fasting through the month of Ramaḍān, almsgiving, pilgrimage to Mecca, and the basic profession of faith ("There is no god but God, and Muḥammad is the Messenger of God"). He recommends in addition a number of other activities, such as meditative reading of the Qur'ān, the use of litanies, invoking blessings on the Prophet, among others. But the mere performance of an act, required or recommended, is never sufficient. It is rather the quality of intention, recollectedness, and attentiveness that is the criterion of authenticity. Given that, Ibn 'Abbād is interested in assessing the actual benefit of deeds of piety for the individual and the community. He looks always for the interior transformation and the enhancement of the individual's relationship to God and to others, with the more obvious external effects subordinate to the less readily discernible affective and moral changes within the individual.

If one can speak of a hierarchy of acts, or a set of criteria by which to set priorities as to the most important religious and devotional activities, I believe the following "principles" implicit in Ibn 'Abbād's advice may provide a useful summary. First, the seeker ought always to attend to the religious deeds incumbent on all Muslims. However, one must keep a wary eye on the interior quality of the act. It is fascinating, for example, that the Pilgrimage, which in some ways symbolizes more than any other activity the life of the spirit well-lived, is the focus of one of Ibn 'Abbād's lengthiest and most searching reflections on the need for a proper inner disposition. In certain cases, the desire to make the Pilgrimage may be a veiled form of self-centeredness. In that case, making the journey would be vitiated by impurity of intention. In other instances, the journey may be a thinly disguised excuse for sidestepping more pressing obligations right at home. Letter 6 examines this issue in detail.

Second, other nonrequired deeds of piety and private devotion are critical to a vibrant spiritual life. However, if the seeker is inclined toward such activities to the detriment of the required duties, then the performance of those supererogatory acts is suspect and may well be inappropriately motivated. In addition, such an important practice as spiritual reading of the Ṣūfī classics can be counterproductive if it is a merely intellectual exercise. Similarly, the reading of the Qur'ān remains fruitless if one is preoccupied with proper pronunciation and enunciation, and so forth.

Third, even one's ordinary occupation can be performed in such a way as to be truly devotional and spiritually profitable. Letters 10, 11, and 14 address the concerns of a teacher of small children who is beset with fears that his occupation may be coming between him and his Lord. Ibn 'Abbād reassures him that his labor is not only not reprehensible but a positive blessing, so long as he realizes that the scruples he is experiencing are not from God.

Finally, Ibn 'Abbād also mentions some occupations that, while they are ostensibly religious, are to be avoided. The aspirant on the Path should leave aside the intellectual curiosity that might lure him into speculative or legal studies. Such involvements are best left to those who have made a profession of them. Letter 4 makes Ibn 'Abbād's position on the matter very clear.

The man to whom Letters 7 through 15 are addressed often asked Ibn 'Abbād to compose some prayers like those of his spiritual predecessors in the Shādhiliyyah order. Nwiya has edited a marvelous meditation on the Divine Names, and I include here a translation of a small portion of that prayer as a sample of one of our author's own favorite devotional practices. It was evidently composed shortly after the period during which these Letters were written.

> O God, direct me toward You through Yourself; grant me, before I come to meet You, strength enough to remain worthy of You.
>
> O Merciful, be merciful to me in your grace and clemency, preserving me from adversity and hardships in relation to You.
>
> O compassionate, show me compassion in allowing me entry into Your Garden [Paradise] and gracing me with nearness and the sight of You.
>
> O Sovereign of this world and the next in perfect and utter Mastery, bring me into the presence of glory and of the kingdom great in power and deeds.
>
> O Holy, remove from me my faults and shortcomings, cleanse me from my sin and sinfulness.

O Source of Peace, keep me safe from every kind of harm and make me one of those who approach you with a pure heart.

O Faithful, keep me faithful on the Day of Awesome Terror, and grant me increase of faith in You to the greatest of my capacity.

O Glorious, place me in your glory among those who come humbly before you, and cause me to strive for the deeds of the glorious ones in your presence.

O Protector, place me under your protection as one who witnesses and sees, and as one who holds fast to your faithfulness and your covenant.

O All-Powerful, bring my state into conformity with your will and let me not lord it over Your servants.

O Majestic, make me among those who are humbled before your magnificence, obedient to your decrees and judgments.

O Creator, create in my heart a love of obedience, and keep me, as one of your creatures, from all injustice and partiality.[13]

The seeker's response to God's presence as revealed in any given "moment" may, in short, take any number of forms. What is needed above all is the kind of self-knowledge that allows an individual to respond, both interiorly and exteriorly, in such a way that the response, first, expresses an awareness of utter poverty before the One who is All-Sufficient; second, advances the struggle against the centrifugal tendencies of the "lower self"; and third, opens the aspirant ever more to God's light in the heart. The question of how the aspirant can "lock into" the bearings of authentic spiritual growth and avoid wandering off course is of great concern to Ibn ʻAbbād. He offers several important observations.

The Path as a Way of Life. "Contemplative vision" [*mushāhadah*] is probably the single most important term Ibn ʻAbbād employs to describe an overall attitude or comprehensive method requisite to the spiritual life. The term refers to a way of experiencing, thinking, feeling without which neither "proper demeanor" [*ḥusn al-adab*] nor "thinking well of God" [*ḥusn aẓ-ẓann*] nor being a "son of the moment" [*ibn al-waqt*] is possible. Letter 9 explores the implications of "contemplative vision" and the lack of it, from several different angles. There Ibn ʿAbbād describes a variety of "moments" and religious activities and explains how the loss of contemplative vision has led his addressee to his current inability to see beneath the surface of his experience. Contemplative vision would allow him to evaluate his circumstances and his responses to them more accurately.

Elsewhere, Ibn ʿAbbād says that there are means to attaining this contemplative vision, but that mere human effort is of no avail, for it is God who decides how a seeker will gradually interiorize this attitude. One can dispose oneself toward it, however, by allowing oneself to be led by God, acknowledging God alone as the cause of all things, and remaining faithful to the Revealed Law. To the question of what can be taken as a sign that contemplative vision has become a habitual mode of living, Ibn ʿAbbād responds that a person who has achieved that state has no need of proof. But if a seeker simply must have a sign, he allows that a peaceful conscience, free from agitation and scruples, will serve; that, however, is a kind of negative indicator and is to be regarded as a lesser indicator.[14]

Ibn ʿAbbād does not have a term that corresponds precisely to the opposite of contemplative vision—he speaks mostly of its loss or lack—but in this instance the "inauthentic" clearly means an attitude that predisposes one to *shirk*, self-centeredness [*daʿwā*], and "thinking badly of God" [*sūʾ aẓ-ẓann*]. A phrase such as "misdirected or false asceticism" might be useful here. Its signs are many: worry about the way things used to be, or fear of what they might become; imposing on oneself excessive austerities and penances and refusing to take legitimate delight in God's gifts; failure to believe that one's actual state is manageable for God; and so forth.

Letter 1 begins with several pages on how God gives the seeker the gift of contemplative vision in stages. And in his commentary on Ibn ʿAṭāʾ Allāh's *Book of Wisdom*, Ibn ʿAbbād quotes the founder of his order, Abū ʾl-Ḥasan ash-Shādhilī, ending the passage with a famous "Sacred Tradition" [a *ḥadīth* or saying attributed to God] that aptly describes the result of contemplative vision. Speaking of how the servant comes to God only after abandoning all initiative, desire, and choice, Shādhilī says:

> When God wishes to have him reach Him, He facilitates it in this way. He makes manifest to him some of the sublime attributes and holy qualities whose divine epiphany hides from the soul of the servant his own attributes and qualities. This serves as a sign that God loves him. Thus He suggests to him the following divine tradition related by the Prophet: "When I [God] love him, I become his own ear with which he hears, his eyes with which he sees, his hand with which he gathers, and his foot with which he walks."[15]

In that state the servant has surrendered his will, wishing only what his Lord desires, and is united with God not by any human effort but through God's gracious mercy. Ibn ʿAbbād notes that contemplative vision as a habitual disposition or level of religious experience is rare indeed.

Assessing and Facilitating Spiritual Growth. Ibn ʿAbbād deals with a wide variety of problems in these Letters, from the qualms of conscience and scruples that can plague a beginner to the more subtle issues that arise as the aspirant advances along the Path. As a spiritual director he is primarily concerned with helping his directees name their immediate experience and its causes, and proceed from there. He observes that some difficulties are the result of laziness, negligence, or spiritual torpor. Sometimes excessive interest in the study of legal casuistry can lead to scepticism, neglect of religious duties, loss of fervor, hardness of heart, and so forth. People who commit errors and sins are of two types: there are those who become terribly discouraged by their inability to live lives free of sinfulness; and there are those who minimize the seriousness of their faults, or absolve themselves altogether of guilt, by appealing to the notion that God has foreordained all things and has thereby relieved the person of both freedom and responsibility. To the first type, Ibn ʿAbbād replies that one ought to give oneself the benefit of the doubt, turn to God in confidence, and give more thought to God's favors than to one's own shortcomings. To the second, he warns that sorrow for sin is necessary, for God does not desire mediocrity.

Ibn ʿAbbād's astuteness and depth as spiritual director, however, becomes most evident in his manner of diagnosing problems more subtle than the ones that describe the human condition in such a general way. Some of the historical background of the tradition of spiritual direction from which Ibn ʿAbbād came will be included in the next major section of this Introduction. The following are some of the elements of that tradition more immediately evident in or suggested by the Letters.

First there is the matter of the need for and availability of personal spiritual direction. According to Paul Nwiya, one important result of the shift toward secondary works in the study of religious law during Ibn ʿAbbād's time is that, among Ṣūfī's, the living tradition of one-to-one contact between the spiritual guide and the aspirant was being supplanted by the use of books. One could claim as his spiritual master any author whose books he had read, just as he could claim to have studied law with any jurist whose books he had studied.[16] Ibn ʿAbbād himself was introduced to the Ṣūfī way through silent meditation and reading, and these he considered the true masters of Ṣūfī initiation. Even when he was a disciple of Ibn ʿĀshir in Salé, he was quite independent; but his shaykh did not hesitate to intervene when he felt Ibn ʿAbbād was heading toward some excess or other.

In Letter 16, our author discusses in a very balanced fashion the question of whether a seeker absolutely must have a spiritual guide [*shaykh*]. No one can simply decide to attach himself to the right director, for a truly learned and perceptive guide is always a gift from God. It is God who decides whether, and when, the aspirant should have individual personal guidance. The process of finding a guide cannot be reduced to a set formula or left to the seeker's whim.

Second, even when a seeker does find a spiritual master, God Himself remains the primary director, guiding the heart with His light. In other words, direction occurs from within the person. Numerous Ṣūfī writings indicate that aspirants can be said to experience God's guidance in two very different ways. God guides some along an active, purgative way. Through long periods of renunciation and discursive meditation, the "wayfarer" [*sālik*] is led upward, from the effects of God's actions in the world, to God's Names, to the contemplation of His Attributes, and finally to God's very Being. God guides others along a more passive, illuminative Path. One who is "drawn" or "attracted" [*majdhūb*] moves quickly and effortlessly, beginning at the Divine Essence and descending to creatures, whom he experiences as having their being "in God." Both ways are God's gifts. The difference is that the first type sees God in creatures while the second sees creatures in God.[17]

Third, given the understanding that God is always the real director of the spirit, certain characteristics of the human relationship need to be kept in mind. The shaykh must treat the seeker like a son, and the aspirant must be totally docile, concealing nothing from the master. The director must never be authoritarian and must be certain he understands what the directee has said before he offers his advice in reply. In Ibn 'Abbād's time there were two types of shaykh. One type provided "instruction" [*ta'līm*] in basic character formation and fundamental requirements of the Revealed Law and the Ṣūfī Path. An aspirant could enlist the services of more than one "instructing shaykh" at a time. The second type provided "education" [*tarbīyah*] rather by example and personal association than by using more standard pedagogical methods. His direction was generally more "directive" and individualized and involved teaching the aspirant his own invocation [*dhikr*], leading him through a forty-day retreat, regulating his daily order (sleeping, eating, times of silence, etc.), and imposing certain ascetical practices. Only one such director could be had at one time. According to Ibn 'Abbād, an aspirant will generally make more rapid progress under a shaykh who is a *majdhūb* than under one who is a *sālik*.[18]

Fourth, whether the seeker gets help from a living director or from the spiritual classics such as those Ibn 'Abbād recommends in his Letters, an awareness of certain signs and touchstones is indispensable for spiritual progress. Already several centuries prior to Ibn 'Abbād, Muslim spiritual writers had developed sophisticated and intricate typologies of spiritual development. Using the metaphors of "stations" (more permanent and achieved in connection with human effort) and "states" (fleeting and purely God's gift), they described the Path as marked off by arrival at certain distinctive levels of spiritual growth. These are meant to serve as general indices of the quality of the seeker's relationship with God, and each has its own unique affective (rather than rational or intellectual) tone. Ibn 'Abbād speaks often of the "stations" of hope, fear, patience, love, resignation, gratitude, contentment, intimate knowledge of God, and so forth. Each is said to have its peculiar manifestations or effects in the aspirant's behavior. Just as such vices as arrogance, hypocrisy, anger, conceit, envy, and rancor are the signs that mark the inauthentic life, so the stations and states are the milestones on the journey toward the authentic.

Ibn 'Abbād is truly expert in the art of discernment of spirits. He distinguishes authentic discernment from scruples and other forms of harmful interpretation of the interior life. The main difference is that the latter continue to badger the aspirant even after he has heeded them, whereas praiseworthy discernment, once heeded, leaves the seeker in peace. The Letters go into considerable detail as they discuss the addressees' alternating experiences of "contraction" and "expansion," desolation and consolation. Though there is not sufficient space here to delve further into Ibn 'Abbād's method, the reader will readily pick out the clues and concrete applications of the method at work in these Letters. Now, before exploring the context and sources of Ibn 'Abbād's spirituality, a short look at how he views the goal of the spiritual journey.

c. The Mystic Truth [*Ḥaqīqah*] as Goal

As Ibn 'Abbād indicates several times in the present Letters, some of his contemporaries who occupied themselves with the study of religious law [*fuqahā'*, "jurists"] considered the goal of the Ṣūfī Path incompatible with the requirements of the Revealed Law. He expresses his amazement that the jurists could so divide and compartmentalize the faith as to think the Revealed Law and the Mystic Truth are opposed to each other, and see a lack of continuity between the external, apparent dimension of the Revealed Law and its interior, less obvious meanings. In Letters 1 and 30 of the "Larger Collection" (RK), Ibn 'Abbād makes several very clear statements concerning the interrelationships of the Revealed Law, the Path, and the Mystic Truth. First and most directly, "The Revealed Law is the Mystic Truth and the Mystic Truth is the Revealed Law; anyone who violates the Revealed Law goes against the Mystic Truth and whoever goes against the Mystic Truth transgresses the Revealed Law."

Second, he describes the Ṣūfī Path as the interiorization of the Qur'ān and the Example of the Prophet.

> Sufism essentially amounts to the servant's conducting himself according to his Lord's good pleasure and His love for the servant. Sufism has two parts: doctrine and action. The doctrine purifies the beliefs of people of faith and the intentions of those who are obliged to practice the Revealed Law. Action in turn tends toward more appropriate conduct in the presence of the Lord of the Universe, so that one assumes the attitude of a servant before Him at all times and in every circumstance. In short, Sufism is tantamount to the true religion and the Straight Path that our Prophet Muḥammad came to preach. . . . If that, then is Sufism, one can hardly imagine that any-

> one who believes in God and the Last Day could neglect it or substitute something else for it.

Herein, according to Paul Nwiya, lies Ibn ʿAbbād's originality.

Third, the spiritual director summarizes in one fascinating paragraph the meaning of the Mystic Truth:

> The substance of the Mystic Truth comes into being when a human being regards himself as nothing, both in himself and his knowledge, awarenesses and all his qualities. Now only the Laws revealed by the Prophets and the Messengers are able to conform to such a Reality. Their revelations contain certain truths that the intellect can arrive at unaided and others that are beyond the power of reasoning. All these truths are, nevertheless, professed by the faithful as one single entity, and it is their unity that nullifies all [merely human] reasoning and opinion. For the unity of that which is intelligible and that which surpasses reason gives rise to a third reality which is neither intelligible nor beyond reason, and is thus outside either of these categories; and if it is neither of these, then the human being, with his knowledge and awareness, is reduced to nothing in the face of it. He thus becomes like a blind person to whom the way is shown and who lets himself be guided. Now the Mystic Truth is just that.[19]

Fourth, in Letter 3 of this translation, Ibn ʿAbbād says quite simply, "Their goal is to focus their hearts on their Lord and become totally immersed in experiencing and being near to Him." Toward that goal the seeker moves through ever-increasing gifts of what I have translated as "intimate knowledge." The term *maʿrifah* has frequently been rendered as "gnosis," with its related active participle [*ʿārif*] translated as "gnostic." I have preferred "intimate knowledge" and "mystic" to avoid the connotations of elitism, foreign to Ibn ʿAbbād's thinking, often associated with "gnosticism" and its cognates.

Finally, if Ibn ʿAbbād were using our working definition of spirituality to help orient his directees, he might very well call the Mystic Truth "The Authentic" or "Authenticity Itself." "Mystic Truth" is, alas, only slightly less clumsy; but so, I believe, are "Divine Reality" or simply "The Reality," terms frequently used in translations. "Mystic Truth" has the benefit of preserving both the connotations of "truth" in the word's root [*ḥaqq*], and the idea that it is the goal of the kind of experience that can fairly be called "mystical" (so long as one keeps in mind Ibn 'Abbād's decidedly nonelitist usage of classical terminology).

2. The Sources and Historical Context of Ibn 'Abbād's Spirituality

Up to this point I have attempted to provide a sketch of Ibn 'Abbād's spirituality as specifically *Islamic*, with some indication of those features that mark it as distinctively "'Abbādian" as well. In this section the focus shifts to more characteristics of the latter sort, namely, qualities and attitudes that define Ibn 'Abbād's as one of a number of spiritualities that have developed within the larger Islamic tradition. From here on the reader will be asked to step back more deliberately into the world of the fourteenth-century Moroccan Muslim. It is a world populated by unfamiliar personalities who wrote books long lost and debated issues now obscure in their antiquity. But it is equally a world of which enough is known to allow us to discern important threads woven into Ibn 'Abbād's Islamic heritage and to appreciate something of the religious, intellectual, and cultural forces that shaped his world view.

In the earlier section on Ibn 'Abbād's view of history, passing mention was made of the political, economic, and social situation. The following pages will consider four facets of the history of Islamic spirituality as they relate to Ibn 'Abbād's religious background. First, some general background on the history of Sufism to the thirteenth century will highlight several variant emphases within the tradition. Second, a look at developments in North African and Spanish Sufism will provide the context for the third facet, namely, the origins and growth of the religious order to which Ibn 'Abbād belonged. Special attention will be given to the founder of the Shādhiliyyah Order, Abū 'l-Ḥasan ash-Shādhilī, and to Ibn 'Aṭā' Allāh, third head of the order. That order's arrival in Morocco will, finally, set the scene for Ibn 'Abbād's own life.

a. The History of Sufism to the Thirteenth Century

Paul Nwiya has proposed a three-part analysis of the material.[20] The first period, which Annemarie Schimmel calls the "formative period,"[21] runs from the time of the Prophet—or, using Sulamī's count of the "five generations," beginning with Ḥasan al-Baṣrī (d. 728)—down to about 950.

The earliest Ṣūfīs sought to interiorize their response to God, and to foster in themselves an ever keener awareness of the changes this interiorization effected within the depths of their beings. They used the language of the Qur'ān to express their new discoveries, but developed a "symbolic hermeneutic" (Nwiya's term) as distinguished from the literalism of the Sunnī jurists. Both the Ṣūfīs and the jurists were directing their attention to the same Revealed Data, but they used different modes of expression to describe their findings. Nwiya believes that the major discovery of the early Ṣūfīs was that both in the Qur'ān and in God's "signs" in creation as a whole, one can find an inner meaning whose implications go far beyond those of the exoteric, literal, apparent meaning.[22]

Ibn 'Abbād's letters mention a number of Ṣūfīs from the formative period, all of whom will be described briefly in notes as they appear in the translation of the Letters. Among them are: Abū Yazīd al-Bisṭāmī, Bishr al-Ḥāfī, Dhū 'n-Nūn Miṣrī, Al-Ḥallāj, Ḥasan al-Baṣrī, Ibn Khafīf, Ibrāhīm ibn Adham, al-Junayd, Ibrāhīm al-Khawāṣṣ, al-Muḥāsibī, Nūrī, Ruwaym, Sahl at-Tustarī, Sarī as-Saqaṭī, Shiblī, Sumnūn al-Muḥibb. Of the personalities Ibn 'Abbād mentions by name or quotes in the letters translated here, a very high percentage are Ṣūfīs from the formative period.

Nwiya labels the century and a half from 950 to 1100 the period of "elucidation," Schimmel, that of "consolidation."[23] If in the first period the Ṣūfīs began to call attention to both the inwardness of their experience of God's revelation and the diversity of the experience's manifestations, the second period witnessed the standardization of Ṣūfī vocabulary and practice. Collections of the writings, deeds, and sayings of the earliest Ṣūfīs led to the development of typologies of personal religious experience. Those "manuals" also provided for the wider public a wealth of information about some of Islam's most engaging personalities.

For the benefit of those who began to feel that some Ṣūfīs were a bit too eccentric, given their occasionally bizarre behavior and statements that sometimes appeared to border on blasphemy or self-deification, treatises in defense of Sufism began to appear. Ibn 'Abbād mentions two such works several times: the *Food of Hearts* [*Qūt al-Qulūb*] by Abū Ṭālib al-Makkī (d. 996); and the *Treatise on Sufism* [*Risālah*] of al-Qushayrī (d. 1072). Although he does not mention Abū Naṣr as-Sarrāj

(d. 988) in these Letters, he does cite him by name (referring to material in the *Kitāb al-Luma'*) in his commentary on Ibn 'Aṭā' Allāh's *Book of Wisdom.*[24] These were three among many in a line of writings that preceded another work that profoundly influenced Ibn 'Abbād, *The Revival of the Religious Sciences* [*Ihyā 'Ulūm ad-Dīn*] by Abū Ḥāmid al-Ghazālī (d. 1111). These treatises on the interior life in effect systematized typologies of spiritual development that had originated in real-life observation of the ways God leads His servants. Once systematized, the typologies were open to misapplication. Instead of using them as general guidelines and descriptions of the spiritual life, some were inclined to impose the levels and categories in cookie-cutter fashion on all and sundry aspirants to the spiritual life. Still, the benefits of preserving the rich Ṣūfī tradition more than outweighed the dangers inherent in codifying real-life experience.

Two trends emerged during the third period of Sufism's history, from about 1100 on. One was a movement toward the institutionalization of what had been systematized in the treatises. The other was a tendency to intellectualize. According to Nwiya, the development of speculative Sufism from the late twelfth to the middle of the thirteenth century constitutes a veritable renaissance of Sufism. For that he credits the Persians, Suhrawardī Maqtūl of Aleppo (d. 1191) and Rūzbihān Baqlī of Shīrāz (d. 1209), along with the Maghribī school of Ibn Masarrā of Almeria (d. 931), which came to an end with Ibn 'Arabī (d. 1240). An excursus into the realm of speculative Sufism would be fascinating, but it is not immediately germane to our study of the very nonspeculative Ibn 'Abbād. No thinking person in any society can totally escape the spell of powerful intellectual currents. For the moment, however, it will suffice to mention that Ibn 'Abbād was surely aware of the intellectual side of Sufism. He refers explicitly several times to one of the followers of the School of Almeria, Ibn al-'Arīf (1088–1141).[25]

The institutionalization of Sufism may be said to have occurred "definitively" when groups that had existed more or less informally since the eighth century became large enough to require a space bigger than a home, and exclusive enough to require a space more private than a mosque. A second mark of institutionalization appeared when the bond between the aspirant and the adept evolved from a teacher-pupil relationship to a master-disciple covenant. A third feature is that requirements for membership were eventually fixed in a written "constitution" or charter for the various orders.

Until the latter half of the twelfth century, the Ṣūfī groups remained rather fluid. Special buildings that had until then served as way-stations for wandering Ṣūfis gradually came to be used as permanent dwellings. Spiritual masters associated themselves with a particular place; and as their reputations spread abroad, Ṣūfis from elsewhere came to sit at their feet and express their willingness to commit themselves to a time of rigorous discipline under the shaykh's direction. J. S. Trimingham explains the relationship between architecture and institutionalization in Sufism:

> Whereas the *khānaqāhs* were little more than hostels for Ṣūfis . . . and *ribāṭs* had an indefinite character as the establishment of a teacher or preacher, not necessarily a Ṣūfī, *zāwiyas* were centres for a genuine teaching shaikh, whose successors consciously carried on his particular teaching and method. Whereas appointments to the headship of *khānaqāhs* was made by secular authorities, the superior of a *zāwiya* was elected by the *ikhwān* [brethern] and it was in these that hereditary succession began.[26]

The names of two men associated with the founding of two of the earliest formally constituted orders ought to be mentioned here. 'Abd al-Qādir al-Jilānī (1088–1166), known as the "shaykh of the East," is often credited with founding the first Ṣūfī order. "Eponymous ancestor" is probably a more appropriate term than founder. The Qādiriyyah Order made its way as far west as Morocco by the late twelfth century.[27] Shihāb ad-Dīn Abū Hafṣ 'Umar as-Suhrawardī (1145–1234) is the second man. He wrote *The Benefits of Intimate Knowledge* ['*Awārif al-Ma'ārif*], a work that Ibn 'Abbād recommends highly, and was the nephew of 'Abd al-Qāhir as-Suhrawardī (d. 1168), who is generally considered the founder of the Suhrawardiyyah Order. Even though the uncle's order did not gain wide popularity in Ibn 'Abbād's part of the world, the nephew's writing merited a place of honor in Ibn 'Abbād's advice to a friend who was looking for profitable reading on Sufism.[28]

Sufism developed largely in three separate geographical areas, each with its own distinctive flavor. The three areas are Iraq, Khurāsān or Central Asia, and the Maghrib. Iraqi Sufism is often associated with the "sober" spirit of Junayd of Baghdad (d. 910); Khurāsānī with that of the "intoxicated" Abū Yazīd al-Bisṭāmī (d. 874). Trimingham characterizes them further as safe/suspect, conformist/illuminate, theist/monist, based on trust/blame, recommending companionship/solitude, directed by an earthly shaykh/spirit shaykh.[29] Maghribī Sufism has received far less scholarly attention than either Iraqi or Khurāsānī, perhaps because Maghribī Ṣūfīs contributed little to Sufism during the periods of formation and consolidation. Moreover, Maghribī developments during the third phase of Sufism's history rarely spread beyond Spain and North Africa. By the time Sufism took firm root in the Maghrib, it had already been flourishing farther to the east for nearly four centuries.

One significant result of this state of affairs seems to be that, whereas in the East Sufism grew up in a kind of sibling rivalry with the sciences of Tradition and Law, a rather conservative school of jurisprudence had been well established in the West for quite some time before Sufism became a force to be reckoned with there. Some of the most prominent Eastern Ṣūfīs were, to be sure, members of the most conservative of the law schools, the Ḥanbalite. But it may still not be a gross oversimplification to say that the institutions of orthodoxy in the West never had quite as much to fear from Sufism as they did in the East. I. Goldziher believes that Western Sufism tended to be less nihilistic than Eastern Sufism, because the former was more immediately linked with the jurists from the outset.[30]

In a similar vein, Annemarie Schimmel observes that "perhaps the western Muslim world was generally more inclined toward a more philosophical or theosophical interpretation of religion, as contrasted to the enthusiastic, enraptured attitude of many of the mystics in the eastern countries—trends that can be observed in the peculiarities of some mystical fraternities as well."[31]

Some of the categories used here to describe Sufism, such as "sobriety" and "intoxication," were invented by the Ṣūfīs themselves. Some are academic superimpositions. What is important to keep in mind is that Ibn ʿAbbād, and many other Ṣūfī sources before him, quotes sayings and cites anecdotes of a Junayd and a Bisṭāmī cheek by jowl without ever suggesting that the advice of the "sober" mystic ought to be heeded, while that of the "intoxicated" mystic is to be disregarded. He uses illustrative material from Ṣūfīs of every sort, and all as though they carried equal weight.

b. Development of Maghribī Sufism

Ibn Masarrā of Cordova (883–931) was the first Western Ṣūfī to begin a "school" of mystical thought. But his style of thinking, with its tendency toward a type of illuminationism, was not widely accepted.

Even in Spain, inclined to speculative thought almost as much as North Africa was to jurisprudence, it was not until a century and a half after Ibn Masarrā that such bright lights as Ibn Tufayl (d. 1185) and Ibn Rushd (d. 1198) began to shine in the intellectual firmament. Nearly all of those Iberian luminaries eventually left Spain for North Africa and the Middle East. Ibn al-ʻArīf (1088–1141) kept the spirit of Ibn Masarrā alive in the so-called School of Almeria, and was the first Western scholar to interpret Ghazālī's writings for Western Muslims. Ibn al-ʻArīf suffered for his convictions, however, and he too died in Morocco.[32] Had it not been for the patronage of the Almoravid and Almohad sulṭāns at the court in Marrakesh, the contributions of many great Iberian Muslims might well have been lost.

Abū Yaʻazzā (d. 1176) has been called the "Spiritual Father of Western Sufism." He came to Marrakesh in 1146. Some years later he moved to Fez, where he and a certain Muḥammad ad-Daqqāq initiated into Sufism a young man from Seville who would come to be known as the "Shaykh of the West." That youth was Abū Madyan (1126–1198), destined to be the spiritual grandfather of ash-Shādhilī. Ironically, the very Almohad sulṭān who did not hesitate to invite to his court scholars famed for their intellectual attainments was afraid of Abū Madyan's popularity. The sulṭān summoned the Ṣūfī to Marrakesh, but Abū Madyan died en route in Tlemcen. He became that city's patron saint.[33]

Apart from his continued general popularity as a saintly presence down through the time of Ibn ʻAbbād, and the survival of his Ṣūfī teaching in a cluster of orders that look to him as their founder, Abū Madyan's chief interest for us here is that he seems to have exercised a significant formative influence on ash-Shādhīlī—at least indirectly. Ibn Mashīsh (d. 1228) was Abū Madyan's pupil, and ash-Shādhilī was Ibn Mashīsh's most famous disciple. Shādhīlī (1196–1258) was born in northern Morocco among a Berber tribe that still exhibited the kind of separatist tendencies one might associate with the Kharijites of former ages. Abū Madyan had attempted to Islamicize the tribe through his Ṣūfī teaching, and Ibn Mashīsh was later murdered by an unreceptive member of that tribe. After ash-Shādhilī received the patched frock [*khirqah*] from another of Abū Madyan's disciples, Abū ʻAbd Allāh ibn Muḥammad ibn Ḥarāzim of Fez (d. 1236), he set out to find the "Spiritual Pole" or "Axis" [*quṭb*, a title bestowed on the man judged most holy in all the world]. One shaykh told Shādhīlī he would find the Pole in the West. When the young man met Ibn Mashīsh in Fez, he knew he had discovered the pivot of the universe. Ibn Mashīsh would later bequeath the august office to Shādhilī.

A. M. M. Mackeen describes the spirituality of Ibn Mashīsh. His theology revolved around four key notions: the unity of God as realized through asceticism; fear of punishment; belief in God's omnipresence; and immersion in awareness of God's attributes. Ibn Mashīsh emphasized the fulfillment of one's obligatory religious duties and detachment from ambition. He taught that the secret of intimate knowledge [*ma'rifah*] is in coming to know the cosmic secret of the Prophet Muḥammad as final cause of all creation. By that means one can realize union with God.[34]

Ibn Mashīsh's only extant writing is a meditation on the Prophet. The subject is one dear to the heart of Ibn 'Abbād, and the text is rare enough to be included here. The translation is that of Titus Burckhardt.

> O my God [*Allāhumma*], bless him from whom derive the secrets and from whom gush forth the lights, and in whom rise up the realities, and into whom descended the sciences of Adam, so that he hath made powerless all creatures, and so that understandings are diminished in his regard, and no one amongst us, neither predecessor nor successor, can grasp him.
>
> The gardens of the spiritual world [*malakūt*] are adorned with the flower of his beauty, and the pools of the world of omnipotence [*al-jabarūt*] overflow with the outpouring of his lights. There existeth nothing that is not linked to them, even as it was said: Were there no mediator, everything that dependeth on him would disappear! [Bless him, O my God,] by a blessing such as returneth to him through Thee from Thee, according to his due.
>
> O My God, he is Thine integral secret, that demonstrateth Thee, and Thy supreme veil, raised up before Thee.
>
> O my God, join me to his posterity and justify me by Thy reckoning of him. Let me know him with a knowledge that saveth me from the wells of ignorance and quencheth my thirst at the wells of virtue.

Carry me on his way, surrounded by Thine aid, towards Thy presence.

Strike through me at vanity, so that I may destroy it. Plunge me in the oceans of Oneness [*al-aḥadīyah*], pull me back from the sloughs of *tawḥīd*, and drown me in the pure source of the ocean of Unity [*al-waḥdah*], so that I neither see nor hear nor am conscious nor feel except through it. And make of the Supreme Veil the life of my spirit, and of his spirit the secret of my reality, and of his reality all my worlds, by the realization of the First Truth.

O First, O Last, O Outward, O Inward, hear my petition, even as Thou heardest the petition of Thy servant Zacharia; succour me through Thee unto Thee, support me through Thee unto Thee, unite me with Thee, and come in between me and other-than-Thee: Allāh, Allāh, Allāh! Verily He who hath imposed on thee the Qur'ān for a law, will bring thee back to the promised end [Qur'ān 28:85].

Our Lord, grant us mercy from Thy presence, and shape for us right conduct in our plight [Qur'ān 18:10].

Verily God and His angels bless the Prophet; O ye who believe, bless him and wish him peace [Qur'ān 33:56].

May the graces [*ṣalawāt*] of God, His peace, His salutations, His Mercy and His blessings [*barakāt*] be on our Lord Muḥammad, Thy servant, Thy prophet and Thy messenger, the un-lettered prophet, and on his family and on his companions, [graces] as numerous as the even and the odd and as the perfect and blessed words of our Lord.

Glorified be thy Lord, the Lord of Glory, beyond what they attribute unto Him, and peace be on the Messengers. Praise be to God, the Lord of the worlds [Qur'ān 37:180–2].[35]

This is the kind of prayer Ibn 'Abbād has in mind when he recommends to his directee that he devoutly call down blessings on the Prophet.

c. The Shādhiliyyah Order

The Shādhiliyyah Order's genesis occurred in two stages, in Tunis and in Egypt. Ibn Mashīsh advised Abū 'l-Ḥasan to go into retreat in a cave near the village of Shādhila, between Tunis and Qayrawān. Shādhilī did so, but would occasionally emerge to preach, and he began to gather a following. In 1240 he went to Tunis. There, with the support of the Ḥafṣid sulṭān, Abū Zakariyyah (1228–1249 rule), he forged the beginnings of the order with the "Forty Companions." Among those were a certain aṣ-Ṣaqallī (not the man Ibn 'Abbād quotes at length in Letter 8) and a still more important figure, Abū 'l-'Abbās al-Mursī (1219–1287). Shādhilī's rapid successes evidently angered local religious scholars, so in either 1244 or 1252, he moved to Alexandria. Aṣ-Ṣaqallī remained behind as spokesman and correspondent in Tunis. The order proceeded to grow apace in Egypt under its first three shaykhs: Shādhilī himself, al-Mursī, and Ibn 'Aṭā' Allāh of Alexandria (1252–1309).[36]

According to Nwiya, Ibn Mashīsh had been accused of heresy. Because he was an Idrīsid, he was associated with Shi'ite views—or at any rate, views regarded as not entirely "orthodox"—that had formerly been linked with the Idrīsid dynasty (c. 788–985). Shādhilī also spoke of a spiritual succession in terms that were difficult for the Sunnī authorities to accept. Al-Mursī later spelled out the precise nature of the succession more explicitly, claiming that the order was neither of East nor West, but derived lineally from 'Alī's son (and Muḥammad's grandson) Ḥasan. Mursī was thus indicating that the succession of spiritual masters in the order was founded, not on the transmission of the *Khirqah*, but on the guidance by which God connects his servants spiritually with the Prophet. This theory was quite different from those of earlier Sunnī orders, and the departure signaled the beginning of a new type of mystical spirituality.

The new theory of succession held that Shādhilī himself was "incarnated" in his successors to leadership of the order. The Shaykh was no longer merely a leader who handed on a doctrine; he transmitted his very self in his capacity as pivot of the universe [*quṭb*].[37] When Mursī took over as shaykh in 1258, therefore, he considered himself above the jurists; for both he and Shādhilī regarded only experiential knowledge of God—not mere intellectual attainment—as the only genuine knowledge. Among the favorite books of both Shādhilī and Mursī were Al-Ḥakīm at Tirmidhī's (d. c. 932) *Seal of the Saints* [*Khatm al-Awliyā'*] and Niffarī's (d. 965) *Book of Stayings* [*Kitāb al-Mawāqif*]. The *Seal* developed a theory whereby sainthood is shown to have a hierarchical structure and a pinnacle [the *quṭb*] or "seal," just as there is a seal of prophethood, namely, Muḥammad. The "Pole" is thus accorded a status roughly parallel to that of the Prophet himself. Niffarī's unusual work likewise supports the idea that a mystic can, like Muḥammad, become close enough to God to converse with Him.[38]

One of the best ways to capture the atmosphere of any spirituality is to experience the tone and mood of the prayers it has produced. In Letter 13, Ibn 'Abbād recommends that his correspondent use the "Great Litany" of ash-Shādhilī, and praises the prayer's benefits lavishly. Here is a translation of ash-Shādhilī's celebrated "Litany of the Sea," which the shaykh used to pray during his many crossings of the Red Sea on his way to and from pilgrimage to Mecca. The litany has remained popular down to modern times. Ibn Baṭṭūṭa, one of Ibn 'Abbād's contemporaries, thought it important enough to include the prayer in his *Travels.* The translation is that of H. A. R. Gibb:

> O God, O Exalted, O Mighty, O Forbearing, O All-knowing, Thou art my Lord and Thy knowledge is my sufficiency. How excellent a lord is my Lord, how excellent a sufficiency my sufficiency. Thou aidest whom Thou wilt, for Thou art the Powerful, the Compassionate. We pray Thee to guard us from sin in our movements and stillnesses, our words and designs, and in the stirring of doubts, of unworthy suggestions and of vain imaginings, that veil from our hearts the perception of things unseen. Verily *the Believers have been tried and grievously shaken, and when the time-servers and the sick-hearted say, "The promises of God and His Apostle to us are naught but delusion,"* do Thou establish us and succour us, and subject to us this sea as Thou didst subject the sea unto Moses, and as Thou didst subject the fire to Abraham, and as Thou didst subject the mountains and the iron to David, and as Thou didst subject the wind and the demons and the jinn to Solomon. Subject to us every sea that is Thine on earth and in heaven, in the world of sense and in the invisible world, the sea of this life and the sea of the life to come. Subject us to everything, O Thou in Whose Hand is the rule over all. *Kāf-Hā-Yā-'Ayn-Ṣad.* Succour us, for *Thou art the best of those that open the way;* forgive us our sins, for *Thou art the best of pardoners;* show mercy upon us, for *Thou art the best of those that show mercy;* give us our daily bread,

for *Thou art the best of sustainers.* Guide us, and *deliver us from the hand of evildoers*, and grant us a *fair wind* according to Thy Knowledge; waft it upon us from *the treasures of Thy Mercy*, and carry us thereon with conveyance of Thy favour, [granting us] therewith preservation from sin and wellbeing in our spiritual and our material life and in the life to come; *verily Thou art disposer of all things.* O God, *smooth for us* our affairs; give peace to our hearts and our bodies, and grant us health and wellbeing in our spiritual and our material life. Be Thou our Companion in our journey, and Guardian of our households in our absence. Blot out the faces of our enemies, and transform them into vile creatures in the place where they be; then shall they not be able to go nor to come against us. *If We will, We shall blot out their sight, and they shall hasten with one another to the Bridge [over Hell]; how then shall they perceive? If We will, We shall transform them in their place and they shall not be able to go forth nor shall they return. Yā-Sīn. Faces shall be deformed. 'Ayn-Mīm. Faces shall be humbled before the Living, the Self-Subsistent, and frustrated is he who bears a burden of wrong-doing. Ṭā-Sīn. Ḥā-Mīm. 'Ayn-Sīn-Qāf. He hath let loose the two seas that meet together, between them is a barrier, they cannot pass. Ḥā-Mīm* [seven times]. *The matter is decreed, Divine aid is at hand, against us they shall not be victorious. Ḥā-Mīm. The revelation of the Book is from God, the Mighty, the All-knowing, Who pardoneth sin and acceptance, Whose chastisement is heavy, the Long-suffering; there is no god but He, to Him is the way* [of all flesh]. *In the name of God* is our door, *Blessed is He* is our walls, *Yā-Sīn* is our roof, *Kāf-Hā-Yā-'Ayn-Ṣad* is our sufficiency, *Ḥā-Mīm-'Ayn-Sīn-Qāf* is our defence. And *God will suffice thee against them, for He is the Hearing, the Knowing.* The curtain of the Throne is extended over us, the Eye of God is watching us, in the Might of God none can harm us. *God is behind them, encompassing! Nay, it is a glorious Qur'ān in a Preserved Tablet.* God is the best in keeping, and *He is the most Merciful of them that show mercy. Verily my patron is God, who hath sent down the Book, and He upholdeth the cause of the righteous. My sufficiency is God, other than He there is no god; upon Him have I put my trust and He is the Lord of the Glorious Throne. In the Name of God*, with Whose Name nothing that is on earth or in heaven shall suffer harm, and *He is the Hearing, the Knowing. Each one has attendant angels before him, watching over him at the command*

> *of God*. "There is no Power nor Might save in God, the High, the Great."[39]

Constance Padwick notes that the Prophet is said to have taught this Litany to Shādhilī in a dream. The shaykh then gathered his followers around him, and told them to have their children memorize the prayer. It was apparently meant to carry a kind of magical, apotropaic power, in addition to its considerable devotional value.[40] Note the difference between the almost talisman-like quality of the litany, and the following prayer of ash-Shādhilī, which approaches God in much the same way Ibn 'Aṭā' Allāh prays in his aphorisms (to be discussed shortly):

> My God, if I ask Thee for succour, I have asked something beside Thee. If I ask for what Thou hast guaranteed to me I show suspicion of Thee. If my heart rests in aught else but Thee I have been guilty of the sin of association [*shirk*]. Thine attributes in their majesty are above contingency, how then can I be with Thee? They are transcendent of causes, how then can I be near to Thee? They are exalted above the dust of earth, how then can my stay be other than Thee?[41]

Several distinctive characteristics of the Shādhiliyyah Order's spirituality emerge from the earliest evidence of the order's existence. In addition to their belief that the Pole or axis of the universe would always be a member of the order, there was the firm tenet that membership in the order is foreordained from eternity. The Shādhiliyyah did not at first have a distinctive ritual or vocal public prayer formula. They did not withdraw from society or wear clothes that would mark them as poor, and they were not a mendicant order.[42] For these and other similar reasons, Mackeen remarks that "it is a fact of basic importance that the Shādhiliyya was born out of an urban surrounding, not necessarily in revolt against it but as an outcome of the existing patterns of politico-religious and economic life."[43]

If one can judge from Trimingham's descriptions of more recent communal *dhikr* [invocation] gatherings of the order, the Shādhiliyyah have evidently drifted over the centuries toward more ecstatic expression and experience;[44] but the mood seems to have been much more sober for at least the first century and a half. Still there has been a fundamental continuity in the order's spirituality. As A. Schimmel writes, the original teaching of the order "appealed neither to the lower classes, who needed more exciting means of getting onto the Path, nor to the poets, but is primarily connected with the middle class, the officials and civil servants who were trained in the Shādhiliyya method to fulfill their duties carefully. It is revealing that one of the few modern orders that still attracts new disciples in Egypt and gives them a thorough training in spiritual education, is an offshoot of the Shādhiliyya, an order that inspired man to a sanctification of his daily life."[45]

An important part of "spiritual education" has to do with the process of "affiliation," or the tracing of one's spiritual lineage back to the first spiritual master. According to a Shādhiliyyah manual from about 1909, there are four grades in the training:

> The first is by the handclasp, the allocation of graduated *dhikr* tasks, investment with the frock and with the turban-tassel; purely as a means of meriting benediction and affiliation.
>
> The second concerns training in the tradition (through a reliable chain of transmitters) and consists of reading the writings of the order without receiving any explanation of the meaning; and this similarly is solely for the purpose of meriting the benediction and the affiliation.
>
> The third is training in understanding (scrutiny of internal evidence) and consists of an exposition of the books in order to grasp their meaning. This likewise does not involve any practice in them [i.e., the actual methods].
>
> These three sections as a rule are the only ones normally involved, and there is no objection to the trainee having a number of shaykhs to guide him to the best of their ability.
>
> The fourth is the undertaking of the actual training [*tadrīb*], receiving instruction [*tahdhīb*] and undergoing progressive development through service, by the ways of self-mortification [*mujāhadah*], leading to enlightenment [*mushāhadah*, rendered as contemplation or contemplative vision" in the Letters translated here] and absorption of self into the Unity [*al-fanā' fī 't-tawḥīd*] and subsistence in it [*al-baqā' bihi*]. This process the as-

pirant must not undertake except with his exemplar's permission.[46]

As a spiritual director and local leader of the Shādhiliyyah, Ibn 'Abbād was concerned with these very issues, although not usually in so systematic or schematic a fashion. His discussion of the role of the spiritual director, in Letter 16, indicates that he had a very flexible notion of "membership" in the order.

As so often happens in human institutions, the "founder" of the Shādhiliyyah bequeathed a spirit rather than a framework for an edifice. He left the institutionalization and propagation of that spirit to his followers. Mursī was the first to put the order in an exclusive dwelling when he gave the group its own monastery and mosque in Alexandria. Ibn 'Aṭā' Allāh was the first to capture the spirit in writing, especially in his biographical sketches of Shādhilī and Mursī and in his *Ḥikam* [*The Book of Wisdom*]. Ibn 'Aṭā' wrote that Mursī's role in the order was "that of propagating the learning of Shaykh Abū 'l-Ḥaṣan [ash-Shādhilī], of diffusing its lights and expounding clearly its mysteries, in such a way that people flocked to him from all over the land."[47] But it was to the enormous popularity of the *Book of Wisdom* that the order owed in great measure its return to North Africa, whence it had once been banished.

Ibn 'Aṭā' was born about 1250 at Alexandria. His father and grandfather were both Mālikite jurists;[48] and although neither of them was particularly enchanted with the Ṣūfī movement initially, the father evidently warmed up to Sufism after he met Shādhilī. Victor Danner suggests that Ibn 'Aṭā' 's father was quite likely a disciple of both Shādhilī and Mursī.[49] Ibn 'Aṭā' himself remained suspicious of the Ṣūfīs for some time, so steeped was he in law and traditional studies. Nwiya theorizes that he eventually changed his attitude as a result of conversations with companions of Mursī. Around 1276 the young Ibn 'Aṭā' met Mursī face to face. That began a relationship that would continue for about twelve years, during which Mursī would guide Ibn 'Aṭā' through a series of personal crises. As mentioned in the earlier section The Presence of God, Mursī explained that the believer can experience only one of four states at any given time: blessings, tribulation, obedience, disobedience. God treats his servants in one of the first two ways, and the servants respond in one of the second two. When one receives blessings, God expects gratitude; when one experiences trials, God expects an acknowledgement of His goodness; if one is disobedient, God expects His servant to seek pardon.

One of Ibn 'Aṭā' 's personal dilemmas was similar to a quandary in which one of Ibn 'Abbād's correspondents also found himself: Should the aspiring Ṣūfī continue to associate with the jurists? Shaykh Mursī assured his advisee, in accord with the distinctive approach of the order, that he need not terminate any of his ordinary involvements. But Ibn 'Aṭā' continued to experience such a severe tension that he believed he must choose to seek either learning or God, but not both. Mursī again guaranteed him that God can transform an individual into His servant regardless of occupation. At length Ibn 'Aṭā' resolved the conflict. After Mursī died, in 1288, the disciple-turned-shaykh continued to teach both law and Sufism in Cairo until his own death in 1309. During his career of over two decades in Cairo, Ibn 'Aṭā' engaged in spirited debate with Ibn Taymiyyah (d. 1328), a Ḥanbalite jurist who was also a Ṣūfī. The intricacies of their exchange of views are not precisely relevant to our present concerns, but one point needs to be made: Ibn 'Aṭā' sought to steer a middle course between monism, of which Ibn Taymiyyah claimed Ibn 'Arabī (d. 1240) was guilty, and anthropomorphism, of which Ibn 'Aṭā' accused Ibn Taymiyyah. When we consider the *Book of Wisdom*, so crucial for an appreciation of Ibn 'Abbād, it will become clearer how Ibn 'Aṭā' steered that course.

The *Kitāb al-Ḥikam* was probably Ibn 'Aṭā's earliest work, and it has without a doubt remained his most famous. Nwiya calls it the "breviary" (liturgical office book) of the order; but the work has been used as a manual of Sufism by other orders as well. It is part of a literary genre that developed during the twelfth and thirteenth centuries, the "renaissance" of Sufism according to Nwiya. The genre may have grown out of the long-standing Ṣūfī practice of recounting the "life" of a great master in the form of a collection of his sayings. Eventually the masters took to recording their own apothegms in single books. Abū Madyan and Ibn 'Arabī were the most famous Ṣūfīs to employ the form before Ibn 'Aṭā', and Ibn 'Aṭā' was almost certainly acquainted with the genre as one or other of his predecessors had developed it.

The *Book of Wisdom* is a book of prayer, but not merely of praise, petition, or repentance. It is also a questioning, searching prayer that never quite hears the final answer and never definitively arrives at a comfortable goal. Everything the seeker finds is cause to continue the search. The *Ḥikam* are both conversation with God and conversation about God. Utilizing Qur'ānic imagery and Ash'arite terminology in combination with the sober caution of Junayd and Muḥāsibī, Ibn 'Aṭā' explores the dual aspect of the mystery of God. God is utterly transcendent, yet He makes Himself known to His servants without ever blurring the infinite distinction between Creator and creature. During Ibn ʿAṭāʾs time, there was ongoing debate between mystics who held that a substantial union between creature and Creator was possible in what was called "unity of being" [*waḥdat al-wujūd*], and those who held that the pinnacle of unity was that of "witnessing" or contemplation [*waḥdat ash-shuhūd*]. Ibn ʿAṭāʾ taught the latter concept, in which the contemplative and the Contemplated retained their identities.

God's presence suffuses all creation as the Light of the heavens and the earth (Qur'ān 24:35). The essence of the mystical experience is the increasing ability to see through apparent darkness in creatures to the Light that has given those created things their very existence. It is a never-ending process of unveiling, of stripping away the imagination's illusion that some object in ordinary experience is God Himself, when in fact it is other than God. The paradox is that the more one feels that God is near, the more one experiences His utter distance. When Ibn ʿAṭāʾ and Ibn ʿAbbād speak of "certitude" in religious experience, they do not mean security, either of the sort that might result from a feeling that one has fulfilled the "whole law" meticulously or of the sort that one might feel in a time of spiritual consolation [*basṭ*, "expansion"]. As Nwiya analyzes the situation, human beings were made neither for consolation nor for desolation [*qabḍ*, "contraction"], but for God. For that reason, God never leaves an individual in either of these two states, but deals with His servant now through consolation, now through desolation. "Each arrival is a new departure," and "every unveiling is a call to penetrate other veils."[50]

Over the centuries, the *Book of Wisdom* has inspired many commentaries. One of the most popular of them is Ibn ʿAbbād's *Tanbīh* [Instruction, indicator]. We shall look more explicitly at Ibn ʿAbbād's writings later on, but it seems appropriate to mention here some of the salient features of his retelling of, and personal reflections on, the *Ḥikam*, so as to highlight the continuity of thought and spirit from one generation of Shādhiliyyah to the next. Ibn ʿAbbād cites the *Ḥikam* in his Letters more frequently than he does any other single work, with the exception of the Qur'ān. Commentators after Ibn ʿAbbād continued to give witness to the power and influence of the *Ḥikam* and of Ibn ʿAbbād's *Tanbīh*, for many of them quote him as though he were the foremost authority. One of those later commentators, Aḥmad Zarrūq (d. 1493), said that the *Ḥikam* are to Sufism what the eyes are to the body, for they contain four types of knowledge essential to Ṣūfī teaching: instruction and exhortation, asceticism, acquired and infused mystical knowledge, and the science of unveiling.[51]

Written between 1370 and 1372 at the behest of two close friends, Ibn ʿAbbād's meditative discourses on the *Ḥikam* reveal several key themes. The foundation of his thought is the twofold notion of God's transcendence and its corollary, the nothingness of all that is not God. This principle immediately gives rise to a moral dilemma. Human actions are totally inefficacious. Furthermore, to regard any action, good or evil, as efficacious is to suggest that creatures are in competition with their Creator. Ibn ʿAbbād therefore puts great emphasis on the passive virtues of trust, resignation, and total abandonment to God's direction and plan. This is what Ibn ʿAṭā' called the "elimination of self-direction." Trust is "the practical realization of a totally theocentric judgment which denies the creature the better to affirm the Creator."[52] In its extreme form, trust can leave the individual quite alone and without recourse to community support. But for all his emphasis on divine omnipotence, Ibn ʿAbbād staunchly defends human freedom. We will return later to several themes from the *Tanbīh* as they relate specifically to issues raised in the Letters.[53]

Before considering the life and works of Ibn ʿAbbād against the backdrop of fourteenth-century North African Sufism, Ibn ʿAṭā''s position in, and view of, the evolution of the Shādhiliyyah Order might be summed up this way. Ibn ʿAṭā' regarded Shādhilī as the divinely ordained successor to the Prophet Muḥammad. God had confirmed the universality of Shādhilī's intercessory role, through wonders that in turn pointed to the shaykh's position as spiritual axis of the universe. Every saint carries on and manifests—in an esoteric fashion accessible only to the initiated—the same Light that the prophets had manifested in a public way. Mursī then inherited the spiritual role of *quṭb* from Shādhilī, and the Shādhiliyyah Order was born. Neither Ibn ʿAṭā' nor Ibn ʿAbbād ever laid claim to the status of *quṭb*, but it is widely agreed that their writings merit both of them the rank of co-founders of the order.[54]

In short, just as within Christianity spiritualities with varying tones or emphases (e.g., apostolic, mendicant, contemplative, cenobitic, etc.) developed and embodied the spirit of various religious orders (e.g., Benedictine, Dominican, Jesuit, Vincentian, Paulist, etc.), so the Shādhiliyyah Order represents one of many Islamic spiritualities. And Ibn ʿAbbād provides us with a concrete example of that spirituality in action.

d. Ibn 'Abbād and Moroccan Sufism

More than a century before the Shādhiliyyah was firmly planted in Alexandria, Sufism had begun to flourish in the Almohad capital at Marrakesh. It was largely ascetic in tone, and revolved around spiritual masters who were also noted jurists.[55] Six Ṣūfī groups, which were not "orders" in the strict sense, developed in Morocco, tracing their spiritual genealogy back to Abū Madyan, Shādhilī's "spiritual grandfather." Then from the late twelfth century to the end of the thirteenth, Morocco witnessed a certain waning of spirit among the larger institutionalized Ṣūfī groups. Factionalism, loss of interior motivation, and formalism in worship were among the signs of decay.

At the same time, however, a major renewal was beginning. "Sufism at the fringe of the Orders," as Nwiya calls it, took the form of a popular devotion based initially in the smaller villages of Morocco. An intensely personal type of piety, it did not center on formal community life as the orders did. Some people chose to live as ascetics in the *zāwiyahs*, but theirs remained an almost eremitical existence. The time was right for the kind of spirituality that would both encourage the pursuit of a vigorous interior life and allow its adherents to continue their involvement in ordinary daily affairs. Not until Ibn 'Abbād had written his *Tanbīh* did the influence of the Shādhiliyyah make itself felt in Morocco. Ibn 'Abbād was the first Moroccan Ṣūfī to be called explicitly a member of that order. But had it not been for the growth of personal devotion outside the structure of the orders, the Shādhiliyyah might not have found so ready an acceptance as it did in Morocco.

According to Paul Nwiya, the most obvious characteristic of the pre-Shādhilī Sufism of Morocco is that it was integrated into the life of official Islam. Ṣūfīs did not hold themselves aloof, either from traditional religious studies or from the more mundane occupations and functions of community life. A second characteristic is that this was a Sufism heavily influenced by al-Ghazālī (d. 1111), whose reputation the reformer Ibn Tūmart (d. 1130) had rescued from the Almoravid attempt at a *damnatio memoriae*.[56] Ghazālī's success in reconciling traditional religious studies and mysticism is especially evident during the time of the Marīnid dynasty (after 1248). The Marīnid jurists were at least not blatantly hostile to Sufism, mystical works were on the sulṭān's list of favored reading alongside classic Mālikite texts, and the rulers displayed a more than passing interest in the spiritual masters of their day.[57]

In the midst of organized Sufism's decay and the renewal of personal piety on a broad scale stands Ibn ʿAbbād, certainly the most important figure in North African Sufism between 1200 and 1400.

3. Ibn ʿAbbād's Life and Letters

Ibn ʿAbbād was born in 1332 in Ronda, a hilltop town in southern Spain, then under the control of the Marīnid dynasty. By the age of seven he had learned the Qur'ān by heart and had begun his study of Mālikite law as codified by Ibn Abī Zayd of Qayrawān (d. 996) in his *Risālah*. In the year 1340, the Marīnid Sulṭān Abū 'l-Ḥasan suffered a defeat in Spain and had to curtail his military enterprises there. The increasing pace of the Christian reconquest made Muslim presence in Spain more difficult. In 1347, Ibn ʿAbbād moved to Fez, the capital of Morocco.

Sultan Abū 'l-Ḥasan (1331–1348) was endeavoring to make his capital a major center of learning and culture. He patronized the arts, endowed new theological colleges, and invited famous teachers. Ibn ʿAbbād's father became preacher at the Qaṣbah mosque, while Ibn ʿAbbād resumed his religious studies. One of Ibn ʿAbbād's most famous mentors, Ash-Sharīf at-Tilimsānī (d. 1369), was widely recognized as a leader in the revival of Mālikism. So learned was he in the science of legal principles [*uṣūl*] that he was accorded the rare right of "independent investigation" [*ijtihād*]. Tilimsānī taught Ibn ʿAbbād first in Tlemcen and again later when the teacher came to Fez at the invitation of Sulṭān Abū ʿInān.

During his first stay in Fez, Ibn ʿAbbād probably resided in the student lodgings of the oldest still-existent theological college, the madrasah of the Ḥalfawiyīn. Under al-Abilī (d. 1356) he studied an Ashʿarite theological treatise, *al-Irshād*, written by al-Juwaynī (d. 1086), who had been one of Ghazālī's teachers, and some legal writings of Ibn al-Hājib (d. 1248). Like Tilimsānī, al-Abilī urged a renewal of Mālikite law; he criticized the rigidity of the state-sponsored schools and spoke out against the stagnation into which they had fallen.

Under the tutelage of al-Maqqarī (d. 1337), Ibn ʿAbbād read Muslim's authoritative collection of Traditions of the Prophet, along with other works he had studied earlier with Tilimsānī. With al-ʿImrānī (b. 1286) he studied Mālik ibn Anas' (d. 795) collection of Traditions, the *Muwaṭṭa'*. ʿImrānī was a famous jurist who is said to have been very much interested in Sufism. Like other Mālikite scholars, he had authored some commentary notes on the *Mudawwanah* of Saḥnūn (d. 854)—by all accounts the most influential work in North African jurisprudence. Al-Barādhiʻī's (tenth c. Qayrawān) classic summary of the *Mudawwanah* was another source of Ibn ʻAbbād's education, probably while he was in residence at the newly completed Bou ʻInāniyyah Madrasah. In Letter 6 he pays Abū Ṭālib al-Makkī the compliment of saying that his *Food of Hearts* is to the spiritual life what the *Mudawwanah* is to jurisprudence: all-sufficient and irreplaceable.

Two other Mālikite scholars need to be mentioned here. Ibn ʻAbbād wrote Letter 16 to Abū Isḥāq Ibrāhīm ash-Shaṭībī of Granada (d. 1388). His *Muwāfaqāt* was a major contribution to a climate of religious studies that might have opened up dramatically except that it had too many old wounds to heal. Finally, Ibn ʻAbbād mentions Aḥmad al-Qabbāb (d. 1375), also in Letter 16. Like al-Abilī, al-Qabbāb worked to inject new life into religious studies that were still reeling from the severe blow the Almohads had dealt them.[58]

Ibn Khaldūn remarks wryly that "Malikite scholars have never ceased writing commentaries, explanations, and synopses of these main works."[59] Ibn ʻAbbād's schooling in religious law was extensive, but highly traditional and rather stilted, in the Moroccan style. Nwiya points out the conspicuous absence of the name of Fakhr ad-Dīn ar-Rāzī (d. 1209) from among the names of those Ibn ʻAbbād read. Around 1300 there was a split between the styles of legal study pursued in Fez and in Tunis. Tunis had become more speculative under the influence of Fakhr ad-Dīn, who, according to M. Mahdi, "effected a new rapprochement between rational philosophic knowledge and religious studies."[60] Fez meanwhile remained more conservative under the influence of Ibn al-Ḥājib.[61]

In spite of his extensive background in traditional legal studies, Ibn ʻAbbād refuses, in his Letters, to deal directly with legal questions, claiming he lacks the requisite expertise.

It is possible that Ibn ʻAbbād was introduced to Sufism by one of his law teachers, for many of them were Ṣūfīs. Few of his teachers would have been formally associated with recognized orders, but they did teach Sufism in private, using the classic works of al-Makkī, Ghazālī, and Suhrawardī.

After the death of Sulṭān Abū ʻInān, Fez apparently experienced in 1358 a period of considerable turmoil. There were to be seventeen sulṭāns between 1358 and 1465, and six different claimants to the sultanate between 1358 and 1367 alone. Shortly after the sulṭān's death,

Ibn ʻAbbād went west, to the Atlantic coast city of Salé. There Ibn ʻĀshir (c. 1300–1362) had become a pivotal personality in Sufism's revival at the fringe of the orders. Pilgrims from all over Morocco came to the master to receive his blessing. Ibn ʻAbbād went on to become the shaykh's best student. He read widely about Sufism and its various branches and styles. At last he decided in favor of the Shādhiliyyah. That is information from Ibn as-Sakkāk (d. 1451), the first Maghribī author to write explicitly about the Shādhiliyyah. He also says that, as a child, he had met the much older Ibn ʻAbbād and often ate with him.[62]

Ibn ʻAbbād went to Salé both to escape the deteriorating living conditions in Fez and to find a measure of spiritual security. His teacher considered him "in a class by himself." Thanks to his independence and desire to pursue his own course, the pupil was not overcome by his teacher's intensity. Ibn ʻĀshir was a very high-strung individual, given to continual fasting and taking food only every other day. This was an old Ṣūfī practice called the "Fast of David," designed to keep the ascetic from becoming accustomed either to fasting or to satiety.[63] In keeping with his love for the writings of al-Muḥāsibī, Ibn ʻĀshir insisted on the practice of examination of conscience. He was decidedly a sober mystic.

In about 1362 or 1363, after the death of Ibn ʻĀshir, Ibn ʻAbbād left Salé for Tangiers. He studied there under the little-known Ṣūfī Abū Marwān ʻAbd al-Mālik. After a stay of unknown duration there, the young seeker returned to Fez. During this next stay in Fez, Ibn ʻAbbād renewed an acquaintance with Yaḥyā as-Sarrāj (c. 1344–c. 1400), founder of the Fez branch of a family that had originated in Ronda, and addressee of several of the Letters. Ibn ʻAbbād also came to be a good friend of Abū r-Rabīʻ Sulaymān al-Anfāsī (c. 1337–1377). It was at the request of these two friends that he undertook his *Tanbīh*, completed between 1370 and 1372.

Ibn ʻAbbād returned to Salé at an uncertain date and remained there until about 1375. Most, if not all, of his correspondence dates from before that year. About 1375 he was appointed Imām and Preacher of the Qarawiyyīn mosque in Fez, the oldest and most prestigious institution of religion and learning in North Africa. Sulṭān Abū 'l-ʻAbbās Aḥmad (1st reign 1373–1384) apparently made the appointment on the basis of Ibn ʻAbbād's reputation for personal integrity, and the celebrity of his *Tanbīh*. The prospect of taking over the post of preacher at a time when preaching had degenerated to little more than a rote exercise for many preachers must have presented a challenge. Reflecting on the state of the art in one of his Letters,[64] he listed the five types of preachers who in his opinion failed to discharge their duty responsibly. Some repeated the very same sermon every Friday; some repeated it with little variation; some preached without relating their message to changing needs; some attended to those needs, but were unable to relate their message effectively to them; and some simply lacked devotion altogether and were ostentatious actors. The authentic preacher counsels and teaches people in accord with their daily pressing needs, and is able to match his style of delivery with the theme he has chosen. Ibn 'Abbād preferred the didactic style to the exhortatory, for the people were in need of instruction. When he did turn to exhortation, he always included himself under the obligation to which he held his audience bound.

One hundred and twenty-four sermons are extant in a unique manuscript, which Paul Nwiya has analyzed. The Muslim Friday sermon traditionally included two sections: The first developed a theme suited to the occasion, and the second treated a standard topic, namely, a prayer for the Prophet, his Companions, wives, successors, and the Muslim Community with its encumbent caliph or sulṭān mentioned by name. Only one of Ibn 'Abbād's extant sermons still contains the second part. But the opening section of each begins with a doxology, a short prayer for the Prophet, and the Confession of Faith, all followed by the body of the address. The entire piece would typically take about twenty minutes to deliver.

Terse, rhythmic, arresting phrases were meant to emulate the rhymed prose of the scripture. Because of the simplicity of the basic Islamic doctrine, the speaker needed to rely on a mastery of the Arabic language, without at the same time delivering merely a beautiful sound devoid of personal impact and moral challenge. Ibn 'Abbād liked to engage his congregation with a direct appeal to conscience, supported by citations from Qur'ān and Traditions, taking care to hold attention by means of appropriate intonation. He tailored his themes to the seasons: During Ramaḍān he would speak of fasting, and of the necessity of first purifying the heart lest the physical act be void of spiritual meaning. During the month of Pilgrimage, the last month of the lunar liturgical year, he would call for an examination of conscience reaching back over the past year. When the new year began, in the month of Muḥarram, he would counsel almsgiving. Ibn 'Abbād did not regard the public sermon as the proper forum in which to treat of mystical subjects. He reserved such matters for his personal letters of spiritual direction.

During the last quarter of the fourteenth century, the Marīnid dynasty was well past its prime. The great city of Fez was enduring major political difficulties and more than a little spiritual restlessness. The picture of Ibn 'Abbād living in his small house adjacent to the Mosque, attracting a train of little children as he walked to the Mosque, and attending to the needs of the people as best he could is one of conviction and hope in a time of instability and uncertainty. Toward the end of his life, he wrote to a friend, Abū 'l-'Abbās al-Marrākushī, that he was tiring of Fez and of his obligations, but that he was resigned to his ill health and preparing to die. Nwiya suggests that Ibn 'Abbād remained unmarried until very late in life. Some sources say he never married. If indeed he did marry at the end of his life, he may have done so out of a desire to follow the example of the Prophet, rather than out of personal preference. He never made the Pilgrimage to Mecca.

On June 17, 1390, Ibn 'Abbād was buried in the presence of the sulṭān and many of the citizens of Fez. Though the exact location of his tomb is no longer known, it is said to have remained a goal for pilgrims for many years. Until 1936, the Shoemakers' Guild celebrated his feast annually, for he had become their patron saint.[65]

Ibn 'Abbād's Letters

Ibn 'Abbād was not the first eminent Ṣūfī to employ correspondence as one of his chief means of communication. Abū Naṣr as-Sarrāj (d. 988) preserved fragments of letters written by a number of famous mystics to others who had become quite advanced on the Ṣūfī Path.[66] Because those letters were addressed for the most part to accomplished mystics, their content tends to be rather esoteric and too sensitive for general consumption. Some of the letters are addressed to groups of Ṣūfīs. A. H. Abdel-Kader has collected and translated several letters of Junayd, likewise written to Ṣūfīs well along in the spiritual life.[67]

Two other very famous mystics wrote letters comprising a second category, correspondence with government officials. In a recently translated selection of letters by Ghazālī we hear him "reprimanding the Saljuqi sovereigns and their ministers against all compromises with corruption, nepotism, favouritism, injustice and bribery which were the main ills of the society in those days."[68] The Persian mystic Jalāl ad-Dīn Rūmī (d. 1273) maintained analogous epistolary relationships with several local rulers at the Turkish Seljuk capital at Konya. About one hundred and fifty of Rūmī's letters are extant, as yet untranslated into English.[69]

A third type of Ṣūfī correspondence is that between a master and a disciple. Paul Jackson, S.J., has recently translated *The Hundred Letters*[70] of the Indian Ṣūfī Sharaf ad-Dīn Manīrī. Manīrī wrote his Persian letters during the late thirteenth and early fourteenth centuries. Fragments of letters from Ibn al-'Arīf and ash-Shādhilī to their disciples have survived. Like Ibn 'Abbād's letters, they are nonesoteric and largely practical in tone and content.

What is unique about Ibn 'Abbād's correspondence is that here we have two fairly complete collections of intact letters designed to explain the fundamentals of mystical spirituality to individuals who were struggling with specific personal problems. The two collections include fifty-four letters in all, thirty-eight in the "Large Collection" (RK) and sixteen in the "Small Collection" (RS) translated here. All of them were composed between about 1365 and 1375 from Salé to friends in Fez. Nwiya has also published some letters written after 1375, in appendices to both of his editions of the Small Collection. He says the letters are such a privileged source that they "give us a knowledge of Ibn 'Abbād such as we possess of no other Muslim mystic."[71]

The thirty-eight letters in the Large Collection were probably written over a two or two-and-a-half year period, from 1372 to 1374. The first thirty-one of them are addressed to Yaḥyā as-Sarrāj, to whom Ibn 'Abbād also wrote Letters 7 through 15 in the present translation. It is evident from RK that Yaḥyā and Ibn 'Abbād deepened their relationship considerably during the latter's 1370–1372 sojourn in Fez, for in one of the RS, Ibn 'Abbād indicates that he feels he is not well enough acquainted with his addressee to deal with certain questions of a very personal nature. The later letters in RK give a very different image of their relationship, although they give much more information about Yaḥyā than about Ibn 'Abbād.

From the later letters we learn of Yaḥyā's struggle to make a living, and of his crisis of conscience about whether he could be involved both in the exoteric science of Tradition and in the esoteric concerns of Sufism. There Ibn 'Abbād advises him to set aside the Tradition studies, for the general decadence of many people dedicated to such studies was such that Yaḥyā could hardly hope to be influenced for the better by them. Yaḥyā had a tendency to go to extreme solutions, and once he even sold his copy of Mālik's collection of Traditions, the *Muwaṭṭa'*. He later regretted the sale. In the long run, Yaḥyā was unable to escape the attraction of Tradition studies. Two years after Ibn 'Abbād's death he composed a compendium of Traditions that Ibn ʿAbbād had passed along to him.[72]

Ibn ʿAbbād's RK also give some information about the kinds of questions to which the learned in and around the court of the sulṭan turned their attention. Ibn ʿAbbād leaves no room for doubt that he personally has no use for such speculations, but he nevertheless tries to respond to the issues his correspondents ask him to evaluate for them. Paul Nwiya has summarized several of the major questions discussed there.

Some people debated about whether the soul would experience anguish or pain upon leaving this world and passing through the *barzakh*, the region that separates this world from the world of pure spirits. Ibn ʿAbbād confesses he does not have a clear answer, but he does offer an analogy with the commonly held notion that the soul leaves the body during sleep. Since the soul does not experience sorrow then—suffering is something connected with the body—the same must be true when the soul leaves the body and passes through the *barzakh*.

Others argued about whether saints are able to see angels. Ibn ʿAbbād holds that this is possible, since some believed it was possible to see God. Furthermore, some of the Companions of the Prophet saw angels, even though they did not see them "in their natural form"; and since all Muslims share the blessings of the Prophet as the Companions did, the privilege must in theory extend to all. He adds that Abū 'l-Ḥasan ash-Shādhilī saw an angel in the form of a large white bird, but no saint is reported to have seen an angel in its natural form, for that is reserved to the prophets.

Another issue is related to the Jewish community in Fez. The Almohads had disenfranchised the Jews, but the Marīnids had restored many of their former rights. The Jews were the only non-Muslims in Fez, and they enjoyed religious freedom, so long as they practiced their religion in private. It is quite likely that the next question originated among the Jews who had converted to Islam: Is Muḥammad superior to Moses as a prophet? Ibn ʿAbbād's answer is that it is blasphemous to claim that Moses is superior to Muḥammad. Muḥammad had claimed superiority in clear terms, but he had not done so merely out of a desire to advance his personal cause. Ibn ʿAbbād reasons that, if the Prophet had wanted to curry favor with the Jews in Medina, he would surely have been better off acknowledging Moses' leadership of the prophets. That he maintained his own superiority even in the face of fierce opposition is proof of the veracity of his claim. Earlier prophets had foretold that one greater than themselves would arise. Any Muslim who claims that Moses is greater is equivalently admitting that Muḥammad had no mission to convert non-Muslims, and acknowledging Judaism's preeminence over Islam. Finally, the Qur'ān states that not all of the prophets are equal; but since that inequality does not imply imperfection in any of the prophets, there is no point in going to extremes in praising Muḥammad to the detriment of the other prophets' images.

The learned of Fez raised many other questions about personal moral and spiritual status as well. They asked, for example, whether the poor person who suffers much tribulation in this life is superior to the rich person who has not a care in the world. They debated about whether the person who renounces all his goods and gives them away is better than one who gives only out of his surplus. In all such cases, Ibn 'Abbād's basic principle seems to be this: The outward appearance of a person's condition is not important; what really matters is whether the individual is inordinately attached to his condition, whatever it may be.[73]

The last seven of the RK are to unidentified addressees. Two of them are noteworthy in that they appear to be directed to an individual who has drifted away from the practice of religion. In the first of the two, the writer's tone is relatively mild; in the second he is much more stern.[74]

Nwiya describes the sixteen letters of the RS as "little treatises on spirituality . . . and not merely friendly letters whose allusions are rendered incomprehensible by the loss of the letters to which they respond, as is the case with the Large Collection."[75] Ibn 'Abbād's use of summary superscriptions underscores the treatise-like quality of the letters. The first six are written to Muḥammad ibn Adībah, a jurist who apparently lived in Fez after emigrating either from Andalusia or Tlemcen. Ibrāhīm ash-Shāṭibī (d. 1388), a jurist of Granada noted for his work in legal principles, received Letter 16, which dates from around 1375 in Fez. The first fifteen of the RS are from Ibn 'Abbād's first stay in Salé, probably before 1368.[76] I have included in the heading of each letter the name of the addressee, according to Nwiya's attributions.

Ibn 'Abbād of Ronda

LETTERS ON THE ṢŪFĪ PATH

In the Name of God,
The Gracious and Merciful,
And may God bless our Leader and Master
Muḥammad
And his Family and Companions
and give them peace.

LETTER 1

To Muḥammad ibn Adībah. A letter in response to a question someone raised concerning an issue in the book *The Food of Hearts*,[1] in the chapter "Fear." The letter also includes some other useful information the seeker[2] will need in associating with certain individuals.

I send you warm greetings. And I ask my powerful and glorious Lord to give us both complete success, guidance toward the straight Path, and a guarantee that our hopes will be fulfilled and that our deeds will be proper.

I received your letter in which you sought a clarification of a question posed for you by the book of Abū Ṭālib, that healing treatise. To attempt a thorough explanation of its contents, as you have requested, would require an unveiling of well-guarded mysteries and the publication of hidden knowledge. That would be quite risky and would pose great potential harm. Moreover, a penetrating analysis of the attributes and essence of God would be exceedingly difficult for me. One can arrive at such truths only with the lights of certitude, and only the most upright are led along that Path. Which of us can claim to live that way or belong to such a society? Our passions blind us; we are at a loss as to how to conduct ourselves; the merest traces of a campsite[3] stop us in our tracks, so that we squander our provisions and thus fail to reach the destination. Our enemies and whims murder us with their artifices and seduction; our sight is blinded and our hearts darkened. It would be presumptuous of us to desire a full experience of what you have asked me to explain, to follow the road of unveiling and clarity of vision. That would be to disregard our capacity and fall into the folly of pretensions[4] that dishonor the intelligent and prove the ignorance of the ignorant. Falsehood does not gain in stature by such means.

2

Were we to enter the realm of the jurists,[5] we would find that they likewise cannot slake our thirst or show us the way to understanding through their use of reason and their inflexible opinions. All of that is regressive and inappropriate behavior, for it leads to denial and a lessening of faith. Our only alternative in this matter is to defer to those who are worthy of the undertaking. We must content ourselves with our lot and seek a revelation from the Revealer, the Wise. We must seek guidance toward the Straight Path (1:5) of those who affirm the divine transcendence and deny anthropomorphism.[6] That Path is uniquely safe from misfortunes and will preserve the likes of us from foolish misdeeds. It involves proper demeanor[7] alongside the saints and the spiritual masters, conduct that elevates one to the highest degrees of sainthood. As al-Junayd said, "Believing in what we have learned: This is sainthood."[8] Even so I feel obliged to respond to you. So let me speak of the matter insofar as I understand it, by discussing what seems appropriate under these circumstances, in an attempt to remove doubt and obviate the acceptance of an untenable position. I shall limit my attention to that. If I should arrive at the Mystic Truth,[9] it will be as a result of divine assistance. If I fall short, human deficiency will be the cause. In either case our powerful and glorious Lord will be praised.

This is a serious matter that is part of the science of acknowledging the unity of God's uniqueness. It is consonant with the principles of the Ṣūfīs; it epitomizes the spiritual meaning of sincerity; and it originates with the individual who is possessed of certitude, faith, experience, and clear vision. It cannot be explained except by living it and no one can make a case for it except by giving example of it.

Al-Ghazālī concurred with the view of Abū Ṭālib and expressed the matter in a similar way. Both have spoken of the [divine] strategem and have described it at considerable length. And God Most High has predicated it of Himself in various passages in His Book, in the same way that trials and temptations and cunning are associated with Him. All of these terms express aspects of His will and knowledge, and indicate that His holiness, transcendence, and sublimity are beyond comparison and devoid of anthropomorphism.[10]

Let me begin here with some prefatory remarks. The Exalted Creator has fashioned and constituted the human person with both perfection and imperfection, all of which is minuscule when compared to Him, may He be praised. Then He predisposed the human being for intimate knowledge[11] of Him and of His attributes and Names. By that means He raises the individual above the limitations of intellect, through which one comprehends the empirical sciences, and leads him to contemplate the signs in nature and in created beings. Marvels and wonders manifest themselves to anyone who looks upon these things.

They compel him to acknowledge the Fashioner, the Originator, the Creator, the First Principle as possessing the qualities of life, knowledge, power, and will—even as one regards oneself after performing a masterly and exacting task. Then the individual looks also at himself and sees there the qualities of perfection in hearing and sight and speech, so that the experience of the divine power impels him to ascribe the same qualities to the Creator and Originator.

3

One then discerns the immense disparity between the recent and the eternally ancient, the creature and the Creator.[12] This prompts him to affirm transcendence and deny anthropomorphism. At this point one comprehends all that is accessible to human understanding about the transcendence of his exalted Creator. He ascends therefrom to the highest degree and utmost extent of his ability to affirm and see. This is the process by which one examines and reflects and is led to the Cause by means of His effects. And the process will suffice to lead every ordinary intelligent person to the rudiments of the intimate knowledge that is requisite for salvation and spiritual progress. One may, however, continue to experience doubts in one's faith, and not experience the expansion of the core of his being and the purification of the heart.[13]

Then God Most High singles out certain of His servants by manifesting Himself to them through His light, something that is most evident to them. They travel by that light along the way that their intimate knowledge of Him indicates most clearly. They contemplate His wondrous attributes and essential Names in a way that the first group of people do not. They comprehend the majesty of the divine presence and the holy lights in a way that eludes the grasp of those who seek evidence. To these the chosen servants say, "How is it that you seek information about what cannot essentially be demonstrated? When is He so hidden that one lacks evidence of Him? How can He be lost to us when there are traces that lead us to Him? Can anything other than Him be manifest in a way that is not within its natural power until He makes it manifest? How can He in whom every feature is recognized be recognized by His features? Or how can He whose Being precedes every other being be distinguished as a specific entity? And how can one gain access by some remote means to Him who is 'closer than the jugular vein' (cf. 50:16)? And 'Does not your Lord suffice, since He is Witness over all things?' " (41:53).[14]

Through intimate knowledge of Him, they arrive only at the

names; because of His transcendence they do not attain to the farthest limit of praise and magnification. Still they contemplate that Being in comparison with which all else is nothingness, that permanence in comparision with which all else is negation, the experience of which is false, the perception of which is illusion, the memory of which is forgetfulness, and whose increase is diminishment. They see thus with the eye of certitude and clear proof the truth of the one who said, "God existed before all things, and He exists now independent of all that depends on Him."

Once they arrive at this station, they have come into the grasp of the King, the Knower. He frees them from slavery to sensible knowledge and causes them to die to all other things.[15] Their inmost thoughts are purified and God, may He be praised, is manifest to them through His most excellent Attributes and Names. He gives them a knowledge of what He will so that they assume the posture of servants before their Master. They come to rest in the place where the One who knows their every secret thought watches over them. They align themselves in rows of service along with those who "set the ranks and hymn His praise" (cf. 37:165–166). They attain the most excellent ranks of the servants and they sing with the tongue of their spiritual state,[16] saying, "How many were the desires of my heart . . . "[17] And how delightful for them to be chosen for the dwellings of the beloved ones, with that "beautiful life's end" (3:14, 13:29) foretold for them in the Mother of the Book![18]

4

The difference between these two paths and their methods can be clearly explained this way.[19] At the heart of the first path is the intellect's search for evidence and its inability to understand except by a kind of analogical reasoning and comparison.[20] That is as far as empirical study will lead one. The second path, however, rests on the light of certitude, by which only the Clear Truth is manifest. That is the most sublime thing that can descend from the heavens into the hearts of chosen believers, who comprehend thereby the Mystic Truth of the Attributes and Names.

Once you have grasped these introductory remarks, you will understand that the kinds of objections you have raised in relation to Shaykh Abū Ṭālib collapse of their own weight. This issue is intimately bound up with a way of thinking that has nothing to do with analogical understanding or a rational ordering. Furthermore, those objections are associated with a more widespread way of thinking, for their approach to this question does not go beyond the confines of reason.

Now about Abū Ṭālib's statement, "There is no end to the wiles of God, for His will and decrees are boundless." He is referring here to an aspect of God Most High's knowledge, speech, will, and judgments as transcending understanding and comprehension. It is on that account that the Prophet and Gabriel, peace be upon them, feared the strategems of their powerful and glorious Lord even in the face of reassurance.[21] This is a necessary fear. One can scarcely imagine escaping it, for it is one of the requirements of faith and of the knowledge of the divine Attributes and essential Names. Therefore, the person who has a greater share in the Attributes and Names will be subject to a greater fear. As one of the mystics has said, "A person who possesses intimate knowledge of God Most High does not rest comfortably in it, for such knowledge shakes one's security. Only scoundrels consider themselves safe from the wiles of God" (7:97). And someone else has said, "Fear your Lord with a fear by which you are safe from every thing, but caution your heart against feeling safe from God Most High in some thing."[22] In other words, there is no reason to fear any thing; but one is never secure from God Most High.

Surely the surface meaning of God's saying "I have made both of you safe" was not intended to dissolve their fear; for the apparent meaning of the words does not obviate the interior need of the quality of fear. As Shaykh Abū Ṭālib had said, the statement applied to a specific quality that God Most High has already specified by His knowledge. This is an aspect of the transcendence of God's speech, and there is no point in contradicting it since rational methods cannot prevent God from saying things our understanding cannot fathom. The trial and testing of Muḥammad and Gabriel is instructive for us in this discussion. It will profit us to examine their state in considering the realities of the divine Attributes, to see how God alters the states of His elect, as in the story of Abraham, peace be upon him.[23]

5

God's promise of strengthening is quite plausible to the intellect. But how is one to discern the nuances? In addition, there is in the experience of Muḥammad and Gabriel something of a manifestation of their utter dependence on their powerful and glorious Lord. This station to which God elevated His Prophet, peace be upon him, in the majority of his states, is an exalted one. And it is more perfect than a demonstration of independence. Poverty is more appropriate to the condition of servanthood than is independence; for, as the Ṣūfī leaders have described it, independence is one of God's prerogatives. The point is that the two beloved ones, peace be upon them, came to understand, through the disclosure of the attribute of independence and the experience of His majesty and grandeur in this state, that what God Most High wanted from them at that moment was an admission of indigence and an awareness of lowliness and fragility. That is why He dealt and spoke with them as He did.

Abū Ṭālib says further that "God Most High is not constrained by any rules, and no human strictures apply to Him." This is a reference to another aspect of the divine essence's transcendence of creaturely limitations. He possesses action and perfect sublimity absolutely. No decrees bind Him, for it is He who issues decrees. How then could He be bound by decree or subject to restriction, and thus fail to give full proof of His veracity in word and deed? For it is He who declares sincere everyone who possesses sincerity, and He who gives full realization of the Truth to everyone who possesses Truth. His every word is Truth itself, the Mystic Truth whose articulation goes beyond mere outward expression. Therefore, if its meaning is hidden from us or its implications elude us, it is because God Most High would not be God otherwise. This lays to rest those objections to what Shaykh Abū Ṭālib has said. God could not possibly be described as other than veracious. What we have here is thus merely a difficulty in understanding His manner of expression.

Abū Ṭālib goes on to say, "If the words are changed, He himself is the substitute for them," and so forth. It is a sound and remarkable statement about the meaning of the divine unity that escapes rational understanding. God does not, as some have imagined, require permission to abrogate what He has said.[24]

I am not certain of the authenticity of the Tradition Abū Ṭālib cites, nor do I know which of the traditionists transmitted it. However, Abū Ṭālib supports it with his view that since the widely known Tradition does not contradict the Book and the Prophetic Example, it is applicable and authoritative, even if there is some question about its chain—that is, about the integrity of the transmission process and the one who transmitted it. Neither Aḥmad ibn Ḥanbal nor 'Abd ar-Raḥmān ibn Mahdī nor others mention it in the "Chapter of Knowledge."[25]

6

In any case, it is my opinion that no such corroboration is needed to clarify the Tradition and dispel doubts about it. It would be surprising to find someone refusing to accept this Tradition on the grounds that he did not understand it and was convinced that it was absurd and derived from an unreliable chain of transmission. Indeed, God Most High's reassurance to Muḥammad and Gabriel cannot be doubted. Their high rank and lofty estate, and God's raising them to an immeasurably exalted place of repose, are sufficient proof of that.

Their fear of God's ruse may also be understood as an intellectual problem. All that remains of the question and answer is the form of speech, and that is what makes the matter accessible. Our response concerning this Tradition is none other than the answer always given concerning this intellectual difficulty. Al-Ghazālī deals with this question and comments on this Tradition by introducing another Tradition about the prayer of the Prophet, peace be upon him, to his Lord on the day of Badr: "If you destroy this band, there will be none to serve you." He made this prayer in the context of his powerful and glorious Lord's promise of help and victory.[26] The implications of this Tradition in the collection, and the commentary on it, are similar to what has been said about the first Tradition, except that in the first the characteristic of indigence is more evident.

The story of Moses, peace be upon him, and his fear after being reassured, is another variation on this theme of God Most High's transcendent knowledge, speech, will, and decrees, and of Moses' evident need of his Lord, and of the loftiness of his station.[27] This is the significance of Shaykh Abū Ṭālib's statement "Moses did not feel secure" down to the words "because Moses had an intimate knowledge of His hidden strategems and His undisclosed attributes." Abū Ṭālib's observation "and as for His knowledge, it is subject to no decree" refers to the utter uniqueness of God Most High with respect to the decree insofar as being under decree is a form of coercion. Now it is God who is the Victorious One; but if He were in any way subject to a decree, then He would be the one judged and would become the vanquished one. But God is infinitely above such a thing.

7

God's second address does not, as you have imagined, carry the same implications as the first. The second evidently encompasses one of the mysteries of God Most High that inevitably resulted in Moses' peacefulness, repose, reassurance, and lack of fear. This exemplifies His beneficence and graciousness in effecting His will in Moses, peace be upon him. It is to this that Shaykh Abū Ṭālib called attention when he said, "So he was filled with trust in the One who was speaking to him, even though he had not rested easily in the initial manifestation." Do you not see how God Most High brought Moses to the deeper understanding of His intention to make him secure, by using a sentence in which the subject was emphasized and by adding the definite article to the predicate—which is in the superlative form and occurs after the intensified pronominal subject? So much for the external differences between the two statements.[28]

In a similar way the story of Jesus[29] illustrates the transcendence of God's knowledge and speech, and indicates appropriate behavior in that station that literary elegance and orderly exposition could not describe. That is entrusted to those masters whom God chooses to use. I shall therefore go no further in commenting on this question; and I ask forgiveness of God, may He be exalted and glorified, for what I have left out. Indeed no one can arrive at a full understanding of that station I have been describing except the elect who have experienced it firsthand. As for me, I have fallen as far short of that as one can fall.

You alluded to some statements of Abū Bakr al-Khaṭīb[30] that disagree with Abū Ṭālib concerning the Ṣūfīs' opinions on the divine Attributes. Those argumentative statements came subsequent to Abū Bakr's praise of Abū Ṭālib, and it is difficult to explain how the disagreement and the praise go together. If the objector intended his later remarks to imply innovation on the part of Abū Ṭālib, as though he were debating with someone who disagrees concerning the foundations of the attributes, their timelessness, their overall interrelationships, or their transcendence, then Abū Bakr certainly missed the point. Nothing Abū Ṭālib has said warrants such a conclusion. How then is Abū Bakr's difference of opinion consonant with his praise of Abū Ṭālib, if at the same time Abū Ṭālib deserves his stinging rebuke of his spiritual state and wrongdoing more than he deserves Abū Bakr's praise and adulation? If, on the other hand, Abū Bakr merely disagrees without intending a judgment of heresy, as in the amicable debate between the literalists and the spiritualists, then that is acceptable and the antagonist possesses no conclusive proof against his adversary.

What I would like you to do is to stop at that point in al-Khaṭīb's book, write the passage down in full, and send it to me so that I can study it. I am delighted that you are getting involved in these sciences and investigating them, even though you are far from home and separated from brothers and familiar circumstances. Ground yourself solidly in that study and be diligent at it, and you will find the results very worthwhile.

8

You need the kind of instruction whose import can be fully comprehended only through intelligence and experience, and from which one can be distracted only by negligence and dissimulation. These are dangers you will encounter in this learning process, especially among people who are characterized by one of these three qualities: pride, innovation, or unquestioning acceptance of authority. Pride is a curse that prevents one from perceiving the divine signs and admonitions. Innovation is an error through which pride causes one to fall into serious troubles. And unquestioning acceptance of authority is a trammel that prevents one from achieving victory and arriving at one's destination. The individual who possesses any one of these characteristics is subject to poor judgment and is in continual struggle and turmoil. How much more is that the case with the person in whom these qualities are combined!

Do not let yourself be influenced by people of this sort. And do not let your association with them be an obstacle to your understanding in this learning process, so that your piety is weakened and the doors of guidance and success close before you. When one of these people proposes nonsensical arguments or claims to be in some state or station, the result is sophistry, lies, deceit, and delusion. This is seductive both for the one who speaks and the one who listens, for it claims to enrich every gullible and ignorant person. All of that is vanity upon vanity. Herein lies one of the most convincing proofs of the superiority of the knowledge I have been talking about. It opens its door only to the pure and God-fearing servant and lifts its veil only to the heart that is repentant and undefiled by the contradictory notions proposed by other forms of knowledge.

Therefore do not consider any of the proponents of the law to be more competent than someone from this school of Knowledge. For exoteric learning is diametrically opposed to the Mystic Truth. It leads to inappropriate behavior and depravity in one's way of living, and culminates in a ruinous emptiness for those who engage for it. The mystics, on the other hand, contemplate that which is hidden from others and come to a full realization of truths that are beyond the grasp of others. They are like the people of whom the poet said,

My night has become a sunny dawn because of your face,
even though dusk has come to the sky.
Many are they who remain in the darkness of their night,
while we are in the dazzling brilliance of your face.

9

Ash-Shiblī said, "Do not consider yourself learned, for the learning of the religious scholars is suspect."[31] When a question is posed to you, do not approach it in a purely intellectual fashion. You ought rather to deal with it peacefully, setting aside rational objections, so that the simple truth of it, that can calm your heart and expand the core of your being, may be unveiled for you. You will need a pure intention and sincere desire to puruse this learning, for it is a noble learning by which the servant is led to an intimate knowledge of his exalted and glorious Lord and to the experience of His blessings. Through it the servant is brought to the ultimate happiness of meeting Him along with His elect and beloved ones. Al-Junayd has said, "Had I realized that God possessed a knowledge under heaven more noble than this learning we expound with our companions and brothers, I would have run straight for it." All of this is founded on sincerely taking refuge, on the awareness of one's need, on perseverance in supplication, and on self-effacement, in the presence of the King, the Mighty One. Through these means the core of one's being is expanded and the bolts of locked secrets are thrown open. And there is no help and no strength except in God.

Anyone who accepts this instruction and acts in accord with its explicit details and implications will find happiness in this world and in the next, and will be joyful.[32] However, if one continually procrastinates and runs from the telltale warnings, then he will never equal the wise person in well-being. Let us therefore ask our Lord, may He be exalted and glorified, to illumine our spiritual perceptions and purify our hearts, so that in His beneficence and bounty He will give us a share in the mercy He bestows on His servants.

And, first and last, may God bless our Master Muḥammad and his Family and give them perfect peace.

LETTER 2

To Muḥammad ibn Adībah. A letter on treating the causes of sins and vices that characterize a man with a highly developed spiritual life.[1]

10

I received your letter and I am well acquainted with the spiritual states you say you are experiencing. My brother, I want you to know that, given your present time and circumstances, none of those things is either a cause for alarm or reprehensible. One who seeks to purify his heart under such circumstances can scarcely find a path to travel toward that goal, but that his Enemy lies in ambush for him to cut his journey short. In order to achieve that, the Enemy has mustered armies of Satans like himself, not to mention female demons, and has laid snares and traps. Using subtle tricks and ruses he veils this world's charms, delusions, and promises of security from those who are wary. Should the seeker stumble over one of them unawares and without the aid of spiritual insight, the Evil One seizes the opportunity to deploy his armies against him. He sends out his demons to beguile the seeker with all sorts of vanities and affectations that can blind his heart's vision. These things block the seeker's way to the Path of his Lord, leaving him bewildered and without guidance along the way, for he can find no signposts. How can one take a straight course toward purity of heart under such conditions except with the support and prior solicitude of his powerful and glorious Lord?

I wrote to you previously to respond to the questions you had raised when you were here. In that letter I included some sections of use to the seeker on his journey, going into considerable detail as to how he should deport himself in all his spiritual states.[2] Those were my best insights on the matter. No reasonable person will doubt the soundness of what I said or have any misgivings about its implications as a remedy for whatever ails him. After I sent that letter I received a letter from you. Because of your tone and because you did not respond to my letter or say anything about receiving it or offer any reactions to it or indicate whether you remain in your former state of mind, I suspected my letter had not reached you. In any case, I offer my present response to your last letter in the hope that our Lord, may He be exalted and glorified, will grant success. I am writing in light of your questions, as is fitting, and in the hope that my reply will be of some help.

11

The gist of your letter can be summed up in three statements: First, that you are characterized by sins and faults; second, that you are unable to eliminate them or prevent them from happening; and third, that you subsequently experience embarrassment and mental confusion. These last two can actually be reduced to the first, for the inability to keep from committing sins or undo them is a fault, as are the resultant confusion and partial loss of certitude. In short, you are a man with faults.

It is essential that you examine with the eye of spiritual insight these faults of which you have spoken either directly or by implication. In other words, you must not merely consider them in a superficial way, for then you would tend to exaggerate them and thus interpret your way of living as foolish and evil conduct. You would imagine faults where there are none and see a disease in what is really a cure. The servant's intimate knowledge of his spiritual states in discerning the good from the evil, and the relatively good from the relatively evil, is one of the most important and rarest kinds of knowledge. There is very little market for it these days. Those individuals whom many people currently regard as possessing such intimate knowledge in its most developed form are in fact dealing with hypothetical matters and formal learning, which have nothing to do with the Mystic Truth. Under these circumstances the seeker can only become more perplexed, confused, and affronted as he views the scene.

All of that is a result of the paucity of true mystics who are capable of leading one to the love of the Path. One cannot but regret and grieve over the loss of the likes of these. Their absence in our time is underscored by the words of one of our ancestors in the faith:

How sad the dispersal of those who were the beacons and
citadels.
The rain-clouds, the cities, and the valleys' towering cliffs.
How sad the demise of security and repose.
Nor will the nights turn to day for us until fate has run its
course.
Now our hearts are all ember, our eyes all tears.[3]

LETTER 2

There are two ways of approaching the examination of the faults you describe. The first is to regard those faults as qualities that God has designed and created in you. The second is to consider them as imputed to you by the Revealed Law. Someone's saying "They were intended by Him, but they are not to be attributed to Him" suggests these two approaches.[4]

The first approach ascribes neither praise nor blame to the human person. It is the Creator, may He be exalted and glorified, who is in every way to be praised for these things. Your part is to be content with His decree and submit to His judgment and will. Set aside your restlessness about that now, and turn your attention to what you ought to be examining.

12

According to the second point of view, faults are indeed blameworthy. You ought to repent of them and experience sadness and compunction for them. If you do so successfully, you will reap the abundant reward of lasting benefits and win your Master's good pleasure for having done what He commanded. This does not imply that you need to worry if illness or fatigue beset you in the course of events. However, if you are not sufficiently penitent, and your human nature overcomes you and your passions take hold of you, then hasten, hasten to seek refuge in your Lord. Acknowledge your poverty and need of His favor, entering His presence humbly and contritely as one who is in dire straits. You must nevertheless not approach this state as you say you have—as though you were drowning in a wave, or food for beasts, or a tortured prisoner, or one who is condemned to death. Once you have entered the state of repentance, rejoice, for you will already have attained a status so lofty that its worth is known only to the saints. Anyone who attains this state is worthy of having his request answered and his desire granted. The Promise must be fulfilled in justice, and our Lord, may He be exalted and glorified, does not renege on His solemn Promise. One learned man who shares this point of view goes so far as to say that one who possesses this state need not even ask anyone to pray for him. He said, "The fulfillment of a request is encompassed by one's own prayer, not by someone else's."

A story tells how a woman approached al-Junayd and said, "Pray for me, for a son of mine is lost." He replied, "Go, and be patient." She departed but returned later, saying, "I have done what you told me." Junayd said, "Be patient." She answered, "I have run out of patience and can bear this no longer, so pray for me." Al-Junayd said, "If you are telling the truth, go and you son will have returned." So she went off. Later she came back, thanking God. Someone asked Junayd, "How did you know that?" He said, "Through the word of God Most High. 'One who is in need may be sure of an answer when he calls upon Him' " (27:62).[5] The mark of one who is hard pressed is his lack of reliance on his lower self and his nondependence on his own resources and strength, coupled with the sudden realization that nothing in his ordinary experience, but only God his Master, is capable of unveiling or warding off.

One of the mystics has said, "That which you worship is the first thought that comes to your mind when you are suffering anxiety." Another, commenting on the words of God Most High, "One who is in need may be sure of an answer when he calls upon Him" (27:62), said, "The needy person is the one who enters his Master's presence with his hands raised in supplications, envisioning no particular gift from God as though he had a claim to it, and says, 'My Master, give me whatever you have for me.' "[6] That is a needy person, even though he attains in this state the privilege of nearness to God and the special gift of love. Since one is able to profit thus even from indigence, the perplexity one experiences pales in significance.

13

If the answer to your prayer is not apparent to you and you are not steadfast in repentance while you continue in the state I have just described, namely, being in need of God's gifts and not relying on other means, then one of two things will happen. Either you will go to pieces with anxiety and be severely agitated, or you will be patient and resigned. In your case there is no reason why you should come undone with agitation. You have already become secure and have arrived at the Mystic Truth of faith, so you have no reason to fear that you will come to such a pass that you must choose between the two states. Therefore all that remains is patience and resignation. And in this state even the lack of a response is a response.

Ibn 'Aṭā' has said, "If God opens the door of understanding for you under the form of deprivation, deprivation itself becomes a gift."[7] He also said, "When He gives you a gift, He wants you to be aware of His kindness; when he deprives you, He wants to show you His overwhelming power. And in all of that He is causing you to understand and presenting Himself to you in His bounty."[8] In this state you will experience contemplations[9] and degrees of progress in which you will find increase and refreshment. God willing, this state will be means for reaching your goal and recovering from your malady as you come to contemplate your glorious and majestic Lord in His Attributes of grandeur, exaltation, and the plenitude of sovereignty and absolute independence that are His prerogatives. At the same time you will perceive the effects of His decrees and judgments in yourself, and see yourself as the theater of His Attributes and Names. As you turn this over in your heart so that it becomes your primary concern, you will be renewed, God willing, in the advanced states of following the Prophetic Example and in such lofty stations as love, contentment, intimate knowledge, and fear. There is no doubt that these perfect Attributes and divine gifts lead the individual to whom they are evident and who is well-founded in them to the conviction that it is God he desires, God who brings near, gives graciously, and loves.

This contemplation then leads one on to still more advanced states and stations, such as the stations of patience, gratitude, hope, shame, and repentance. All of this happens in an instant, so that you are restored where you were only broken and return to the One from whom you had once fled. Abū Hurayrah said in his collection of Traditions, "The Messenger of God, may God bless him and give him peace, said, 'By the One who holds my soul in His hand, even if you did not sin, God would come to you and make of you a people who would sin and ask God's forgiveness, so that He could forgive that people.' "[10] Ibrāhīm ibn Adham said, "One dark night while it was raining and thundering, I was making my ritual circumambulation of the House. The circuit was empty. So I approached the door and said, 'O God, protect me from ever disobeying you.' I heard a voice saying to me from within the House, 'O Ibrāhīm, you have asked me for protection, and so do all of my servants. But if I were to protect them all that way, to whom could I then be Gracious and Forgiving?' "[11]

On the other hand, if you remain blind and deceived and do not sincerely seek refuge and acknowledge your indigence, you will continue to despise your actual spiritual condition because of a strong urge to alter your spiritual states. You will detest yourself and grieve over your negligence and dissipation. If this should happen, you must undertake devotional works of both heart and body. Such works will point the way on the Path to your Lord and the malaise you endure will not hinder on the Path. A man of great stature has said, "Travel toward God even though you are lame and broken."

14

But a still more direct Path to Him is accessible to you. Remain in the station of gratitude by acknowledging all that is due to Him, and ask for more. In that way you can carry in your heart the grandeur and sublimity of your Lord and His qualities of perfection and transcendence. At the same time you will be aware of the extent of your own baseness, shame, and insignificance, and of your lower self's true lowliness and inadequacy. Look then at the graces God has bestowed upon you in whatever form they may take. Once you have scrutinized them carefully you will have begun to realize the full extent of His bounty to you and you will begin to give thanks for it. Your intimate knowledge of the scope of His grace is itself gratitude, and is the key to every good thing and the source of superabundance in every kind of good fortune and uprightness. Our Lord, may He be exalted and glorified, has said, "If you give thanks, I will indeed give you more!" (14:7). And again, "Be mindful of the bounties of God and perhaps you will be successful" (7:69).

For the servant in the presence of his Master, nothing is more beneficial than this; for it is the "Straight Path" (1:5) from which Satan tries to distract and divert the wayfarer. In this connection the Most High has said, "I shall indeed lie in ambush for them on Your Straight Path" on down to the words "and You will not find most of them grateful" (7:16–7).[12] And a saying of the Prophet, may God bless him and give him peace, goes, "Consider those who have less than you do, not those who have more than you do. This will better assist you not to make light of the grace God has given you."[13] You are no doubt aware of your Lord's inestimable largesse to you in both your religious practice and your mundane affairs. By no means the least of these graces is your aversion to your present spiritual condition as you have described it. That is one of the effects of faith, according to the saying of the Prophet, may God bless him and give him peace: "A believer is one whose good deeds delight him and whose evil ones trouble him."[14] How many people there are in far greater difficulty than you, who still experience no repugnance in their hearts, and who actually take delight and rejoice in their condition!

As I see it, you are still in the beginning phases of this malaise. Your Lord has been merciful and gracious to you in that He has turned matters around so that you might give praise for the effects of his working and, God willing, profit from it without recourse to your own abilities and strengths. You ought to delight in your Lord's generosity to you. Let it absorb you completely and relieve you of excessive introspection. Thus you will be worthy of your Lord's contentment with you. God, may He be exalted and glorified, inspired one of His prophets, saying, "Attain to the grace of wisdom and the hidden grace, for I love that." The prophet replied, "O Lord, what is the grace of wisdom and the hidden grace?" God said, "The grace of wisdom is this: If a heavy burden falls upon you, know that it was I who made it fall; then ask me to lift it from you. And the hidden grace is this: If you should possess no more than a worm-eaten bean, know that it is my way of keeping you in mind; then give thanks to me for it."

15

Therefore take a positive approach to this condition by which your Lord has graciously given you a lesson. With gratitude to your Lord, occupy yourself in being satisfied with it and in desiring more of the same. Regard as an abundant grace and vast wisdom whatever anxiety, restlessness, depression, and anguish you are experiencing. Turn your thoughts toward the reward it will bring you in your Lord's estimation of you, may He be exalted and glorified. A story tells how a certain shaykh saw a young man entering Mecca after the season of Pilgrimage had ended. The youth was defeated, broken, and sad as one who had been completely cut off. So the shaykh said to him, "Thus and so many times I have made the Pilgrimage. Therefore give me this affliction you are suffering and I will give you all of these Pilgrimages."[15] That should convince you that God has, by means of your present spiritual condition, defended you against such severe dangers and grave offenses as hybris, vanity, and all kinds of arrogance. Into this same category, likewise, falls everything you experience that might disquiet your soul and pain your heart.

It is precisely your suspicion that you are on the verge of damnation that is your safety and prize, according to the opinion of the most advanced mystics. For if you were not in that frame of mind, you would be like a sick man in need of healing. A man once said to Ḥudhayfah, may God be pleased with him, "I fear that I am a hypocrite." Ḥudhayfah replied, "If you were a hypocrite, you would not be afraid of hypocrisy."[16] The most important thing the seeker needs to do is to keep watch over this attitude, and take care to see that he possesses it, if he is to purify his actions and succeed in his efforts. That will be an index of the soundness of his intention and the sincerity of his desire.

How many are the people who strive to serve God through external deeds of obedience while manifesting such evils as vanity, arrogance, conceit, and, for all their apparent effort, continue to walk the road of separation and distance from God! How numerous are those who abandon and reject this world and act against their lower selves to the point of secluding themselves from the world, while even the most dissolute and disgraceful person enjoys a higher standing with his Lord than does the first type! For the person who experiences distance even in nearness to God is the one who is blessed with nearness by reason of his fear, and thus ascends to high rank. On the other hand, the person who discerns nearness in distance is deceived by his sense of security and is thus brought low. As Ibn 'Aṭā' has said, "It may be that He will open to you the door of obedience without opening to you the door of acceptance; or perhaps He will ordain sinfulness for you, so that it may be the means by which you come to Him." That is the meaning of the saying "Many a sin has afforded the sinner entry into the Garden."[17] Now if you add to that your perception of hidden faults and of what the lower self has concealed from you in the form of passions that could overcome you, that is the greatest of graces. It is analogous to the way shrewd people make their enemies trip over their own words; but this state defies comparison.

Perhaps you will say, "But surely that can only strengthen the case against me?" It is up to your Lord in every instance to raise objections against you, whether you are aware of the evidence or not. And how fortunate that it is also the Master's prerogative to exonerate His servant! So if you could let go and refrain from some of that, it would be a plentiful grace whether or not it involved a change in your lot. Even if change is involved, the condition toward which the change takes you will always be a lesser one, more easily bearable than the one it supersedes. Therefore take advantage of the disparity between God's assessment of you and your own assessment. Perhaps that will be a step toward refraining altogether from imputing guilt to yourself. Once you have learned this secret, you will not fret about adversity or be overly preoccupied with anxieties; as I have already suggested, you will rather count them as graces.

16

"But," one might object, "the absence of moral concern over these things—even to the point of considering them graces—will result in diminished contrition, which will lead in turn to the violation of the very principle you have laid down, namely, that all those things that upset the soul and disquiet the heart are more excellent. In other words, it would lead to a rejection of what is more excellent, as you have been describing it. Furthermore, it would lead to an underestimation of disobedience and sinfulness and to a slackening of fear and remorse."

My response to the first objection is that the lessening of contrition is laudable in this case. It is preferable to the condition you have described, for this diminishment does have beneficial results; and harm may come from failing to lessen contrition. As for its positive benefit, it effects a discovery of the bounty of God, and of specific graces, as well as a perception of God's superabundance and beneficence. One is thus elevated to the stations of certitude and to all things conducive to the likes of them. Nothing whatever can compare with this most advantageous outcome. As for the danger in failure to lessen contrition, a person risks harm in one of two ways if he persists in a state of heightened contrition for a protracted period, so that his heart and mind are preoccupied with it: The first way is that he may be led into hopelessness and despondency, two of the gravest evils. The second is that scruples may overwhelm and vex his mind. It is crucial to protect and defend the intellect against the onset of scruples, for the intellect supports the traveler along his way. A deficient intellect is never a good friend.

Given my response to the first objection, the second objection—that one is led to regard disobedience and sinfulness as negligible—vanishes. The state of mind I have recommended is actually far more conducive to restraint and repentance than are fear and compunction alone. I advocate a disposition in which contemplation leads one to stations in which he can more rapidly rid himself of his passions. That attitude is akin to awe before one's exalted and glorious Lord. Awe is a quality the servant fosters by becoming aware of the abyss between his Master's power, sublimity, and supreme sovereignty, and his own vileness, lowliness, and utter insufficiency in obeying his Master. I have not the slightest doubt that, as a result of this awe before his exalted and glorious Lord, the servant can arrive at a more accurate estimation of the enormity of rebelliousness than he could achieve through his fear of the Lord.

The reason for that is that in the state of fear one focuses only on himself and on how he would fail to attain his goal if he should fall into sinfulness. In the state of awe, on the other hand, the servant looks at his Lord in His majesty and transcendence, and then takes care lest God should see him doing what is hateful to Him. There is a saying, "Those who avoid sinfulness because they are wary of His punishments are numerous; but those who so behave out of awe before His careful scrutiny are few." The attitude I recommend focuses on that which is sought. What you have described is a focus on the seeker, and, in the opinion of the mystics, there is a vast difference between the two.

17

In addition, what I am talking about is associated with the qualities of servanthood. It is an integral part of the station of contemplation of the Lord in that it teaches one how to conduct himself appropriately in the presence of his exalted and glorious Lord by focusing his attention on Him. One who possesses the characteristics of a servant has all his needs fulfilled, as is indicated by the words of the Most High, "Is not God enough for His servant?" (39:37). An individual for whom God is sufficient will surely have God for his healer and restorer.

Finally, the objector's misgivings about the possible diminution of fear are groundless. Proper fear arises from the servant's intimate knowledge of his lower self's blandishments and sinfulness. One who possesses intimate knowledge of his lower self sees that it is his worst enemy,[18] for all of its enticements open the door to harmful consequences. Then the individual incurs the lower self's wrath and vindictiveness. The lower self beguiles him and causes him to fall into evil under the guise of good without his being fully aware of it. The lower self promises him aid but instead leaves him in greater need, for it wishes only to hurt and destroy him. What enemy could be more hostile than this?

Our Lord, may He be exalted and glorified, has told us precisely that in an expression as clear and forceful as it could be: "Indeed the lower self enjoins evil" (12:53). Its evil qualities are such that one cannot conceive of being liberated from them except through the mercy and providence of God Most High. As the Most High has said in that same passage, "unless my Lord be merciful" (12:53). In view of all this, how can one imagine that fear would be diminished? There is no reason for the objector's concern. Quite the contrary. Fear will more than likely be heightened because of an increasingly intimate knowledge of the Mystic Truth. That is one of God Most High's greatest graces to His servant: Grace itself becomes a means for discovering grace, apart from any direct correlation to the servant's works. Many people have missed out on this and do not enjoy the benefits I have been describing. And above and beyond the benefits already mentioned, blessings are increased and multiplied, as the mystics have said: "The stations of certitude by no means cancel one another out; rather, they reinforce one another in surety and firmness."

Once these two splendid qualities of awe and fear are fully realized in the servant, he receives through them a noble heritage whereby God, may He be praised, casts a light into his heart. The most direct advantage of this light is that it makes the servant aware of his minutest faults and hidden weaknesses. The light becomes a standard for him and an aid in obeying his exalted and glorious Master. Ibn 'Aṭā' has said, "The light is the army of the heart just as darkness is the army of the lower self. So when God comes to the aid of His servant, He reinforces him with brigades of light, and cuts off from him the reinforcements of darkness and of all that is other than God."[19] Ibn 'Aṭā' regards the light as a guardian, ever present and watching out for the servant in every conceivable situation: whether in instant obedience coupled with zeal, spiritual insight, and steady discernment, or in rebelliousness from which the lower self is unable to free itself because it is defeated and captive and has thus become predisposed to disobedience, or in cases more ordinary or where desire overtakes a person, so that he finds no delight or lightness in the gifts received, but rather finds them hateful, burdensome, and disturbing.

18

Another of the light's benefits is the servant's intimate knowledge of the power of the lower self. That knowledge banishes all haughty and boastful behavior, whether in relation to one's Lord or toward one's fellow servants. The servant thereby takes on the qualities of humility, meekness, docility, submissiveness, and compliance toward God; and compassion, refraining from injury, tolerance, sincere admonition of Muslims, love of what is for their good, and giving them delight. In brief, the servant conducts himself appropriately in the presence of his Lord, may He be exalted and glorified, in the hope of increasing every grace from Him and of decreasing in himself all vanity of action and pride of opinion about himself. He realizes that only God's bounty and excellence can help him and that his only recourse is to His generosity and blessings.

Asking God's forgiveness and receiving His pardon is the servant's uppermost desire. As someone has said, "The attention of one who possesses intimate knowledge is focused solely on seeking forgiveness."[20] About those who please Him the most, the Most High has said, "There has been many a prophet beside whom countless men have fought without fainting at what befell them in the way of God, and who were not weakened or defeated. And God loves those who persevere" (3:146). He continued, "And all that they had to say was, 'O Lord, forgive us our sins and wasted efforts' " (3:147). The story is told of how Ibn al-Mubārak came upon some friends of his one day and said, "Yesterday I was impudent with God Most High. I asked Him for the Garden."[21] Such are the excellent spiritual states of people like these, and their lofty qualities. Our Lord desires that we should profit from wishing for the same states and qualities.

Since the blessings I have been describing are yours, why do you not take advantage of them? Why do you cheat yourself of them, frittering away your precious time second-guessing your Lord, and disdaining what He desires for you until you end up in the condition you have described? Ibn 'Aṭā' said, "The individual who desires at a particular moment that something should occur other than what God has made manifest at that moment is holding fast to ignorance."[22]

Let your recollection therefore be filled with thoughts of God's strength and power. Let your manner of seeking forgiveness be such as will efface from you the vestiges of impurity that have infiltrated your inner self, so that you more and more call out as God's prophet Jonah, peace be upon him, did in the darkness, "There is no god but You, glory to You. Indeed I am among the wrongdoers." Then the Most High said, "So we heard his prayer and saved him from anguish, and that is the way we rescue believers" (21:87–88). One of the learned has said, "Every believer who speaks as Dhū 'n-Nūn spoke, when the believer is afflicted with anxieties or confronted with serious affairs, God will save him as He saved Dhū 'n-Nūn, according to His words, 'that is the way We rescue believers.' "[23]

19

We have thus far been examining to what extent your spiritual states are sinful and disobedient. I turn now to the faults you mentioned, such as agitation of the lower self in time of tribulation; anxiety arising from the onset of trials, distress, and failure; and the lack of patience. Those are weaknesses imprinted upon your humanity and firmly rooted in its natural disposition. They are in no way blameworthy. It may be, in fact, that under certain circumstances they are actually of positive value, so long as the servant acknowledges in the midst of them his weakness and inadequacy, lowliness, poverty, and need. As Ibn 'Aṭā' has said, "Your finest moment is the one in which you see clearly the reality of your indigence and are reduced to a state of submission."[24] He also said, "When hard times come, seekers have a festival day,"[25] for they are likely to find an abundance in lean times that they do not find in fasting and ritual prayer. That is the way God Most High tests some of His elect.

A story tells how, when Abū 'Uthmān al-Ḥīrī was with his teacher, Abū Ḥafṣ, he reached for a raisin. Abū Ḥafṣ grabbed him by the throat and tried to shake the raisin out of him. When Abū Ḥafṣ had calmed down, Abū 'Uthmān said, "O Teacher, I know that the things of this world are of no consequence in your opinion; so how is it that you got angry with me over a raisin?" Abū Ḥafṣ replied, "You have foolishly put your trust in a heart that is not ruled by its master."[26]

Someone else has said, "I was once traveling with al-Khawāṣṣ. We stopped to camp under a tree, and a lion came and lay down nearby to rest. I was terrified, so I climbed the tree and clung to a limb till dawn for fear of the lion. But al-Khawāṣṣ paid no attention to the beast. The next night we stopped to rest in a mosque. Al-Khawāṣṣ fell asleep; but when a bedbug happened to cross his face, he stomped on it. I said, 'This is strange indeed! Yesterday a lion did not make you flinch and tonight you are afraid of a bedbug!' He replied, 'Yesterday I was transported out of myself; tonight I have been returned to my senses, and that is why I was afraid.' "[27]

Sahl ibn 'Abd Allāh, may God be pleased with him, said, "God burdens the elect with indigence. He causes them to feel an innate need for created things, and then places in their hearts a resistance to them. He thus forbids people to hold on to creatures, so that they will return to Him. When the elect return to Him desperate and submissive, He gives them sustenance in ways they had not counted on."[28] It is related that a man saw in the Christian Quarter a certain mystic who had taught the acknowledgement of God's unity, detachment, and total reliance on God Most High. Utterly poor and in dire need, the teacher asked his former pupil for something. In response, the latter recited these verses:

When we are in the position of guide,
    it places us above every master and slave.
But when the tables are turned on us.
    Our humiliation surpasses that of the Jews.[29]

20

On the other hand, what is blameworthy is the lower self's seduction of the heart and imposition upon the heart of the lower self's nature. Lack of certitude is the cause of that, and those things that are classified as sins are the result.

Give some consideration to what I have been talking about. Then when some of these matters of which you complain close in on you and overcome you, put into action the qualities of servanthood, petition, and supplication of your glorious and majestic Lord by addressing Him in prayer. In time of need you must call out to Him. "O You who are rich, to whom can the poor man go but to You?" In time of weakness, "O You who are strong, to whom can the weak man go but to You?" In time of inability to act, "O You who can do all, to whom can the powerless go but to You?" And in time of humiliation, "O You who are revered, to whom can the despised man go but to You?" A man who possessed intimate knowledge said, "One who perseveres in that receives a sure response."[30] And Ibn 'Aṭā' has said, "Come to realize your own qualities and He will lead you to know His. Come to realize your weakness and He will lead you to His strength."[31]

Take advantage of the encouragement of certitude and be intent on it if you would devote yourself to investigating the science of the Ṣūfīs. Make that certitude the foundation of your endeavors. Venture into that study as a necessary duty and pay no heed to anyone who would divert you from it or denigrate Sufism, whether in person or in writing, whether directly or by insinuation. It would be a shame for a person of intelligence and understanding to be introduced to a subject and receive no help in it, and all the more if a detractor should turn him aside from it, as I have just suggested.

In an earlier letter I wrote concerning which of the Ṣūfī writings you ought to read. I mentioned that the foremost among them is Shaykh Abū Ṭālib's book. Your desire to study and investigate this book should be tantamount to a desire to seek out that which will bring your malaise to an end and cure your disease. I refer here to *The Food of Hearts.* It will help you attain every goal you seek. Begin by associating with a man of certitude and solid spiritual maturity and attending to those matters that are harmful to you and that constrict the core of your being. I know of no one nowadays who is so amply qualified as my master Sulaymān,[32] may God bless him. So accept from him whatever you find conducive to enriching your heart and nurturing your relationship with your Lord.

Learn to invoke blessings upon the Prophet, may God bless him and give him peace; for I have noted that certain mystics have alluded to that blessing as a means of strengthening one's certitude.[33] Therefore redouble your efforts in that practice.

21

This is my view of means appropriate to the relief of your malaise and the cure of your illness, provided you take action on it. But if you do not put this into practice, and thus find no compensation from among the attractions of the Merciful as you pursue your course—except in external means—then I believe you could strive for a thousand years and never satisfy your desires or find what you are searching for. Your progress in those things would remain but a distant hope. Once you have given yourself over to all of these practices I have recommended, and your heart has surcease from its perplexities, then you will already have begun to approach the awesome mercies of God.

Then, of course, you must persevere in these practices for the rest of your life. Everything I have been discussing in this letter is meant to instruct you in a simple manner of proceeding to achieve your intended aim, with the help of our exalted and glorious Lord. It is a spiritual method. It involves no physical actions except such as are required in the ordinary course of things, and no psychologically taxing labor. In this respect the essence of the method is readily grasped and easily understood. Definitive attainment of the goal, however, requires absolute dependence on God, may He be exalted and glorified, and focusing on Him with undivided attention along the road of perseverance. This will provide immeasurable delight, and it is the beginning of what the Ṣūfis are talking about. One who is steadfast will come to a full realization of that.

Sahl ibn ʿAbd Allāh said, "The servant must in all circumstances take recourse to his Master. His constant returning to Him is the servant's finest spiritual state. When he disobeys he says, 'O Lord, forgive me.' And when his rebellion is over he says, 'O Lord, turn to me.' And when He has done that the servant says, 'O Lord, find me acceptable.' " Commenting on the words of the Prophet, may God bless him and give him peace, "He makes things easy, so do not make them difficult," one of the mystics said, "The saying means, 'Lead them to God and to none other than Him; for anyone who leads you to this world has deceived you, and anyone who leads you to works alone makes you weary, and anyone who leads you to God has befriended you.' "

22

Only the person whose heart is alive with faith is able to travel this Path. The sure sign is that such a person is awake, alert, and sensitive in his religious practice when vicissitudes and obstacles arise, whether in the form of contraction or expansion. The person whose heart is dead, and who is thus impervious to those things and is totally absorbed in pandering to his passions in his evil state, is forbidden to look upon any of this. Such a person is progressing only in an intimate knowledge of wickedness, and will discover in his manner of acting only error and harm. He should avoid the deadly poison and occupy himself with the warnings against disobedience that have been handed down to us in the Book and the Prophetic Example and the words of the learned. And he should bear in mind the law's limits and sanctions in both the physical and spiritual realms. There is no other cure for this type.

Apart from what I have already pointed out in this inadequate and piecemeal description, I have nothing else to say on the subject. Rely on this and put it into practice, for it is an efficacious way of proceeding, God willing. "And God was victorious in His affair" (12:21). "If God is your helper, none can overcome you; and if God does not aid you, who else is there to give you assistance?" (3:160). All things return to Him. Therefore serve Him and put your trust in Him, for God is sufficient for the one who trusts in Him.

LETTER 3

To Muḥammad ibn Adībah. A letter explaining the unquestioning acceptance of authority, and innovation, and the bad faith and malice they involve.[1]

23

Greetings. I received the letter in which you informed me that you had received my earlier reply. You mentioned that it moved you and responded to your need to clarify your thinking and settle your convictions. You also asked in that letter that I explain a bit more fully the "unquestioning acceptance of authority" and "innovation" of which I had spoken in my previous reply.

First of all, these two concepts are censured by the Revealed Law and constitute a serious defect in one who subscribes to either of them. Blind acceptance of authority is really a species of innovation, about which I will speak later, and is tantamount to conformity with the opinion of another without supporting evidence or proof. For example, a person may attribute authority to an individual purely on the basis of that person's high rank, or to a whole community of people on the basis of its multitude or antiquity. God Most High has denounced the first type in many verses of the Qur'ān, for that attitude was in evidence among the factions of the unbelievers. "And they say, 'If only this Qur'ān had been revealed to some great man from the two towns!' " (43:31). They were referring there to specific great men from the two towns, namely, al-Walīd ibn al-Mughīrah of Mecca and Mas'ūd ibn 'Umar of aṭ-Ṭā' if.[2]. They were in that way discounting the true greatness of Muḥammad's prophetic calling and holding him in derision because he was Abū Ṭālib's orphan. In the words of the Most High, "When the unbelievers look at you, they think of you only in derision" (21:36).

24

When the Prophet, peace be upon him, called the unbelieving Quraysh to the true religion, they demanded signs of him. They wanted him to revive for them one of their most outstanding men, Quṣayy ibn Kilāb.

They asked the Prophet, peace be upon him, what he brought; but they followed the opinion of Quṣayy unquestioningly and returned to him. And when Abū Ṭālib was near death a number of the Quraysh were with him, including Abū Jahl. The Prophet, peace be upon him, came to visit Abū Ṭālib and invited him to confess the unity of God. Then the Quraysh said, "O Abū Ṭālib, will you abandon the faith community of 'Abd al-Muṭṭalib?" So the Prophet, may God bless him and give him peace, encouraged him again; and again the Quraysh tried to dissuade Abū Ṭālib. In the end he remained with the faith community of 'Abd al-Muṭṭalib. Then this verse was revealed, "Indeed it is not you who guide whomever you would like; rather it is God who guides whom He will" (28:56). All of this exemplifies blind acceptance of authority on the grounds of prestige. God Most High described people who act that way when He said, "Behold we found our fathers already adhering to a religion" (43:22). In other words, they swore by their ancestors because they had put them on a pedestal.

Concerning the people of Ṣāliḥ,[3] upon whom be peace, the Most High has said, "Are we to follow a single human being from among us?" (54:24). So they refused to follow that one man. The point is that if a large number of people had been sent to them they would willingly have followed them. This is blind acceptance of authority on the basis of numerical strength.

About Pharaoh and the people of Noah,[4] peace be upon him, the Most High said, "We know of no such thing among our ancient ancestors" (28:36). In other words, if Noah had been talking to them about their ancestors' and forefathers' belief in the mission of their prophet, then the people would have accepted the authority of their predecessors and followed in their footsteps. This is unquestioning acceptance of authority on the basis of antiquity.

God did not excuse the riffraff of the unbelievers, either from their blind acceptance of the authority of their leaders or from the misguided leadership of their chiefs. On the contrary, God considers them all to be in error and makes them share in a common warning and punishment. Because of their extreme obtuseness and invincible ignorance, God Most High has likened such people to asses and cattle (7:179; 25:44; 47:12), judging them on the basis of their lack of knowledge and understanding.

You must understand that this despicable attitude of uncritical acceptance of authority has made its sparks fly even in our own time. Its ill effects are widespread. You will note, for example, how the individual who has no true wisdom but merely claims to understand grimaces and frowns when he hears of something relating to true mystical knowledge or of something known to people who give true witness to their faith. Out of the depths of his ignorance such a person says, "If this were true, surely someone would have seized upon it before now and passed it along from generation to generation." You will also see the person who aspires to be a Ṣūfī,[5] but who has no inkling about questions of legal judgment or about what is permitted and forbidden, and who is alienated from his fellows and is fooled by his own charlatanry and deceit. Because such a person's ignorance is so extensive, he says, "These externals and guidelines are for the consumption of the common people. My Master so and so could not read or write and was not affiliated with any legal school."

You will also encounter the lazy libertine who persists in grave sins, imitating the errors of the ancients and the mistakes of the religious scholars, all the while considering that to be solid, true, pure religious practice. Ignorance thus spreads among the people so that they no longer look to the One who is above even their religious leaders, whom they follow like lemmings. They think nothing of sacrificing themselves for their leaders' legal support and practices. People like this are numerous, but I need not multiply examples. My point is simply that you should be aware that social dealings with the likes of these will dull your heart and keep you from the goal you seek. Therefore exercise caution in these matters.

25

You should know further that every question seeks a true answer. There is, therefore, an alternative to unquestioning acceptance of authority, to the extent that one searches for the evidence on which a given question is based, whether in relation to required matters such as the articles of the faith, or nonrequired matters such as are not essential to belief. Blind acceptance of authority in these issues is to be censured, whether or not one's personal inquiry is successful. However, this does not hold true in cases where the general populace accepts without question the authority of those who make a profession of studying the various brances of legal science. In that case one seeks a correct answer of the sort only a professional jurist is likely to arrive at, and which is therefore accessible to the general public only by acceptance of another's authority. Nor does this hold in relation to such things as Qur'ān interpretation, study of the Traditions, history, grammar, linguistics, medicine, and so forth. For even if one seeks a firsthand knowledge of the thing, one must still accept the authority of some professional in these fields. Nevertheless, servile acceptance of authority is essentially blameworthy and cannot be relied upon without deleterious effects. Have you not noticed how the stupid person becomes even more obstinate in matters of faith as a result of blind acceptance of authority in matters relating to his faith, whereas a person whose reason is sound does not share that fate? God, may He be exalted and glorified, knows best.

As for innovation, many verses and Traditions testify to its sinfulness. For example, God, may He be exalted and glorified, has said, "Have nothing whatever to do with those who depart from their religion and create a schism" (6:160). Commentators on the text have noted that these are people prone to caprice and innovation. The Most High has said, "They were not divided until knowledge that caused rivalries among them came to them" (42:14). In other words, those people knew they were in error in provoking division and discord and promoting rivalry. The Most High also called them "devils of humankind and jinn who use guile to make their arguments convincing" (6:113). Guile here means elegant and embellished rhetoric. There are other verses like these. Whenever the Qur'ān speaks of the sinfulness of following caprice and reliance on empty arguments, and forbids these two things, it is referring precisely to innovation.

The Prophet, may God bless him and give him peace, said, "Whoever adds to our religion what does not belong to it is a rebel." He also said, peace be upon him, "None of you is a believer unless you desire to adhere to what I have brought." And again, "Novelties are malicious, and every innovation is an error." And the Prophet, peace be upon him, said, "The children of Israel are divided into seventy-two sects and my community will split into seventy-three, all but one of which are destined for the Fire." The people said to him, "And what is that one, O Messenger of God?" He replied, "The one to which I and my Companions belong." Another version says, "Seventy-two are in the Fire and one is in the Garden, and that is the Community. Indeed, many will depart from my Community after being taken in by these whims as a dog goes along with the pack; and not a trace or remnant of them will survive unless they enter my Community."[6]

26

A man said to Ibn ʿAbbās, "Give me advice." So Ibn ʿAbbās replied "Be an adherent and do not be an innovator."[7] And Ibn Masʿūd said, "If you are a follower and do not seek innovations, you will have done enough." He also said, "Anyone who would follow the Example of the Prophet should act as did these deceased Companions of Muḥammad, may God bless him and give him peace, for they were the best of this Community, the most sincere of heart, the most profoundly learned, and the least pretentious people. God chose them to be Companions to His Prophet, may God bless him and give him peace, and to hand on His religion. Therefore imitate their behavior and special qualities, for they possessed straight guidance."[8]

Shurayḥ said, "The Prophetic Example takes precedence over your analogical reasoning. Follow it and do not be innovators and you will not stray from the tradition you have received."[9] And Sha'bī said, "As for the position concerning the abode of death, if you raise an objection to it you will destroy it."[10] A man asked Mālik about a certain issue, and Mālik replied, "The Messenger of God, may God bless him and give him peace, said thus and so." So the man said, "And is that your opinion as well?" Mālik answered, "Let those who disagree with what the Prophet has said beware lest strife befall them or the punishment of Hell come upon them."[11] And Sufyān ath-Thawrī said, "Iblīs prefers innovation even to outright rebellion. For one can repent of rebelliousness, but one cannot repent of innovation."[12]

Numerous sayings and Traditions address this question. Innovation means any attempt to add to, or propose an argument against, the truth taught through the Messenger of God, may God bless him and give him peace, claiming that the innovation is the true straight path in the realm of legal decisions as to the correctness or error of knowledge or action. Its variations are endless. I have mentioned only a few of them here, for it would be unprofitable to go on about them at length. By way of concrete historical example, however, I propose the following:

God Most High sent Muḥammad, may God bless him and give him peace, as a Messenger to all humanity and as a guide for them the abode of peace. In the pre-Islamic age[13] there lived ignorant people and erring miscreants who were disunited in their opinions and fragmented in their desires. Their proud intelligence recommended to them only heedlessness in their manner of conduct. For all their abundant intellect they attained only to the worship of stone and sun and moon. But God Most High was kind to them in that He sent them a messenger from among them. He was the rarest and finest of them, and God gave him the most perfect qualities and the most excellent character, bestowing on him the most precious gifts and behests.

In the Prophet's being and attributes there was a brilliant sign and an overwhelming authority, so that the fires of error were extinguished at the rising of his lights. Traces of former ignorance were obliterated when his footprints appeared, and strife ceased. It was a time of concord when believers in the religion became brothers and were aligned in obedience to the Lord of the Universe. They sold their souls to the One who owned them and who had freed them, and they were content to live without the objectives and values of this world. They delighted in this splendid pledge of fidelity and said, "We have won inestimable and ineffable blessings." They considered companionship with His Messenger, may God bless him and give him peace, the richest of treasures and the most powerful of defenses. Because of their love for the Messenger, they guarded their association with him with their lifeblood. Their hearts were intent only on him so that they preferred him to all things else.[14] Adults and children alike surrendered to his good pleasure and swore allegiance to him even to suffering violent death, and were one in their praise of the Prophet. "Indeed those who swear allegiance to you are in reality swearing allegiance to God" (48:10). It was a noble, exalted, glorious time, and I could go on about the excellence of their deeds and spiritual states.

27

All that I have said thus far is attested to in the passages of the Book which hand down to us the faith of those people of intelligence. They were, in short, uninamous in the worship of their Lord and united in seeking aid and defense in the exalted word of God Most High. For God Most High brought them together in obedience to a single religious law only that they might become familiar with one another through common adherence to it, and that they might become as one person. God Most High has said, "The believers are nothing else but brothers" (49:10). And again, "The believers, men and women, are one another's protecting friends" (9:71). Therefore the Prophet, may God bless him and give him peace, commanded obligatory unity and forbade disobedience. As the trustworthy Tradition says, "If anyone should witness his commander doing anything distasteful, he should be patient; for anyone who separates himself even a hand's breadth from the Community and dies in that state will die the death of the pagan."[15]

At the end of a lengthy Tradition the Prophet, may God bless him and give him peace, said, "I enjoin on you five things my Lord commanded me: unity, attentiveness, obedience, making the emigration, and fighting in the way of God. Anyone who leaves the Community by so much as a hand's breadth has slipped the yoke of Islam off his neck until he returns. And anyone who adheres to pre-Islamic beliefs is among the people of Hell."[16] By the words "slipping the yoke of Islam off his neck," he meant any breach of the bond of Islam, forsaking the Prophetic Example, and following an innovation.

Sha'bī has said, "Some people from Kūfah went out to the desert to devote themselves to serving God. They decided to build a mosque, and then erected a building. When Ibn Mas'ūd came to visit them they said, 'Greetings, Abū 'Abd ar-Raḥmān. We are delighted you have come to visit us.' He replied, 'I have not come as a visitor, and I will not leave until the desert mosque has been demolished. You are not acting in accord with the guidance of the Companions of Muḥammad, may God bless him and give him peace. Do you not understand that if others do what you have done there will be no one left to fight the enemy, or command the good and forbid the evil, or establish the limits of law? Come back. Learn from those who know more than you do and teach those who know less than you do.' So saying he won them over; and he did not leave until we had torn down their edifice and brought the people back."

After God Most High had taken away His Prophet, upon whom be peace, according to His good pleasure, and had given him the ultimate grace and kindness, He appointed the Rightly Guided Caliphs[17] as successors in his Community to reconcile and show the right way. They followed and defended the Prophet's religion and his Example, and shone with his dazzling lights and resplendent signs. This state of affairs perdured through their lifetimes, until God Most High took them to Himself. But when the era of excellence and justice waned and the age of goodness and refinement passed, the lights of certitude were extinguished along with it.

28

Then the qualities of the "lower selves enjoining evil" (12:53) waxed strong and spread abroad. Caprice and innovation were renewed; the unity of the religion was rent; disputes and factionalism arose so that every group and enclave had its own school of thought. People engaged in mindless innovation and fell under the sway of unbelief and error. They strayed from following a single path; relationships disintegrated; people opposed each other in hatred, enmity, envy, and spite. These scandals even went to the extremes of violation of the inviolable and the shedding of blood. And these abominations then led some to discard modest clothing and expose themselves indecently. In trade for their religion they bought what was worthless and flaunted the wrath of Him to Whom they would return.

This process has continued down to our own time, so that it had been our lot to drink from the very same cup. "For we are God's and to God we shall return" (2:156). Our Prophet, God bless him and give him peace, is reported to have said, "I am a security for my Companions. But when I am gone, my Companions will discharge their mission and my Companions will be a security for my Community. Therefore, after my death, my Community must carry out what they decide upon."[18] He said other things like that as well. And these are the very times of discord that the Prophet, may God bless him and give him peace, has described. He enjoined seclusion and withdrawal from the public at such times.

Here I shall cite some of the Traditions of Discord[19] relating to those trials and ordeals, drawing on the Prophetic Traditions and calling to mind the dazzling evidentiary miracle [the Qur'ān], with their warnings of happenings as yet undisclosed. The Messenger of God, may God bless him and give him peace, said, "How will it be for you in that time when people are sifted as in a sieve, so that there remains only the dregs of humanity, whose oaths and pledges of fidelity are hopelessly muddled, when people are at odds with one another and have become like so?"—then he knotted his fingers together. They asked, "How will it be for us, O Messenger of God?" He replied, "You will hold fast to what you approve and cast aside what you disapprove. You will pay heed to only what pertains to the few of you and disregard the interests of the majority."[20] And in a Tradition of 'Abd Allāh ibn Mas'ūd, he said, may God bless him and give him peace, "What will you do when discord has seized you, so that you adopt a way of acting espoused by the minority and disregarded by the majority, and when if even a part of the Prophetic Example is left unfulfilled it will be said that the whole of it has been abandoned?" They asked, "And when will that be, O Messenger of God?" He answered, "When your Qur'ān reciters are many but your religious scholars are few; and when your commanders are many but the believers among you are scarce; and when this world looks urgently for the works of the next world and yet comprehends only what is other than God." 'Abd Allāh ibn Mas'ūd added, "And we have already arrived at that point."

LETTER 3

29

Commenting on the words of the Most High, "You are responsible for your own souls" (5:105), the Prophet, may God bless him and give him peace, said, "Command the good and forbid the evil; but when you see greed victorious and passion in control and this world preferred, and when you see every knowledgeable person fascinated with his own opinion, then take care of yourselves and leave the common throng. For indeed the days of patience are coming. Then patience will be like grasping live embers. A single person who acts rightly in those days will receive the reward of fifty who act like him." Someone said, "O Messenger of God, the reward of fifty of them?" He replied, "The reward of fifty of you."[21] And he also said, may God Bless him and give him peace, "Do your good works before dissension comes like portions of a dark night, when a man will wake in the morning a believer and end the day an unbeliever; or he will end the day a believer and wake up an unbeliever who has exchanged his religion for this world."[22] Al-Ḥasan said, "This means that he starts the day respecting his brother's life and property and possessions, and ends the day considering them fair game."[23]

The Prophet, may God bless him and give him peace, said, "You live at a time when if a person neglects one tenth of his duty he perishes; but a time will come when anyone who fulfills one tenth of his duty will be saved. Indeed days of patience are coming, when patience will be like grasping live coals. The performance of simple acts of worship in that time of turmoil will be as meritorious as coming to me as emigrants."[24] Ibn ʿAdī said, "We went to visit Anas ibn Mālik and complained to him that we never encountered any people who had made the Pilgrimage. So he said, 'Among the generality of people one is more wicked than the next, until you come to meet your Lord. I heard this from the Messenger of God, may God bless him and give him peace.' "[25]

According to a Tradition from Ḥudhayfah, "The Messenger of God, may God bless him and give him peace, related two Traditions to us, one of which I have seen realized, the other of which I am waiting to see. He related to us how trustworthiness had descended into the inmost hearts of humanity. Then the Qur'ān was revealed, so they recited the Qur'ān and acted according to the Prophetic Example. Then he related to us how that situation deteriorated: Trustworthiness is removed while a man sleeps; then he wakes to find it has been taken from his heart. Its traces remain like a scab or blister caused when a hot coal rolls over your foot. He sees a swelling but there is nothing in it. Trustworthiness is so diminished that it will be said that among the tribe of So and So there is a trustworthy man, and there is a trustworthy man in the tribe of So and So. I have seen a time when I did not care which of you I was doing business with; for if he were a Muslim, his Islām would cause him to deal fairly with me; otherwise, the ruler would make him do so. But today I would buy nothing from any of you except So and So."[26]

Another version of this saying has been transmitted this way: "A man will sleep for a while and trustworthiness will be removed from his heart, so that only the faintest trace of it remains. Then he will sleep again, and again trustworthiness will be taken away leaving a mark like the blister that remains after a hot ember rolls over your foot. The ember leaves a blister, but you notice that the blister gradually disappears until nothing is left of it. People will awake in the morning and engage in business with each other, but scarcely one of them will live according to trustworthiness. And a man will be told how intelligent, how knowledgeable, how patient he is; but in his heart there will be not even a mustard seed's weight of trustworthiness!"[27]

Still another Tradition says: "People used to ask the Messenger of God, may God bless him and give him peace, about the good; but I (Ḥudhayfah) used to ask him about evil because I feared it might overtake me. So I said, 'O Messenger of God, once we were in the age of paganism and evil, the God brought this good age to us. Will evil follow upon this good?' He said, 'Yes.' So I asked, 'And will there be good after that evil?' He replied, 'Yes, but there will be smoke in it.' I asked, 'What will be the smoke in it?' He answered, 'People will follow a way of life that is not mine and give guidance that is not mine, so you will recognize some good in them as well as some evil.' I asked again, 'And after that good will there again be evil?' He said, 'Yes. People will stand at the gates of Hell inviting; and they will throw into Hell anyone who answers their call.' I said, 'O Messenger of God, describe those people for us.' He said, 'They will be our fellow countrymen and they will speak our language.' So I asked, 'What advice can you give me if I should live to see that?' He said, 'Adhere to the Community of Muslims and its leader.' 'But what if they have no Community and no leader?' I asked. He said, 'Then separate yourself from those factions, even if in doing so you wind up clinging to the root of a tree until you die.' "[28]

30

From Usāmah ibn Zayd we have this: "The Messenger of God, may God bless him and give him peace, looked down from one of the fortifications of Medinah and asked, 'Do you see what I see?' They answered, 'No.' Then he said, 'I see dissensions occurring between your houses like rain failing.' "[29] Another saying is, "Believe me, there will be dissensions, and then more dissensions in which the sleeper is better off than the one who is awake, and the one who is awake is better off than one who is sitting, and one who sits is better off than one who stands, and the one who stands is better off than the one who is walking, and the one who walks is better off than one who runs. Anyone who looks upon those dissensions will be mesmerized by them; so anyone who can find shelter or a refuge should take cover in it."[30] He also said, may God bless him and give him peace, "It will not be long before a Muslim's best possession will be the sheep which he will herd to the mountaintops and the places where rain falls, as he flees from the discord and takes his religion with him."[31]

Consider this along with what I have already cited from Ibn Mas'ūd concerning those who secede, and the contrast between the eras will be evident to you. Ibn Mas'ūd said that in his time "clarity has vanished from this world and only opaqueness remains, so that today death is a boon for every Muslim." There are many other Traditions of Discord as well.

One of those sayings tells how "there will come a time when people will be misguided in their religion, but they will not be aware of it. A man will wake in the morning a religious person and end the day not knowing what religion is about. In that time many people's intelligence will be snatched away. Humility will be the first thing taken, then faith, then fear of God." Someone asked Ibn al-Mubārak whether justice would be in evidence after two hundred years. He replied, "I was discussing that with Ṣamād ibn Sulmah, and he became agitated and said, 'If you can die before two hundred years are up, do it! For in that time there will arise dissolute princes, unjust ministers, disloyal chamberlains, and disreputable Qur'ān reciters, whose conversation among themselves will be reprehensible, and whom God considers foul-smelling.' "[32]

Now if all this was true in their day, do you not believe it is so today? In these peculiar times the intelligent person must take counsel with himself and flee from the children of his race. He must find an upright and true companion who walks the path of the pious ancestors in the faith, who leaves aside what is incompatible with the clear way of proceeding, and who relates Traditions accurately and follows the Prophet's way of life. For God Most High does not exempt any age from the duty of defending and proving the religion in opposition to heretics. God Most High rouses in people a sense of His truth and leads them thereby along His Path.

31

The Prophet, may God bless him and give him peace, said, "No faction that abandons my Community is in the right, and no one who disagrees with my Community will harm it unless God commands it." Speaking about knowledge and the religious scholars, ʻAlī, may God be pleased with him, said at the end of a Tradition from Kamīl ibn Ziyād aṭ-Ṭawīl, "O God, let not the earth lack for someone who is concerned with your proof on earth, whether that proof be evident and well-known or hidden and obscure, lest God's proofs and evidences disappear. Where are such people and how numerous are they? They are few in number but their power is great. God guards His proofs until those who contemplate them recognize them and implant their images in their hearts. Then He urges them on to the knowledge of the Mystic Truth of faith, so that they pursue the spirit of certitude. They regard as soft what those who live in luxury consider hard, and they are intimately acquainted with all that the ignorant are estranged from. They live in this world in bodies, but their spirits are intent on the highest abode. These are God's successors on earth, who call people to His religion saying, 'Look here! Look here!' in the hope that they will look. O Kamīl, I ask God's forgiveness for both of us." And at the end ʻAlī said, "And even if such people continued to diminish in number until there were only one left, that one person would constitute the Community."[33]

Someone reportedly asked Ibn al-Mubārak about what was required to constitute a community assembly. He replied, "Abū Bakr and ʻUmar." Someone said, "But Abū Bakr and ʻUmar are dead." "Then So and so and So and so," he replied. Someone said, "But they are also dead." Then he said, "Abū Ḥamzah as-Sukrī is an assembled community." Explaining the meaning of the term assembly or community, Sufyān ath-Thawrī said, "If on some mountaintop there were a single person of understanding, he would constitute the Community." This corroborates what I have already said.

But I have digressed, so let me return to my subject. Everything I have been discussing in this letter has reference to one of the varieties of innovation. Whatever its causes may be, innovation results in dissension, controversy, schism, and fragmentation. Such things occur among those who engage in idle talk arising from the intensity of their divisive fanaticism. They distinguish the liar and the one who speaks the truth. Let us analyze the matter further. Divisions, among liars, result from a destructive desire and the seduction of Satan. The cause of the division among truthful persons is their adherence to the requirements of the faith and commands Muslims must follow. Among truthful persons, however, division occurs for different reasons, as for example in the case of a dispute between Ṣūfīs and jurists over legal questions and the principles of the Revealed Law. Their differences of opinion in those matters, however, are a mercy; for God in His mercy does not wish to coerce us in the practice of the faith.[34]

This last sort of disagreement occurred also among the exalted company of the Ṣūfīs, but with a kindness and mercy that were devoid of enmity and hatred. For all of them were in search of the truth and traveling the road of sincerity. ʿAwn ibn ʿAbd Allāh said, "How excellent it was when the Companions of the Prophet, may God bless him and give him peace, were not at odds with each other, so that when they concurred on something and a man departed from their position he was departing from the Example of the Prophet. But if they did express variant opinions and a man adhered to any one of their views, that man was adhering to the Example of the Prophet."[35] The secret of that is, as I have already said, that the point is to follow a probable opinion rather than to have forced uniformity.

32

The same may be said of the difference of opinion among those who are learned in esoteric matters relating to the heart's progress and the stations of lover and beloved. This is entirely a controversy as to the relationship between the Mystic Truth and the variation in individuals' spiritual states and degrees of sensitivity. Each of the various opinions articulates the mystical experience that occurs in the context of a given individual's capacity. The ability to discern the person who tells the truth from one who lies is very elusive. Anyone who desires that must redouble his efforts in observing the regulations of religious practice and in investigating the life and Traditions of the Prophet, in order to comprehend them in his heart and be secure from unquestioning acceptance of authority by seeking success and confirmation from his Lord.

I had previously cautioned you against people who practice the type of innovation associated with articles of the faith, the exoteric and esoteric sciences, and the actions that are altogether contrary to the Prophetic Example. In fact, that includes all the varieties of innovation. One of the religious scholars has said, "Friendship with innovators ultimately steals away the heart's lights and the goodness of one's actions, so that one inherits God's hatred and distance from Him." Sahl ibn 'Abd Allāh said, "Whoever treats an innovator gently robs the Prophetic Way of its sweetness; and whoever smiles at an innovator deprives his own heart of the lights of faith." And one of the religious scholars has said, "Repenting of innovation does not grant success; for even if a person then discovers part of the Truth, he still does not come to the meaning of the Mystic Truth."

In addition to these numerous kinds of innovation in knowledge and action thus far included in my description of innovation, there are others. They include scruples, exaggeration, extravagance, obstinacy—all of which are blameworthy and are in no way part of the Prophetic Example. Once you have assimilated what I have been saying, you will understand that the only people who have successfully adhered to the Prophetic Example have been this select group of Ṣūfīs, at least up until the introduction of novelties among them in more recent times. The Ṣūfīs' foremost concern has been with those very things that are lacking in people who wander off in error, namely, struggling against the lower self to keep from following their passions, and complete abandonment of this world. Their goal is to focus their hearts on their Lord and become totally immersed in experiencing and being near to Him.

That goal includes all the duties of religious practice, the stations of those who possess intimate knowledge and certitude, and their spiritual states vis à vis the Prophetic Example. Their lofty stations are their inheritance for holding fast to the behavior sanctioned by the Revealed Law. No just person could suspect that they have broken away from adherence to the Example of the Prophet as their most exalted destiny. And yet they are castigated for precisely that, while in fact it was to them that the Prophet, may God bless him and give him peace, referred when he said: "Indeed God, may He be exalted and glorified, has some servants who become thin and whom He makes healthy with His mercy and restores to well-being. And when they die He takes them to His Garden. They are those on whom dissensions fall like the pieces of a dark night, but they are safe from them."

LETTER 3

33

Abū 'l-Qāsim al-Junayd, the master and leader of the Ṣūfīs, has said, "All paths are closed to God's creatures, except to those who follow in the footsteps of the Messenger, may God bless him and give him peace." He also said, "Anyone who does not memorize the Qur'ān and copy out the Traditions is not to be imitated, for all of our knowledge is set down in the Book and the Example of the Prophet." He said further, "This knowledge of ours is based on the Traditions of the Messenger of God, may God bless him and give him peace."[36] Sahl ibn 'Abd Allāh said, "Our principles are based on six things: The Book of God, the Example of His Messenger, eating permitted foods, refraining from injury and avoiding sins, repentance, and the pursuit of justice." Abū 'Uthmān al-Ḥīrī said, "Anyone who makes the Example of the Prophet his rule in word and deed speaks with wisdom; anyone who lets passion rule him speaks as an innovator." God Most High has said, "And if you obey him you will be guided . . . " (24:54). Ibn 'Aṭā' said, "When a person conforms himself to the Example of the Prophet, God illumines his heart with the light of intimate knowledge."[37]

No station is more exalted than the following of the Beloved One, may God bless him and give him peace, in his commands, actions, and personal qualities. Abū Ḥamzah al-Baghdādī said, "One who knows the Path of God has no trouble following it. And the only guide toward the Path of God is imitation of the Messenger in his actions, spiritual states, and words."[38] Abū Bakr aṭ-Ṭamastānī said, "Whoever takes as his companions the Book and the Example of the Prophet, and leaves behind his lower self and the created world, making an Emigration to God in his heart, is upright and just."[39] And Abū 'l-Qāsim an-Naṣrābādhī said, "The fundamental principles of Sufism are adherence to the Book and the Prophetic Example, abandonment of innovation and whim, holding in high esteem the strictures of the spiritual masters, discernment of the guiles of the created world, perseverance in private devotions, and forsaking the pursuit of luxury and futile interpretations."[40]

Abū Yazīd al-Bisṭāmī said to one of his companions, "Come, let us go see this man who has made himself a reputation for saintliness." The man to whom he was referring was renowned for his asceticism. He continued with the story: "So we went. When the man came out of his house, he entered the mosque and spat in the direction of the niche. Abū Yazīd turned away without greeting the man, and said, 'This is not representative of the behavior of the Prophet, peace be upon him. How could this man be exemplary in what he prays for?' "[41] Abū Yazīd also said, "I took a notion to ask my Lord, may He be exalted and glorified, to remove my desire for food and for women. But then I said to myself, 'How can I ask God for this when the Messenger of God, may God bless him and give him peace, did not do so?' So I did not ask for it. Then God, to whom be glory, removed my desire for women to such a degree that I did not care whether I was looking at a woman or a wall!"[42]

Ja'far ibn Nuṣayr asked Bakrān ad-Dīnawarī, ash-Shiblī's servant, "What is your opinion of ash-Shiblī?" Bakrān said, "He once told me, 'I had gotten a dirham unfairly, so I gave it as devotional alms on behalf of its owner; but my heart was never more distracted than that.' Then once he told me to perform his ritual ablution for him. I did it but I forgot to comb his beard. He was unable to speak, so he grabbed my hand and ran it through his beard. Then he died." Ja'far wept and said, "What can you say about a man who never in his life had to be reminded of the behavior prescribed by the Revealed Law?"[43]

34

Many other such stories are told about the Ṣūfīs. I have mentioned enough of them that God might make us profit from their blessings and gather us among their ranks and make their Path accessible to us. Anyone who travels their way, and prefers their Path to that of the jurists, will catch up to them and come into conformity with them in speech and thought. And God Most High knows best.

This, then, is what I wanted to say about the meaning of blind acceptance of authority and innovation. I have found none of the religious scholars mentioning a specific limit or regulation on them, but I have made inferences from their intended meaning and their implied generalizations. Perhaps what I have said is sound, but it is God Most High who grants success in accuracy, according to His kindness and generosity.

I have decided to conclude this letter with a quotation from that greatest of religious leaders, al-Ḥasan ibn Abī 'l-Ḥasan al-Baṣrī, may God be pleased with him. He calls attention here to ancient and neglected ways of proceeding which the person of lofty aspirations must learn to treasure. I thought I might in this way summarize what I have been saying and bring to completion my stated purpose.

Commenting on the words of God, may He be exalted and glorified, "Indeed you have in the Messenger of God a good example" (33:21), Ḥasan, may God have mercy on him, said:

> God Most High surely chose Muḥammad, may God bless him and give him peace, for knowledge, and revealed His Book to him and sent him as a Messenger to his people. Then He gave the Prophet a place in this world wherein the people of this world might look to him, and gave him power in the world. Then He said, "Indeed you have in the Messenger of God a good example." But, by God, the tribesmen scorned that example, so God put them far from Him. The rescue, the rescue! The revelation, the revelation! Upon that you will arise! In that you will rejoice! The cords of this world are cut off from you and its doors are locked to you. It is as though you were a cavalcade of horsemen at a standstill—a call from any one of you is its own answer. This world's conditions depended on the pledge of the Messenger of God, may God bless him and give him peace; but you involved yourselves in the world's sinfulness. So, by God, all that we know of what remains is the final accounting.
>
> When God, may He be exalted and glorified, sent the Prophet, He said, "This is a Prophet, this is my favorite. Adhere to his Example and his Path." Before the Prophet no door was bolted; before him no gatekeeper arose. He did not take his breakfast in bowls, nor did he rest; rather, he was always going out. Whoever wanted to meet the Messenger of God, may God bless him and give him peace, met him. He would sit on the ground and put his food on the ground and he dressed in rough clothes. He rode a donkey that followed after him and licked his hand. And the Prophet said, "Whoever despises my Example is not part of me." Many are those who shun his Example and depart from it. Infidels! Sinners! Their food is usury and rancor. My Lord has declared them foolish and despises them. They claimed there was nothing wrong with the way they ate and drank and adorned themselves. They gave their own meaning to the words of God, to whom be glory. "Say: who has forbidden the adornment of God which He has brought for His servants and the good things He has provided?" (7:32). But these things are for the friends

of Satan, and he has made those things the playground of his belly and his digestive tract.

35

The Companions of the Messenger of God, may God bless him and give him peace, acted in accord with the Book of God and the Example of His Messenger, may God bless him and give him peace. They practiced what they preached and preached what they practiced. When night fell on them, they stood on their feet and covered their faces. Their tears ran down their cheeks. They desired freedom for their slaves. And when some of this world's goods were offered to them or made available to them, they took as much of it as they needed and left the surplus for the next life. They gave thanks to their Lord for it and sold the remainder for the good of their souls. And if those good things were taken from them, they rejoiced and said, "This is part of God's attentive predilection for us, may He be exalted and glorified." If they did something good, they were pleased and besought God to accept it. And if they did evil, they felt remorse and asked God's forgiveness. They always behaved that way. And, by God, only through forgiveness were they free from sin or blessed with the Garden.

People came to be desirous of the faith and hastened toward it. Believers strove for good deeds and feared that they might not be acceptable. But after them there came people who did evil, feeling secure and having no fear that they might be caught in their deeds. Among the people of this Community were individuals who might live fifty years without ever having a garment to fold, with nothing to put between themselves and the ground, and who did not order their families to prepare any food that appealed to them. When such a person entered his house, he entered gaunt and feeble. When this invitation to faith came to them, they accepted it sincerely; and into their hearts there came a certitude about it. Their hearts and bodies and eyes became submissive to the invitation, as though they had seen what they had been promised. And, by God, they were in no way a people given to dispute, or vanity, or affectation.

A command came to these people from God Most High

and they believed in it, so that God Most High described them with the highest praise in His Book when He said, "The servants of the Merciful are those who walk upon the earth modestly"—the word modesty in Arabic means gentleness, tranquillity, and dignity—and He continued, "and when the foolish address them they answer, 'Peace' " (25:63). These are the noble, the Godfearing, the patient. If they are wronged they do not retaliate. If they are treated ignorantly, they respond with nobility, and they are patient until God takes up their cause. That is how the servants of God deal with others.

Their nights follow their days, and their nights are better. For they spend the night prostrate before their Lord and standing upright on their feet before Him, veiling their faces. Their tears run down their cheeks because of separation from their Lord. That is why they keep night vigil before Him and that is why their days are less important. "They say, 'Our Lord, turn away from us the punishment of Hell, for its punishment is anguish' " (25:65). All things pass away, and so will anguish; but so long as the heavens and the earth last, anguish is inevitable. These people give witness to God, beside whom there is no god. The faithful labor but do not tire.

And you—may God mercifully grant you this faith; for God has no better gift for His servant either in this world or in the next. Believers are patient, docile, God-fearing, and reverent. By God, a servant cannot comprehend his Lord in such a way that he becomes haughty or presumptuous or conceited. A servant does not seek this gift without working for it and exerting himself for it, giving witness to God both in private and in public ceaselessly until his death. Then his Lord hears the praise of His people: "They say 'Our Lord is God,' and then they are going in the right direction" (41:30). By God, they are upright in intimate knowledge of Him and they hasten to obey Him: "The angels descend upon them, saying 'Do not fear and do not be sad: hear the good news of the Garden promised to you' " (41:30). They leave the world behind to its people but that does not leave them sad; nor do they compete with its people for this world's glory. Noble, understanding,

> and wise, they are the lamps of guidance who lead away from all dark earthly discord. The people of earth do not recognize them, but the people of heaven know them.

I will cite no more here of what Ḥasan said. His words are marvelous gems and lofty thoughts, as excellent as any can be. Even the most eloquent tongues cannot express such things fully, and one who contemplates these matters cannot but be overawed. With that we have concluded the issues and purpose at hand. How numerous were Ḥasan's praiseworthy spiritual stations in assisting the religion and in vanquishing apostates, in guiding the wayward to the right paths and in instructing the ignorant! May God give him recompense and great reward for that. And may He give us success in following in Ḥasan's steps and in being illumined by his lights.

LETTER 4

To Muḥammad ibn Adībah. A chapter on the conduct of those involved in the legal sciences, and on the innovations and misdeeds for which they are responsible.[1]

37

You should understand that innovation abounds nowadays among people of this ilk, and the results are divisiveness and far-reaching harmful effects. Corrupt intention in their methods of investigation and ignorance of the law's uses and applications are the cause. The perversity of their intention has sent them plummeting into the abyss of deceptions; and because of their ignorance of the true meaning of the science, their hearts lack the ecstasy of the light. They have become the epitome of fading vision and will become aware of their shame on that day when inmost hearts are put on trial. You need only observe their actions and gain an intimate knowledge of their spiritual states in order to be persuaded of the soundness and accuracy of what I have said about them. Hearsay is no substitute for eyewitnessing and nothing clarifies like seeing for yourself.

In short, anyone who engages in these sciences with malicious design and guile in his heart is deluded from the outset. Naturally, then, such a person proceeds to make all kinds of unacceptable interpretations, and in the process the characteristics of his reprehensible lower self gain strength. This state of affairs results inevitably in a multiplication of evils and setbacks, but all the while the person thinks it is his Lord who has empowered him to do it!

Suppose that one of these jurists were to engage in his work with what he claims is a pure intention. He is convinced that his Lord will reward him for his study and learning. He thinks he is spending his time as he should and that he is free of evil motives. Then his accursed enemy plunders him, overpowering him with all sorts of guile and half-truths, reminding him only of the excellent qualities of the learned and the advanced status of the jurists and intellectuals. Meanwhile the poor fellow is unaware that he has been duped by a phantom. He has played into the enemy's hands by rejecting the very things that are binding on him and for which he is responsible.

38

Still another jurist might set about his task with sound intention. He is serious about fleeing from these sinful defects, putting the issues in their proper perspective, and keeping in check the motives and tendencies of his lower self. This man, however, can find no one to give him guidance in his present state so that he can remain in it; and circumstances compel him to seek the company of people he does not know. Before long an interior fever begins to spread in him and signs of hypocrisy begin to appear in his outward conduct. Perversity replaces probity, and the path of success and fulfillment becomes unclear to him, "except for those who believe and do good works, and they are few" (38:25).

From the Master of Humankind, may God bless him and give him peace, we have received the Tradition, "The most hypocritical people among my community are the Qur'ān reciters."[2] Al-Ḥasan ibn Abī 'l-Ḥasan said, "When a man goes in search of knowledge, it soon becomes apparent in his humility, his clothing, his gaze, his speech, his gestures, his ritual prayer, his guidance, and his asceticism. If the man is to reach the final gate of knowledge, he must act in accord with knowledge. Things will go well for him in this world, insofar as that is possible; and if not here, then he can expect that in the next life." He went on to say, "God does not accept fasting or ritual prayer or the freeing of a slave or a Pilgrimage or a lesser pilgrimage or participation in a holy war or alms or a just deed, from an innovator. Indeed a time will come when people will confuse the truth with falsehood. When that happens nothing will avail but a cry like the cry of a drowning person. So help yourselves to knowledge; but knowledge will not keep its people safe."[3] Al-Ḥasan, God be merciful to him, is referring here to the search for knowledge, devoid of spiritual insight, that was evident in his day.

Sufyān ath-Thawrī has said, "Beware the many seductions of the deceitful scholar! And beware the humility of the hypocrite!" Mālik said, "I went to see 'Abd ar-Raḥmān ibn Hurmuz. He had violated the law in private and spoke of the revealed laws of Islam, and of how he was afraid because of what he had done. And he wept copiously." Mālik went on, "Now Ibn Hurmuz was a man I liked to emulate. He spoke little, expounded few legal opinions, was firm in his observance, circumspect in his conversation, severe in dealing with libertines, and was one of the most learned of debaters."[4] Mālik continued, "I went to visit Rabī'ah and found him crying. So I said to him, 'May God give you courage, why are you crying?' He replied, 'O Mālik, unbelievers and reprobates are expounding the law and speaking out on our religion!' " And Mālik concluded, "How well Rabī'ah understood our situation."[5] Someone else said, "I noticed that Sufyān ath-Thawrī was sad, so I asked him about it. He said, 'We have come to the point of having to deal with the children of this world.' So I asked, 'How so?' He answered, 'One of them remains with us until he becomes identified with us. Then he leaves us to become a laborer or a chamberlain or a steward of a tax collector. Then he says, "ath-Thawrī handed this Tradition down to me . . ." ' "

39

Perhaps you will ask, "How can the student and the teacher be travelers on the road of the Example of the Prophet and adhere to what is required of this community of faith?" The interrelationship between the teacher's instruction and the pupil's study comes down to this: The Prophetic Example as regards the student's investigation requires that, in matters of specific legal duty, he put his trust in the most knowledgeable and God-fearing teacher he can find. As regards the teacher's instruction, the Prophetic Example enjoins kindness toward the student, a genial disposition toward him, and the most eloquent instruction the teacher can give. Even in matters that do not involve specific legal requirements the Prophetic Example presupposes that the intention of both teacher and student is sincere, and that they avoid forbidden and reprehensible actions, and that they not take liberties in meeting the external requirements of the Revealed Law. If they should go against any of those requirements and think they have performed a good deed, then they are innovators and their opinion is heresy, for it is not consistent with the way of our ancestors in the faith. If, on the other hand, they acknowledge their sins and desire to be saved from them, but merely lack the capacity, then they are not innovators but disobedient people who have set aside the more excellent course of action.

Here are some of the more common transgressions of the student. He might study with someone who is fond of having a great throng of followers, or against whom there is some evidence, or who allows reprehensible things to go unchecked in his classes. These latter may include slander, fighting, posturing, contentiousness, and shouting, either in the mosque or in the course of listening to Traditions of the

Prophet, God bless him and give him peace. They may also include contradicting one of the religious scholars in a belligerent way, hurting a fellow student by false accusation, breach of propriety, refusing to abide by the view of the majority, and other things of this sort. In general terms, this includes unkind behavior by harassing him with questions or contradicting what he says, or lording it over one's peers and fellow students, or mistreating in word or action those nearby in the class, or thinking badly of them, and so forth.

As for the teacher, he may fail by accepting students whose minds are clearly subject to impure intention or evil thoughts. Indeed it is precisely the lack of regard for this matter that accounts for much of the corruption in our time. The teacher may also err by seating himself in a place elevated above his companions without sufficiently cogent reason; or by being indulgent with bad conduct, whether directed at the teacher or at another student; by failing to speak strictly at times and even ordering a student to leave the class, in accord with the teacher's understanding of the requirements of the religion; or by favoring the wealthy and the children of this world with places nearest him, to the exclusion of the poor and indigent—an action that is in no way related to religious requirements.

The teacher may also be at fault for not giving students advice when it is appropriate; or for failing to include in his classes the recollection of God Most High, the recitation of verses from His Book and of the Traditions of the Prophet, God bless him and give him peace, and the tradition of the pious; or for not invoking blessing upon the Prophet, God bless him and give him peace, or not invoking God's forgiveness and mercy and seeking refuge in Him—for these things are explicitly prescribed for all. In fact the teacher ought to make these things the foundation of the class, give careful attention to them, and consider them among the class's greatest benefits.

40

Such matters are the surest index of the teacher's alertness of heart and purity of soul. If he truly possesses an ample portion of the knowledge of certitude and a solid share in the spiritual states of the mystics and the spiritually successful, then he should speak to his students about this precious learning of his to the extent that they are able to grasp it. He should let them see some of his noble spiritual states so that theirs might thereby be strengthened. He should point out to them the interrelationship of the Revealed Law and the Mystic Truth and clarify their understanding of the mysteries of the clearest Path, about which they would like to know. By his interest and by the way he speaks the teacher should prevent the students from giving their attention to all that is novel and ephemeral, and help them realize the meaning of the words of the Prophet, God bless him and give him peace: "The truest verse the poets ever spoke is this: 'Are not all things empty that have not God in them?' "[6]

Such was the way of our devout forefathers in faith and the counsel of our authoritative religious scholars. Anyone who emulates and follows them gains great success in his lifetime and attains everlasting righteousness as a last result in the presence of his Lord. Anyone who turns aside from following that exemplary conduct and parts company with our forefathers has bartered the next world for this world (cf. 2:86) and will incur the wrath of his Master and be subject to the judgment of the word of God Most High: "Say: Shall We tell you who will be the greatest losers in their deeds? Those whose efforts in this life are wayward even while they believe they are doing good" (18:104–5). And God is our refuge from that.

LETTER 5

To Muhammad ibn Adībah. A letter to console the heart of a friend afflicted with anxiety over someone's objections concerning the letters of his friend.

41

Praise to God alone.

I send you warm greetings. I find it necessary to write to you since I have become aware of your distress of what Zayd or 'Amr[1] has said about the contents of the letter I wrote you some time ago. I gather that has taken a considerable toll on you.

I want you to know that I dared to attempt that kind of exposition of truth and error knowing full well that I was exposing myself to the invective and censure of long-winded critics. That did not deter me in the least, for I did it with sincere intent and the letter achieved its purpose. Anyone who is persuaded that he can escape people's fault-finding and challenging is deluded. I personally have no fear of the kind of criticism that falls by its own weight. However, I am afraid of the individual who twists my intended meaning and fails to comprehend its essential import. I am convinced that what I wrote on the subject was clear and precise, without being overstated, and that I avoided being blunt where it would not lead to understanding.

Ash-Shāfi'ī hit the mark exactly when he said while giving advice to one of his companions, "I will speak only the truth to you. In any case, there is no way to be safe from the public; so I will keep in view what is in your best interest and then impose it on you as a duty."[2] And a certain wise man has said, "The public can be a far more severe affliction for an individual than even the seven sins or poisonous serpents: One can avoid the latter, but one can never be entirely aloof from the public."

God therefore bestows on us a tranquillity that revives hearts and minds, and a repose that shines with the brilliance of dawn. With those two gifts we care little about people who cast lightening or thunder at us, and we are not much concerned about who stands or sits. On the contrary, we take it all as a cause for reflection, a means of recollection, and a reason for great praise of our Lord, who alone is worthy of it. A certain wise man has said, "Whoever looks at people with his own eye gets into lengthy disputes with them; whoever looks at them with God's eye forgives them."

42

We ought, therefore, to go down the list of those travelers on the Ṣūfī path who have been criticized and accused of error and freethinking and consider their behavior. They are the elect among the saints, accustomed to trials and tribulations by virtue of grace so plentiful that it cannot be measured and for which one can never be sufficiently grateful. But that grace does not diminish by a single atom the integrity of their spiritual states. No one can gainsay them, except perhaps saving with a tearful eye, "How could I ever be like that seeing I am who I am? Can the likes of me aspire to so lofty a status?"

> Nevertheless I am pleased that passion has
> been taken away and I am free of it; it no
> longer has any hold on me.

In the midst of the spiritual trials that make heads bow, let us not be distracted by what is going on around us or be concerned about its harm or benefit.

This is what I wanted to explain to you in order to heal your heart and set your mind at ease. I preferred to do it this way rather than avoid mentioning in this letter what I had written to you previously or suggest that privacy and secrecy are necessary. Do not let any of those things frighten or trouble you. Let me commend to you again the advice I gave you in my earlier letter and confirm the pledge of support that it implies. We ask our powerful and glorious Lord for success according to His good pleasure. May He gather our desires in righteous service before Him, for He is a generous, eternal, merciful King.

LETTER 6

To Muḥammad ibn Adībah. A letter in response to various questions. Individual captions are given in the margins [but here are inserted in brackets] since the topics covered are grouped together. First the question of Pilgrimage and its legal requirements in relation to individuals and circumstances.

43

Praise to God alone.

[Principles related to going on the Pilgrimage.]

These days making the Pilgrimage is something for which people have an increasing desire and [to which they] are very favorably disposed.[1] They prefer the hardship, need, and separation from home that are part and parcel of the Pilgrimage to relaxation, comfort, and staying at home. There are, of course, some who have abandoned their religion and have no desire to make Pilgrimage. And there are others who, once they have carried out the formalities of the intended action, have only one interest and desire, namely, to return to their home countries and rejoin their families and friends. But once they have done that, they again experience the tedium of staying at home. They are overcome by boredom and ennui so that they long even more than before to take to the road. These are all basic and natural human tendencies.

When the intelligent and spiritually insightful person attends to such matters, he must set aside his natural needs and subject his human inclinations to a spiritual critique. He must take counsel with his heart and act in accord with the requirements of religious practice, insofar as they are clearly evident to him. Otherwise he should ask the advice of one who is competent in these matters, rather than follow personal whim. Without spiritual insight and deliberation his actions will be futile and he will succumb to exertion in vain.

The specific legal requirements of Pilgrimage are not unknown to you. So let us look at the subject from a more general point of view. I would say that Pilgrimages are of three types: those that are entirely praiseworthy, those that are entirely sinful, and those that are partly laudable and partly censureable.

LETTER 6

A Pilgrimage that is altogether praiseworthy is that of a person who is knowledgeable, sure, and free from the dictates of the lower self. Such a person is not overcome by his human tendencies. The requirements of religious practice and the light of certitude motivate him. This is a noble state, a most exalted position that only one who has experienced it can fully understand.

44

A story tells of how one of the religious scholars once said, "As I was making my ritual circumambulation of the House, a very old man came up to me and inquired about my homeland. I told him about it, and he asked, 'How far is it from here to there?' I replied, 'About two months.' Then he said, 'You could make Pilgrimage to this House every year!' Then I asked him, 'And how far away is your country?' He answered, 'When I was still a youth I set out from my homeland on a five-year journey.' I was amazed at that, so he went on to say.

Visit the one you love even when the dwelling
    is far from you and is hidden and veiled.
Do not let distance deter you from visiting Him,
    for the lover visits the one he loves.

Another story tells how one day Shaykh Abū 'l-Ḥasan al-Lakhmī was sitting with his companions and discussing the legal aspects of Pilgrimage. They talked at great length about whether the requirement remained in force in their time. Meanwhile a poor man was listening just outside their circle. After they had finished, the man poked his head into the gathering and said to the shaykh,

O my Master,
If you had not the least desire to shed my blood,
    You would hardly give excessive consideration to it.[2]

The characteristics of a Pilgrimage that is entirely blameworthy are quite different from those of one performed with an intention free of hypocrisy and the desire for reputation. The former is motivated purely by idle whim. But these first two types of Pilgrimage occur only rarely and their legal implications are clear.

The Pilgrimage of a pious person who proceeds out of a conviction that contains an admixture of personal goals and passions is sinful in part and laudable in part. Such a person is unaware of the ruses of the Enemy and the guiles of the lower self that influence his decision to go. Neither the good motives nor the evil seem to be predominant. However, motivations for this type of Pilgrimage vary with individuals and circumstances, and this requires some explanation.

45

Both those who have already made one Pilgrimage and those who have not done so may make this type of Pilgrimage. For a person who has not already made Pilgrimage,[3] who is capable of fulfilling the duty directly, and who has sufficient means and no impediments, the journey is both laudable and obligatory. Once he had discharged his duties to parents, family, and creditors, in accord with the specific prescriptions of the jurists, nothing stands in the way of his Pilgrimage. On the other hand, if one fears death or lacks the proper conditions, or is faced with some obstacle, then the obligation is mitigated. The same is true for the common folk, that is, the generality of Muslims who are concerned only with external actions. Similarly, if a person neglects acts of obedience and good works, individual or communal, shirking times of prayer and supererogatory deeds and refusing to do things that are beneficial to others—such as teaching or studying or acting with kindness toward a Muslim—even when he is at home, then the obligation is lessened. Conversely, if a person would, while traveling, either omit some duty or do something forbidden, as he would not have acted had he stayed at home, the obligation is mitigated. Under such circumstances the Pilgrimage would be sinful: The power of the lower self's inclination would result in sinfulness and in the loss of the religious intentions requisite for the Pilgrimage.

Even if a traveler were keenly attentive to observing prescribed duties and avoiding what is forbidden, his journey could still be predominantly blameworthy, either because of the strength of his personal inclination and the consequent lack of the religious intentions just mentioned, or because he cannot be certain of his safety. On the other hand, his journey could be predominantly laudable, to the extent that it helps him fulfill the duty of Pilgrimage itself and avoid juridical error—provided he is physically strong, has plenty of money, and can go by a well-traveled road. In that case he must observe his prescribed duties and avoid occasions of sin along the way. If none of these problems occurs as he goes on Pilgrimage, then the case is all the more clear.

Given this context, a Pilgrimage will be predominantly acceptable under the following conditions: if one is from the more educated classes, or is among those who are more disposed toward the kind of activities needed in struggling against the lower self, purification of the heart, vigilance over one's thoughts, maintaining a healthy imagination, being immersed in considering and being mindful of other matters relating to exalted states and noble stations, and being firmly grounded in the need for interior purification from the major sins of a rebellious heart. These last simply must be eradicated. They include conceit, vanity, envy, malice, dissembling, hypocrisy, deceitfulness in religious practice, evil thoughts about Muslims, a powerful love of this world, and other kinds of folly. If in this regard conditions favorable to making a Pilgrimage prevail, then one must investigate the legal principles involved, so far as he is able.

46

If, on the other hand, the individual is not well grounded in the purification and cleansing I am talking about, or does not consider this necessary for him, and if he lacks either good physical health or sufficient finances, then it would be sinful for him to make Pilgrimage, given his alienation from the rudiments, not to mention the fine points, of the spiritual states I have described as preconditions for Pilgrimage. A strong inclination of the lower self is another impediment. Suppose, for example, that a person had abundant physical strength and the resources necessary to prevent fatigue and overexertion and to take him from desire to fulfillment. Suppose further that his desire to travel was so powerful that it would perdure even if it were possible to free him from the duty of Pilgrimage and to secure the same reward by refraining from travel altogether. In that instance it would be better for him not to go, for two reasons: the strength of his natural inclination; and the risk of losing out on the benefits he would enjoy just by remaining at home, whereas he could not be certain of attaining them on his journey mainly for lack of a secure road.

But what if one had very little desire to make Pilgrimage and his sole motive for going were the fulfillment of a requirement? If that person's lack of inclination and desire to go could be entirely removed, then his making a Pilgrimage would be praiseworthy. His desire is weak, but his hope of achieving his goal through physical health and sufficient resources is strong, particularly if he should join up along the way with devout brothers and agreeable companions, and if he makes his way along a well-traveled road.

All that I have said thus far applies to the person who has not already made the Pilgrimage.

Now consider the case of one who has already made Pilgrimage. If the person is one of the common folk, whose attitude toward good deeds and works of devotion is similar to the attitude I described earlier, then there are several reasons why his going on Pilgrimage would be blameworthy. They include the inclination of his lower self, the risk of losing the goals he has already realized, and his uncertainty as to the perfection of his desire and as to his safety from the dangers he might encounter. Suppose that if he remained home his situation would be different from the one I described earlier. Then his making the Pilgrimage would probably tend to be more blameworthy, because the inclination of his lower self is powerful and he would risk weakening his sense of religious obligation or falling into sin on his journey. It is possible, however, that his journey might be predominantly laudable because of his desire to engage in a particular kind of worshipful act, even if such an inclination is not held in the highest esteem. I am presupposing here that he is free from the impediments mentioned above; but if he knows clearly that he is not free from them, then making Pilgrimage would definitely be predominantly sinful, for nothing is as important as that freedom.

If the individual in question is among those more educated in religious matters, then Pilgrimage is censurable if it involves a loss of the excellent spiritual states he already enjoys, and a consequent diminishment of the words and deeds attendant upon those states. These require an emptiness of heart, a singlemindedness, and a purity of intention that long journeys such as this cannot but minimize. I consider the qualities just mentioned to be of greater consequence than supererogatory acts performed on Pilgrimage, for the former are essential concerns and act as a corrective to one's devotional acts. They are essential for one who travels the way of sincerity and of acknowledging the Divine Unity, and raise one to the stations of the elect. No supererogatory acts of worship can equal these deeds of the heart and no pious actions can replace them.

47

If this type of individual undertakes the Pilgrimage without sincerity, then he is more deserving of blame than of praise. Natural inclination toward the Pilgrimage, together with a catering to the lower self and its objectives, is an indication of insincerity. In this case the lower self desires to fulfill its designs through the devotional works the person performs on his journey. These may include meeting religious scholars and people renowned for their piety, taking advantage of their learning, asking for their blessings and prayers, being of service to one's friends and companions, tallying up the merits of one's meticulous efforts, observing the passing scene of cities and deserts, and making much of the rituals and duties of the Pilgrimage with its clamor and excitement. The true intention of this kind of Pilgrimage remains an ill-concealed desire to see foreign lands, experience the novelty of encountering the learned and the servants of God, freedom from the ordinary cares of home, and relief from the drudgery of mundane concerns, among other such purposes and hidden agenda. The telltale sign that a person is being so deceived is that he could perform many of these same pious deeds, and greater still, while remaining at home; but when he is at home he pays them no heed and is not at all interested in them.

This was the condition of the man who, as he considered making Pilgrimage, made a request of Bishr al-Ḥāfī. Abū Naṣr at-Tamār relates that a man came to bid farewell to Bishr ibn al-Ḥārith, saying, "I am eager to make the Pilgrimage, so give me some instructions." Bishr said to him, "How much money do you have for your sustenance?" The man replied, "A thousand dirhams." "And what prompts you to make your Pilgrimage?" Bishr asked. "Is it entertainment, or a yearning for the House, or a desire to please God?" "A desire to please God," said the man. Bishr asked further, "And if you could please God Most High by staying home and spending the thousand dirhams, and you were sure this would please God, would you do it?" "Yes," said the man. "Then give it to ten people," Bishr said. "Then the person of faith can fulfill his religious practice, and the poor person can get back on his feet, and the father of a family can make his family prosper, and the one who is raising an orphan can give him joy. So if the One God gives your heart the strength to give the gift, do it. For surely your bringing happiness into the heart of a Muslim, and your sending rain to the sighing, and your alleviating the pain of the destitute, and your affirming a man who is weak in certitude are all more excellent than hundreds upon hundreds of proofs of Islam. Go and disperse the money as I have advised you. Otherwise tell me what is truly in your heart." The man said, "O Abū Naṣr, my journey is uppermost in my heart." So Bishr smiled and approached him and said, "When money is gotten through unfair and suspicious business practices, that goads the lower self into conceiving a desire to hasten toward outwardly pious works. But God Most High has sworn that He will accept only the actions of the God-fearing." When Bishr had said this, the man wept.[4]

48

Take the case of a person who is well-founded in the spiritual states I have mentioned and devotes himself fully to fostering them while remaining at home. Suppose that he desired to test his fidelity to those states by enduring separation from the familiar and dependable things of his homeland, resolving to struggle against his lower self in that way. His Pilgrimage would be praiseworthy. Though that struggle is not the primary purpose of Pilgrimage, it is conceivable that one might undertake the journey with that in mind. That remains one of the habits of detached wayfarers. Still, I consider the lower self's inclination toward making the Pilgrimage to be sinful in most cases, arguing from the principle that the lower self's proclivity for acts of worship that are physically arduous is sinful.

[Response to the second question: Concerning how the lower self can be inclined toward that which involves hardship.]

Someone who hears this may be astonished and ask, "How can the lower self be inclined toward that which involves hardship when such a thing is not in its best interests?" The objector does not realize that the lower self sometimes seeks a destiny at which it can arrive only by abandoning its share of comfort. One sees, for example, people so obsessed with the love of fame and wealth and so determined to gratify their desire for them that they risk dangers, plunge into the seas, and place themselves in all kinds of peril. Their hope of attaining their desires urges them to delight in such hardships. Even so, what they gain is not what they had hoped for. There are two sides to this question. The difference is that the goals I have just mentioned are commonplace and well known to most people. The ways of achieving them are clear and not the least bit ambiguous. On the other hand, religious people whose spiritual states are elevated beyond those of the generality of Muslims are dedicated to the other goals I have been talking about. But it is out of ignorance and sheer folly that the lower self performs arduous tasks to attain petty results, even as a person might expose himself to battlefields, slanderous talk, and buffeting so that he might be praised posthumously for his valor and endurance. This is consummate ignorance, for of what use will those things be to the lower self after death?

Such goals are pursued without any concept or purpose and without compensation in the end, as 'Alī ibn Ḥazm said in *The Book of Gov-*

ernment.[5] Still more foolish than these are the people I have met who do not know why they sacrifice themselves. Sometimes Zayd attacks ʿAmr, sometimes ʿAmr Zayd, perhaps even on the same day. They risk death senselessly. They are slaughtered for the Fire or they flee in disgrace. The Messenger of God, God bless him and give him peace, issued a warning about such people when he said, "A time will come upon the people when the killer will not know why he kills, nor the one slain why he was killed."[6]

49

Now the matter at hand is analogous to situations in which the natural inclination of the lower self impels some people to become deeply involved in acts of worship and to apply themselves with great intensity to practices of self-denial. They hurl the lower self into dangerous situations and the fulfillment of duties on the assumption that this will hasten their progress toward the spiritual states they associate with great people. They imagine that by means of these excessive tendencies they can exchange their own shortsightedness for an insight into perfection. They abandon certain worldly goals hoping to bolster the sincerity of their lower self's intentions by claiming they are pursuing religious obligations. Before long they consecrate these actions and periods of devotion, devote increasing amounts of time to them, and lose hold of their set purpose by regressing into baser things than they had originally intended and desired. If the lower self's intentions had been acceptable, its actions would in no way constitute a violation; and the lower self would understand that only adherence to the religion of the original monotheists[7] could bring it to that end. I swear by my life that anyone these days who adheres to that religion and follows its ways will, strange thing, undergo unimaginable suffering and drink a choking beverage such as no person can drink. Therefore[8] his reward will be abundant and his efforts meritorious, for the sound principle is that everything that is a burden upon the lower self is genuinely good.

[Response to the third question: Concerning the positive aspect of hardships on the lower self.]

Let me explain. God Most High has required His servants to worship Him. He has informed us that He has created them precisely for that purpose, in His words: "I created the jinn and mankind only that they might worship" (51:56). Worship is one of the most sublime and magnificent characteristics with which He described His prophets and messengers and one of the noblest titles with which He has named them, especially our Prophet Muḥammad, may God bless him and give him peace. That is why he attained the very highest place and held the loftiest position and will thus appear over the universe on Judgment Day with all of the prophets and messengers under his standard.

One of the most succinct and eloquent statements on this topic is someone's saying, "Worship is the spiritual vision of Lordliness." This expression sums up the meaning of servanthood in the opinion of the Ṣūfis. It relates to the station of doing good mentioned in the tradition of Gabriel, peace be upon him. It has been said, "Worship means being His servant in every circumstance, as though He were your Lord in every circumstance." It is also said that "worship has four characteristics: the fulfillment of pledges, observing the limits of the law, contentment with one's actual condition, and patience in the midst of losses." The point of these and other such expressions is that worship is a quality inherent in the servant, which prompts him to obey the Divine Commands, avoid what is forbidden, and be resigned to the Divine Decrees. Servanthood begins with the station of surrender and ends with the station of doing good.[9]

Only the "lower self that incites to evil" (12:53) can divert the servant from fulfilling this worship according to its stations. Therefore the only way to fullness of worship according to the Divine Commandments is the struggle against the lower self along the Path of this elect company of Ṣūfis. God, may He be exalted and glorified, has said, "Surely We guide to our Paths those who strive by our power" (29:69). And again, "Indeed the Garden will be the place of rest for the one who has restrained the lower self from passion" (79:40–41). And according to a saying of the Prophet, "Your greatest enemy is the lower self that is between your two sides."[10] God Most High inspired David, upon whom be peace, to say, "Your lower self is an enemy; indeed, nothing else in all the kingdom is contentious with me."[11]

50

Al-Junayd said, "I got up one night to keep my period of private night prayer, but I did not experience my usual consolation. I decided to go back to sleep but I could not. So I sat up, but I could not do that either. So I opened the door and went outside, and there was a man wrapped in a woolen cloak lying on the path. When he noticed me, he raised his head and said, 'O Abū 'l-Qāsim come quickly!' 'Right away, good sir,' I replied. Then he said, 'I asked the Inciter of Hearts to arouse your heart.' 'He has done just that,' I responded. 'What is it that you need?' He asked me then, 'When does the disease of the lower self become its own remedy?' I replied, 'When the lower self acts against its passions its disease becomes its cure.' The man was pensive for a moment and then said, 'Had I given you that answer seven times you would have rejected it. But now you have heard it from al-Junayd, so you have listened to it.' Then he turned away from me but I did not know him."[12]

Reflect on this remarkable story. There are countless others that make the same point. It is in the context of trials by which God Most High tests some of His servants that the benefits of such self-denial and religious exercises come to fruition, for those trials cause servants to resist their desires and detest their passions. They profit by bearing those things with patience and exhibiting the character traits servants strive for: humble, self-effacing submissiveness and the acknowledgement of their poverty. People who undergo trials stand as examples. For that reason the prophets are our models, according to the word of God Most High, "So be patient as the stout-hearted messengers were patient" (46:35). They were indeed accustomed to suffering and hardship—Job, for example, peace be upon him. They were cut with scissors and sawn in two, and there were seventy prophets.[13] To say, then, that everything burdensome to the lower self is good is to say that every trial is a grace.

[Response to the fourth question: An exposition of less weighty matters that are praiseworthy.]

One may ask whether this means that every activity that rests lightly on the lower self or causes it to act appropriately through grace and hope is therefore an evil and a cause for distress. Should one enjoy asking for burdens and tribulations and seek them actively since they are actually a good grace, or is such a course recommended?

To the first question my answer is no, for one can find all kinds of deeds of piety that are both easy for souls and praiseworthy, and a variety of graces that are pleasant, entirely positive, and containing no evil. I am referring to the kind of lightness some people experience in such actions as taking a break from their worldly occupations, laying to rest some of the cares of the heart, or being grateful for some grace that surpassed every expectation and which they find pleasant. Some sources of that praiseworthy lightness are, for example, comforting the sorrowful, feeding the hungry, clothing the naked, giving drink to the thirsty, sheltering the orphan, arguing against a rival religion, and so forth. Therefore, the experience of lightness and joy in graces the servant merits by such deeds becomes a means of obeying and worshiping God. These are the graces given to those who give food or drink, clothe, shelter, give transportation, or give in marriage. However, as I shall explain, it is commendable to take delight in these gracious deeds only because they constitute a rebuke to one's natural disposition, and never because they might serve as means to someone's sinful purpose.

[Response to the fifth question: About refraining from desiring and asking for hardships.]

51

So long as no religious prohibition is involved, it is permissible to desire and ask for trials; but it is not allowed if religion forbids it. According to an authentic Tradition from Abū Hurayrah, the Messenger of God, God bless him and give him peace, said, "Do not be eager to meet the enemy; but if you should come upon them, be patient." And according to a Tradition from 'Abd Allāh ibn Abī Awfā, the Messenger of God, may God bless him and give him peace, said "O people, do not be eager to meet the enemy; ask God for well-being. But if you do meet them, be patient and know that the Garden is under the shade of swords."[14] Anas ibn Mālik also reported an authentic Tradition that the Messenger of God, may God bless him and give him peace, paid a visit to a certain Muslim man who had so wasted away that he had become like a chicken. The Messenger of God, may God bless him and give him peace, asked him, "Have you been praying for something or making some request of God?" He replied, "Yes, I have been saying, 'O God, let me not be punished in the next world, rather, hasten that punishment for me in this world.' " So the Messenger of God, may God bless him and give him peace, said, "Glory be to God! That is beyond your capacity and you could not endure it! Why do you not say instead, 'O God, give us good in this world and good in the world to come, and protect us from the punishment of the Fire' "? (2:201). Anas says the man then prayed that way and was healed.[15]

A variation of that Tradition says, "We cannot endure the punishment of God." The Messenger of God, may God bless him and give him peace, never ceased to pray for abundant graces and freedom from trials.

Trustworthy accounts report that one of the Messenger of God's frequent prayers, may God bless him and give him peace, was, "O God, give us good in this world and good in the world to come and protect us from the punishment of the Fire."[16] And another tradition from Abū Hurayrah reports that the Prophet of God, may God bless him and give him peace, used to seek refuge from an adverse judgment, from being overcome by suffering, from his enemies' delight in his misfortune, and from the distress of tribulations.[17] These were only a few of his prayers for safety. In one of the regions where the infidels had done him injury, the Prophet, may God bless him and give him peace, said, "But I am more interested in your well-being."

The wisdom in these sayings is this: Trials are not desirable in themselves, but only when they include some of the benefits I have mentioned, and when they enhance the reward promised to those who are patient in them. But even without sending down trials or burdening people with troubles, God Most High gives all those good things and more to whom He chooses. The Messenger of God, may God bless him and give him peace, is reported to have said, "It is God's prerogative to withhold His rich generosity from any of you who are His servants, until the servant reaches out and takes hold of it." The Messenger of God, may God bless him and give him peace, also said, "Indeed God keeps disease and illness from some of His servants in this world. He gives them health in life, health in death, and health in the Garden to which he brings them."

52

It behooves the servant to ask his Master for pure largesse without the intermediacy of trials and hardship. It follows that he must not make a point of desiring for himself, or asking his Master for, straightened circumstances; for they require a superadundance of strength and unflappable endurance. Creatures are weak and, except by God's help and support, are unable to sustain or fend off even the force of an atom that is able to overtake them. Self-Reliance is out of the question; even to hope for it is the height of presumption. One ought rather to be fearful of relying on and trusting in himself and thus perish as some people have.

When ash-Shāfiʿī, God have mercy on him, became gravely ill he often said, "O God, if it please you to do so, give me more of this illness." So al-Maʿāfirī[18] wrote to him from the south of Egypt, "O Abū ʿAbd Allāh, you are not one of us who suffer trials and then ask for contentment with things as they are! We must above all ask for kindness and health." Ash-Shāfiʿī wrote back, "I ask God's forgiveness and repent before Him." After that he used to say, "O God, give me the blessings I desire."

Then we have this remarkable statement:

I desire You, but I desire you not for the sake of reward;
    No, I want you for the sake of eternal punishment.
I have realized my every desire.
    Except for the delight of ecstasy in agony.[19]

And this saying of Sumnūn: "You are my sole desire, so put me to the test however You wish."[20] When Muʿādh ibn Jabal was at the point of death he said, "Strangle me with Your strangling, and I will have given you a sign that tells you my heart loves you."[21] All of these statements are the result of an overwhelming spiritual state in which the Sulṭān of Ecstasy has taken possession of the speakers.

53

Thus are lovers in the station of love overcome by God, whether through humiliations or through a feeling of expansiveness, so that they speak of things that are shocking at first hearing. Some of what they say seems to be tantamount to unbelief. They are nevertheless justified in all they say and are secure in their exalted stations. As Shiblī has said, "The lover perishes if he keeps silent; the mystic perishes if he does not keep silent." It is reported that when Sumnūn uttered the verse quoted above, one of his companions said to another, "Yesterday when I was in Rastāq I heard the voice of our Master Sumnūn ibn Ḥamzah calling upon God Most High, imploring and begging Him for healing." A second man said, "I also heard this yesterday while I was in such and such a place." A third and a fourth said something similar. The word got back to Sumnūn. He was suffering from a debilitating illness, but he was patient and not in anxiety. So when he heard they were saying these things, when in fact he had neither prayed for nor said any such thing, he realized that they were acting as servants should by keeping his true spiritual state veiled. So he took to walking around among their places of study, saying, "Pray for your uncle the liar."[22] Now this Sumnūn was one of the lovers and had experienced wondrous things in the station of love.

The servant must therefore ask for, desire, and be satisfied with good health. Such attitudes are part of one's proper demeanor. When trials come, one must be patient, yielding, and content with the course of God's judgments, knowing that he is traveling the path of those who are purified by adversity.

From what I have said thus far, it should be clear that the servanthood I have referred to does not consist only in various kinds of struggle and suffering, and that its starting point is in deeds of body and heart. If the seeker finds a spiritual guide who directs him to the road of worship and protects him from its pitfalls, a guide of noble spiritual lineage and high aspirations, then the seeker should cling to the hem of his cloak, follow in his footsteps, and emulate him in word and action. The seeker must realize then that he has found the red sulphur[23] and has won the greater portion of eternal happiness.

[Response to the sixth question: Concerning which books one ought to read on Sufism, and how one ought to go about it.]

If the seeker does not find such a guide, or has a hard time doing so, he should rely on the writings of the Ṣūfī authorities, especially the books of al-Muḥāsibī,[24] as-Sulamī,[25] al-Qushayrī,[26] Abū Ṭālib al-Makkī, Abū Ḥāmid al-Ghazālī, and as-Suhrawardī's *The Benefits of Intimate Knowledge.*[27] These are the primary sources from which people have taken advice and derived every kind of knowledge and learning. For that reason the sayings of the Ṣūfī leaders have been excerpted in letters and anthologies and have been widely passed around among the religious scholars of Islam. These sayings are meant for the seeker once he has established his adherence to a Sunnī legal school and has come to rely on its authority concerning the particulars of his religious practice, in accord with a legitimate religious leader. From that school the seeker should choose the best in the Example of the Prophet, with sincerity of intention and a firm resolve to undertake the course of action that is revealed to him. Then he must strive to realize those things fully in action and speech, seeking help from his Lord in all his spiritual states. Once an individual has taken on these characteristics and has entered upon a study of these writings, one may hope that he will arrive at the goal he seeks and the understanding he desires.

Of the famous literary works I have mentioned, I know of none more likely to quench the thirst, cure illness, and lead to the Path than the works of the religious authorities Abū Ṭālib al-Makkī and Abu Ḥāmid al-Ghazālī. They have incorporated in these two books such mysteries of knowledge and marvels of understanding as will both give delight and make matters easier. For example, al-Ghazālī has categorized, arranged in chapters, illuminated, clarified, refined and polished, and made a compendium of things otherwise scattered among many other books. He gives examples, removes vagueness, and explains subtle mysteries, pointing the way to the paths of reflection and insight.

54

However, his book does contain some abstruse material that is at variance with the opinions of the speculative theologians.[28] The seeker does not need an intimate knowledge of these things, for they are not essential foundations for the rudiments of the Path he is following. Most of that material is in the quarter "Constructive Virtues,"[29] in the chapters on repentance, gratitude, the Divine Unity, and love. A more easily understandable treatment of these issues may be found in the other quarters of the book. When one who is studying this book comes across one of these sections he should simply move on to another, and give the author the benefit of the doubt about what the seeker knows not. He may likewise become acquainted with certain Traditions that deal with similar matters, but he should neither accept nor reject them. The seeker will thus combine the advantages of reading the book with a deferential attitude toward the religious scholars who understand these things.

Abū Ṭālib's book[30] is revered and preferred above all others, for nothing else of its scope is available and I know of no one who has produced the likes of it. In it he sets forth the erudite science of Sufism which defies explanation, and he breaks the seals of its secrets as no one else does. His book unites profound meaning with beauty of expression, and is presented in a manner which attracts the ear and which tongues find sweet. He describes the branches and roots of knowledge and has arranged them according to questions and chapters. In this respect the book is for Sufism what the *Mudawwanah*[31] is for legal science: It takes the place of all others and none can substitute for it.

This work also contains a certain amount of arcane learning that cannot be comprehended through rational analysis and does not conform neatly to traditional legal science, along with some Traditions that belie a way of thinking and a way of proceeding that are uniquely the author's. When the reader comes across these things he must be prepared to suspend judgment about them, as I mentioned earlier, and simply pursue a straight course in hopes that God, the Revealer, the Knower, will open these things to him.

LETTER 6

Of the writings I have mentioned, these two contain all the many benefits the seeker must have, and he will find no adequate substitute for them anywhere. He must search for those benefits in their pages and draw them out of their secret recesses, and seek help by associating with someone who espouses the same way of thinking and can make the seeker participate in his goal and the object of his desire.

[Response to the seventh question: On the seeker's avoidance of associating in Sufism with those who might tend to undermine his spiritual state.]

The seeker must eschew the company, occupations, and actions of two groups of people. The first group includes those who are immersed in the exoteric sciences, such as the study of religious law and the like. He will generally find no peace in such pursuits and so may fall into various kinds of sinfulness, both interior and exterior. Freedom from sinfulness is rare enough under any circumstances. But in the midst of inquiry into rarified legal speculations and gratuitous academic controversy, there is no protection against the dissipation and neglect of the heart. The seeker would spend his life in vain exertion, squandering all his time in profitless and inconsequential endeavors. As he wasted away in the throes of casuistry the merits of his labors would evanesce.

55

The best of those who are currently engaged in these studies are the ones who use them as a structure for educating those who need their expertise in litigation on which the jurist rules. However, they defend their occupation with specious reasoning. For example, one might say, "I am engaged in a necessary task of banishing ignorance and error. From of old and down to this day people have persistently labored to do that, and have held investigation and urgent searching in high esteem, as did Mālik and other religious scholars. I am traveling that same path and doing their work. Am I not in that way a refuge from drowning and a source of guidance for the erring, from the wrong path back to the straight path?" Thus do they steadfastly attempt to prove the sincerity of their deeds; thus do they give counsel and try to make their case clear. But that is one of Satan's suggestions and insinuations, by which he spreads abroad dissension and error. One of the gravest errors into which Satan can lead with his polished rhetoric and twisted argumentation is for a person to forget his lower self and his Master. Satan takes control of the person's rein with the hand of his passions, thereby making him deaf and blind. Discarding his fear and apprehensiveness, the individual is overcome by heedlessness and callousness. So he joins the company of the base and riffraff, bringing forth the fruit of all manner of evil.

Such obstacles as these multiply in a person in proportion to his immersion in legal studies so that it becomes increasingly difficult for him to be free and escape from them. The more a person advances his learning out of avaricious motives, the more he compounds his ignorance and deficiency. He becomes like a person who has built a fortress but has razed a city. High estimation of the lower self is the indicator, along with his amazement at his intelligence and intuition, his haughtiness, and his refusal to accept advice and spiritual counsel. Because his heart is heedless and his ears inattentive, he rejects those things from anyone who proposes them. He scorns his associates and his peers in learning. He falls into the gravest of sin by slandering them in their absence and calumniating them in their presence. Anyone who has experienced their way of operating and witnessed their actions will be convinced of the accuracy of what I have said about these people. Their way clearly has nothing in common with that of our devout ancestors in the faith, whose way was one of brotherhood, familiarity, and mutual openness.

Now if such an unfortunate man should become aware of his negligence and conceit, realize the vileness of his deeds and their consequences, and conceive a desire for repentance, a change of heart, and the justice that is characterized by the highest values, he will also discover that his afflictions are deeply rooted in his disposition and that their darkness extinguishes the lights of his spiritual insight. If he is the sort of person who had formerly been attentive and well guided in the path of vigilance, he will regard the prospect of struggling against his passions with excruciating dismay; but he will proceed to weed out his sinful qualities, even if under unspeakably difficult circumstances. If, on the other hand, the person suffers an adverse judgment so that God leads his knowledge awry, then his blindness will increase. He remains a slave to his passions and loses out in both religious and mundane affairs. And we take refuge in God from that.

56

Anyone whose heart is afflicted with such specious arguments—and giving in to those errors is the worst of all enemies—need only compare, with the steady, unswerving eye of perfect impartiality, the spiritual states of the man I have been describing with those of the religious leaders I have mentioned. He will then see for himself the abyss and disparity between the two conditions and will say, "What a difference!" That is because the religious leaders built their way of life on the foundation of fear of God, piety, sincerity of heart, and openness. That in turn resulted in the acuity of their discernment and the purity of their inmost being. They comprehended truths both hidden and manifest and the sciences of both this world and the next. They found assistance both in the very times in which they lived and in their brothers, and that aid and friendship set their affairs aright for them in ways others did not experience. We know all of this about the spiritual states of those leaders thanks to the continuous retelling of reports from them on the matter.

Secondly, the seeker must avoid those eccentric mystics who do not hold themselves bound by law and who are not disciplined in the formal side of religious practice. The seeker must avoid them even as he shunned the jurist, and more so, for those people do still greater harm. Their spiritual states conform to the passions of the lower self, for they lay claim at once to lofty stations and to freedom from physical works. That runs counter to the opinion of the true mystics and is an abandonment of the love of the Path. The teacher Abū 'l-Qāsim al-Qushayrī, may God have mercy on him, said, "The Ṣūfī spiritual masters agree unanimously that the Revealed Law is to be held in high regard. They characteristically follow the Path of spiritual exercises and are careful to adhere to the Example of the Prophet without violating any of the obligations of religious practice. They agree that any person who fails to engage in spiritual exercises and self-denial and does not build his life on the foundation of devotion and fear is heedless of God, may He be praised, and is deluded even as he prays to Him. Such a person destroys himself and causes the death of anyone who is trustingly taken in by his idle talk."

Al-Junayd has said, "We did not learn Sufism from hearsay, but through hunger, abandonment of this world, and detachment from things familiar and pleasant to us." He also said, "Truly, those who are intimately united with God derive their acts from God and return to Him through them. Were I to live a thousand years, my deeds of devotion would not diminish by an atom's worth unless He prevented me from doing them."[32] Someone saw Junayd carrying a rosary and said to him, "In spite of your eminence you still ply the beads?" He replied, "I do not stray from a path that has led me to my Lord."[33] He used to go into his shop every day, lower the curtain, and pray four hundred prostrations before returning home.[34]

Ruwaym said, "Sufism is the forfeiture of the spirit. If you can be a Ṣūfī in spite of that, do so; if not, then do not get involved in the hoaxes of the Ṣūfīs."[35] He also said, "Even if the whole world had settled for formalism and the Ṣūfīs had focused on the eternal verities, it would still be less risky for you to sit among all sorts of folks than to associate with the Ṣūfīs. Most people claim their souls through the externals of the Revealed Law while Ṣūfīs claim their souls through the truths of devotion and enduring sincerity. So whenever anyone associates with them and argues with them about something about which the Ṣūfīs have more advanced knowledge, God removes the light of faith from the first person's heart."[36]

57

Yūsuf ibn al-Ḥusayn ar-Rāzī said, "When I see a seeker indulging in luxury I know nothing will come of him." He wrote to al-Junayd, "May God not cause you to relish the food of your lower self, for once you have tasted it you will never again have a taste for goodness."[37] Ibn Khafīf said, "Desire makes trouble and restlessness perdure: And nothing is more harmful to the seeker than to reprieve the lower self by giving in to softness and rationalization."[38] Al-Ḥuṣrī said, "People say al-Ḥuṣrī does not advocate supererogatory works. In fact, I oblige myself to periods of private prayer as though I had the strength of youth and as though I would be punished for omitting even a single prostration!"[39]

Add to all that the rending of the veils of the Revealed Law and engaging in slander and quarrels, and the case against the eccentrics is all the stronger and flight from them more imperative. Abū Yazīd al-Bisṭāmī said, "If you should see a man who performs wonders, even to ascending into the air, do not be impressed until you examine how he lives with respect to the command and the prohibition, honoring the limits of the law, and conducting himself according to the Revealed Law." And Abū 'l-Ḥusayn an-Nūrī said, "If you see someone praying before God in a state that removes him from the known bounds of the Revealed Law, do not go near him!"[40] Someone asked Abū ʿAlī ar-Rūdhbārī about a person who listens to music and says, "For me this is permissible because I have arrived at a level in which no trace of conflicting spiritual states remains in me." Abū ʿAlī responded. "He has arrived indeed—in Hell!"[41] And someone said to an-Naṣrābādhī, "What about the person who sits in the company of women and says, 'I am inviolable in their eyes'?" He answered, "So long as people exist, and commanding and forbidding remain, the permission and the prohibition will apply to him. Any who lays claim to inviolability is legally in error."

Abū Bakr az-Zaqqāq said, "I wandered in the desert of Israel for fifteen days. When I happened upon the path, a soldier took me in and gave me a drink of water, and hardness returned to my heart for thirty years."[42] Abū Ḥafṣ al-Ḥaddād said, "Anyone who does not weigh his deeds and spiritual states at all times against the Book and the Example of the Prophet, and does not take account of his sins, is not to be counted in the register of men." Someone asked Ismā'īl ibn Nujayd about Sufism, so he said, "It is patience under the burden of the command and the prohibition."[43] And Abū 'l-'Abbās ad-Dīnawarī said, "They have torn down the pillars of Sufism and destroyed its Path, and have altered its spiritual meanings with the terminology they have concocted: They call food growth, misconduct sincerity, departure from the truth eccentricity, delighting in what is censurable goodness, pandering to the passions temptation, return to this world arrival, bad morals arbitrariness, miserliness endurance, asking questions work, and verbal obscenity disapproval! But this was not the Path of the Ṣūfīs."[44] And there are countless other reports and stories like these about the Ṣūfīs.

[Response to the eighth question: Describing Sufism's moderation in investigating the sciences of Qur'ān and Tradition.]

If the seeker desires to make some study of the sciences of Qur'ān interpretation and Tradition, that is excellent, for Qur'ān and Tradition contain the truths of the faith and the stations of the people of certitude. They have found in those two sources their place of crossing over, the theater of their reflection, the object of their inquiry, a healing remedy for their ills, the defense against their enemies, and the curbing of their passions. In this respect these two sources differ from legal science, even though legal science is derived from and based on them. I have already spoken of the temptations that attend the study of the law. One ought to take from legal science only what is needed for his worship and external acts, and leave the rest aside.

[Response to the ninth question: Description of the lofty spiritual states the seeker must attain to.]

58

There is no question about how the seeker must comport himself interiorly and exteriorly, both in the spiritual states through which he progresses and in those voluntary actions that have a bearing on his wealth or poverty, health or illness, obedience or rebelliousness, recollection or forgetfulness. By recollection I mean the witness and presence of the heart, and by forgetfulness, the veiling and absence of the heart. Both on his way and as he arrives, the seeker must keep watch over these things, for vigilance is one of the firmest pillars and foundations. It is one of the servant's most excellent qualities and encompasses in part the clear acknowledgement of the Divine Unity. Through recollection and vigilance the seeker will refrain from being too rash in acting on the hopes and anxieties that emerge from within him, and will be freed from servitude to sin and from weariness in his actions.

Riches, health, obedience, and recollection are of very high value and dignity. One's interior behavior in relation to these things will consist in his intimate knowledge of his Lord's majesty, grandeur, sublimity, and omnipotence. An intimate knowledge of these words of the Most High will bring that about: "They do not measure the full power of God" (6:92). In order to gain an intimate knowledge of the baseness, inferiority, despicableness, and weakness of the lower self it is sufficient to gain an intimate knowledge of this saying of the Most High: "Has there ever come upon a person a time in which he was a thing unremembered?" (76:1). Once firmly grounded in these two aspects of intimate knowledge, the individual understands definitively that he can in no way merit the gifts I have mentioned. He realizes that, except for God's bounty and munificence, they would be very few; and that, if God were to impose upon him all kinds of distresses and trials through the direst calamities and set him in circumstances that caused him to stray from his religion and fall away from it through his wordly concerns, it would be because he deserved it. Of all that he is absolutely certain. One ought therefore be overwhelmed with joy and gratitude to his Lord. In that way he will be kept from striving for what is beneath his dignity and from being in the spiritual state in which he had been initially deceived.

Riches and health require that in one's external behavior he make use of these two gifts for obeying God, may He be exalted and glorified, rather than for rebelling. Obedience therefore involves sincerity, amendment, and suspicion of the lower self. One may then be confident that his behavior is proper and hope it will be acceptable. The meaning of recollection is that expansion will not lead one into misconduct, that contraction will not prevent one from performing actions that are necessary or that one deems commendable, and that the individual watches over his behavior continually and does not absolve himself from even an atom's weight of his required duties.

Poverty and injury are related to humility and weakness. The interior behavior related to them consists in the intimate knowledge that through these two things God Most High has set one on the path of His most beloved prophets and saints, and that God has considered the individual worthy to approach Him and receive His purification. In this way God teaches the person that one of the grandest possibilities available to him is to be tested in his religious practice and in his everyday life. It is therefore fitting that a person be overcome with joy in his Master for His predilection in putting him to the test and making him one of His intimates, and with gratitude to God for afflicting him with so pleasant a destiny as a sign of God's kindness and attentiveness to him. That prevents a person from morbid preoccupation with the suffering and trials and from settling into sorrow and complaining.

59

There is a story about how a sulṭān arrested the friend of a certain saint. The saint wrote to his friend and said, "Be grateful to God." The man was astonished, so he wrote back saying, "I give thanks to God." Then a Magian was brought in. He had a gastric ailment and was fettered. One of the Magian's feet was shackled to one of the other man's feet. Now the Magian had to get up several times during the night, and the other man had to get up with him. This kept up until the man was exhausted. So he wrote to his friend the saint, who then replied, "Give thanks to God." The man wrote back and asked, "How long will you tell me this? What greater suffering could there be than this?" His friend answered, "What would you do if the belt around his waist were tied around your waist the way the shackle on his foot is fettered to your foot?"

A man said to Sahl ibn 'Abd Allāh, "A thief has broken into my house and stolen my belongings!" Sahl replied, "Be grateful to God. For if the thief had broken into your heart—I mean Satan—and plundered your acknowledgement of the Divine Unity, what would you do then?"

A certain spiritual master was walking along a street when a tub of ashes was dumped on his head. He fell prostrate in gratitude to God

Most High. Someone made a comment about that to him, so he said, "I was expecting the Fire to be poured out on me. What a grace that it turned out to be only ashes!"[45]

A person's external behavior in relation to poverty and injury should consist in perfect patience, asking God to relieve the injury, having recourse to the external requirements of the law and to medical treatment, and flight from the source of injury and peril. If one's intimate knowledge is so advanced that he can dispense with recourse to these remedies under certain circumstances, that is acceptable as well. It is said that the tongues of beginners are forever yelling for help, while the tongues of the spiritually advanced are silent.

Someone asked al-Wāsiṭī whether he called out in prayer. He replied, "I am afraid to call upon God lest I be told, 'If you ask Me for something I already have in store for you, it is because you doubt Me. And if you ask Me for something I am not prepared to give you, you will be all the more disappointed with Me. But if you were truly content, I would bestow on you what I have set aside for you from eternity.'"[46]

A story tells how 'Abd Allāh ibn Munāzil said, "I have not requested anything of God for fifty years, and I do not want anyone to pray on my behalf."[47] He was referring to prayer that is intended to satisfy specific needs of his, not all prayer absolutely; for well-directed prayer that is meant to give evidence of one's service of God, along with prayer for another who is in a lamentable state, are both religious duties required of the religiously educated and the wider populace alike. These latter types of prayer are in no way inimical to the exalted stations of the spiritually advanced. They are in fact a cause of spiritual growth for them, except for one who is totally immersed in some spiritual state about which nothing could be said.

On the other hand, if a person is so filled with certitude that he abandons even ordinary livelihood and medical treatment, well and good; for that is what all of the spiritual leaders have done. Someone has said, "A group of people visited al-Junayd, saying, 'We are looking for sustenance.' He replied, 'If you know where it is, go after it.' They then said, 'We are asking God for it.' Junayd said, 'If you are sure He has forgotten you, then remember Him.' So they said, 'Then we will go home and put our trust in God.' Junayd replied, 'The temptation is doubt.' 'Then what is the trick,' they asked. He answered, 'The abandonment of trickery.' "[48]

Abū Ḥamzah said, "I am ashamed before God because I went into the desert satisfied. I claimed to rely on trust, but I had actually brought provisions with me that night by going forth already satisfied!" Someone said to Habīb al-ʿAjamī, "You have given up your trade." He replied, "But I have found genuine security."[49] When Abū Bakr the Truthful One was ill someone asked him, "Shall we call a doctor for you?" He answered, "The doctor has already examined me and said I was bringing about what I desire." And someone said to Abū 'd-Dardā, "Shall we not call a doctor for you?" He replied, "The doctor has made me ill."[50] Someone said to Sahl, "When is the servant's trust firm?" He responded, "When he is plagued with physical ailments and diminishing wealth and yet is not spiritually distracted, and continues to look to God Most High to take care of him."

60

One's interior behavior in relation to disobedience and forgetfulness will consist in the knowledge that those two things are under the disposition and decree of God, and in the intimate knowledge that there is a gracious favor in the emptying of the servant, in his sinfulness, and in his being mastered by the enticements of negligence and distraction. These things happen because God desires to give him an intimate knowledge of His exalted qualities and an experience of His sacred attributes, including His glory, His justice in removing hindrances, His ownership, His gracious gift of forgiveness, and His acceptance of his servant's repentance. This is indeed awesome, but not surprising; for as the Tradition says, "If you did not sin, God would not guide you." Another Tradition says, "If you did not sin, I fear you would fall into something still more terrible—wonder of wonders!"

Ibrāhīm ibn Adham said, "One dark night during a hard rain, I walked around the Sacred House. The circuit was empty and I was happy. When I had completed the required ritual, I said, 'O God, protect me from disobeying You.' Then a voice spoke to me saying, 'O Abū Ibrāhīm, you ask Me to protect you, and so do all My servants. But if I were to protect them, to whom could I be Gracious and Forgiving?' "

One finds in the states of disobedience and forgetfulness a growth one does not find in obedience and recollection. That is what is meant by the anonymous saying, "Many a sin has afforded its owner entry into the Garden." The sinner has an overpowering experience of God's kindness even in being rebuked. His compunction over the possible loss of his eternal destiny and timeless happiness turns his attention away from the offence of the moment. One of the mystics has said, "The person who has a genuine understanding about God Most High is the one who submerges the difficulties of the present in the kindnesses flowing over him from God, drowning the sins of his lower self in God's beneficence toward him." "Therefore recall the bounties of God and perhaps you may be successful" (7:69).

Only the person whose heart is alive with faith and certitude can experience strengthening and growth through these kinds of interior behavior and spiritual insight. The index of that is that the individual's external actions and physical behavior, of which I shall speak shortly, are free of defects. His advancement does not make him tepid in performing his religious duties. On the contrary, he redoubles his carefulness in those acts and takes a greater joy in their results. Such people therefore gain strength through their exactitude and grow by keeping in mind these divine kindnesses and insights. There are, however, some types of people for whom thinking and reflecting on these matters can be seriously harmful, and they should not do it. Rather they should limit their attention to their external behavior, including such things as beginning repentance; breaking the grip of wrongdoing; attentiveness to fear, remorse, and tears; fleeing toward yearning and prayer; and careful watchfulness over the crucial matters of recollection and presence of the innermost heart.

61

In all of these spiritual states, the seeker's outward behavior must consist in attending to each situation with a special kind of recollection tailored to the situation, and he must use similarly appropriate invocations. In this way one keeps alive his presence and careful attentiveness so that this becomes his habitual way of acting. Once the servant has seen to these requisites and has fully appropriated these most significant insights, he will have been prepared for the station of gratitude and will be entitled to the increasingly firm recollection promised as part of that station. No growth is more exalted than the achievement of, and progress in, these spiritual states. The servant is spared an undesirable destiny and attains to a priceless treasure in his lifetime, achieving his goal by a foreshortened path. Each dawn and in every period of private prayer he gives the One he worships His due. Such a servant finds help in the special privileges for which he has been singled out and which the Giver of all gifts bestows on him.

LETTER 6

[Response to the tenth question: Mentioning how one ought to behave in investigating the theological speculations of the religious scholars.]

The seeker must strive to conduct himself appropriately toward all who are learned or religious. He must not refute them or find fault with what they do, except when what they teach is at odds with the Revealed Law. He should not think ill of them except when he is absolutely certain of his case. When he is considering something said by one of his contemporaries or by others, or becomes aware of something they have done, he should submit it to the critique of the Book and the Prophetic Example, in accord with either the literal or the spiritual interpretation. If the action is in line with those criteria, well and good. If not, he should seek out a legally correct interpretation. If he finds one, that is good; if not, he should suspend judgment on the matter. However, if he then takes a notion to express a contrary opinion, he is duty-bound to set it aside and give it no further attention. All of this pertains only if the legal issue is of direct and crucial concern to him. If it does not concern him, then he ought not engage in proof and counter-proof in demonstrating the validity or invalidity of the issue. The seeker should conduct himself as did the Messenger of God, may God bless him and give him peace, when he said, "An important part of a man's Islām is his abandonment of what is none of his business."

Let the seeker be especially careful about his behavior toward both the elite and the wider public in all of his dealings, as I have been describing the matter. As he becomes proficient in all that I have been talking about, the seeker will gain, by God's leave, an inner strength that will lead him to embrace spiritual exercises and to ascend in the stations and spiritual states. He will become acquainted with the mysteries of the law, as the dazzling light of certitude rises in his heart and he gains an intimate knowledge of the deceptions and delusions in both knowledge and action. He will distinguish between truths and trivialities. He will think only of what pleases his Lord, and he will intend only that which he hopes will secure his well-being and bring him near to God. He will taste the sweetness of faith and certitude, and the works of the God-fearing will be easy for him. The ease of being in this station is wonderful and is different from the kinds of marvelous lightness I spoke of previously. It is one of the ways in which God Most High refreshes some of His servants as a kindness and an expression of tenderness to them.

62

However, this lightness is not a quality inherent in the station of servanthood. As a matter of fact, some servants' burdens are doubled. Contraction overpowers them and they stand before God as people who have resigned themselves to accepting the burden He has laid upon them. Their spiritual state is more perfect than that of the others; for they gain progress in proper demeanor and watchfulness, and are safe from various types of dangers that harass other people. Al-Wāsiṭī, God have mercy on him, said, "Beware of delighting in the gift, for those who are pure know it is a concealment." He also said, "Be careful: The sweetness of pious deeds often conceals a deadly poison." The reason for that is that these things excite the lower self and cause it to trust in, and conform itself to, what is evident to it. That can only lead to carelessness in forbidden matters, for the lower self experiences an increase whose scope it does not grasp and whose dangers it does not comprehend. It was to this, as God knows best, that al-Junayd was referring when he said, "If an upright person were dedicated to God for a thousand years and then suddenly turned away from Him, what he lost would be greater than what he gained." In other words, the person became satisfied with his standing before God and was distracted from his Lord.

A certain spiritual guide said concerning contentment and security, "I am afraid that their sweetness may distract me from God, may He be exalted and glorified."[51] And the teacher Abū 'l-Qāsim said, "The vision of proximity is a veil over proximity, and whoever swears by his lower self, either in itself or by substitution, is duped by it. Some have also said in this connection, 'May God keep you distant from Him,' that is, distant from your experience of nearness to Him. Indeed, attempts to become familiar with nearness to Him contain in them the marks of deception. For God Most High is beyond all intimacy, and to be in the very presence of the Mystic Truth can only bring on perplexity and annihilation. Someone has said concerning this:

My being put to the test in You is that I do not
    care about my being put to the test;
Your nearness is like your distance, so when
    will I get my relief?

The teacher Abū 'Alī ad-Daqqāq recited much poetry like this:

LETTER 6

Your affection is abandonment and your love is hate;
Your nearness is distance and your peace war.

Abū 'l-Ḥusayn an-Nūrī said when he saw one of Abū Ḥamzah's companions, 'You are one of the companions of Abū Ḥamzah, who talks a lot about nearness. When you meet him, tell him that Abū 'l-Ḥusayn an-Nūrī sends greetings and says, "From our point of view, the nearness of nearness is the distance of distance." ' "[52]

To develop fully the things I have been discussing would take a long time and would require the unveiling of secrets we are not in a position to unveil. Once the seeker has arrived at this point, his heart is filled with brilliant light and overwhelming insights, so that a portion of his Lord's indescribable majesty and grandeur and some of the marvels of the worlds of His power and wisdom become manifest to him.

[Response to the eleventh question: A reference to another letter.][53]

63

I have already said all I had to say about the divine ruse, a question which Shaykh Abū Ṭālib raises in the chapter on Fear. I shall venture no further explanation beyond what I said about that in the first letter. Be content with that and reflect on this treatment of the subject. Study it carefully, for it is arranged in orderly fashion, is meticulously argued, and well integrated. I propose this present letter as a course for the seeker's journey toward the way-stations of acknowledging the Divine Unity. I have rounded off the matter to the extent that it can be verbalized, and have summarized all of the insights and types of behavior, a full treatment of which would require volumes. This letter contains a full response to all of your questions apart from those from which I have excused myself. That is what I intended here.

I therefore ask our Lord, may He be exalted and glorified, to give us both success in our actions in accord with our knowledge. May He not regard our deeds as a condemnation against us. Please pray for me as well as for all of our companions who read this. Finally, there is no power and no help except in God, the Exalted, the Sublime. He is our portion and the best of protectors. An may He bless our Master Muḥammad, his family and his Companions, and give them abundant peace.

LETTER 7

To Yahyā as-Sarrāj [probably]. A letter concerning the degrees of patience and resignation among people who are undergoing trials.

64

Praise to God alone.

I received the letter in which you describe your confusion about the matter of patience in the midst of adversity. The issue is actually quite clear and needs no debate. Long-suffering is one of the stations of certitude and is proportionate to certitude's strength or weakness, increase or diminution. Patience involves restraining the lower self from consenting to voluntary acts and words that are opposed to the Revealed Law and the Mystic Truth, under the sway of one's natural tendencies. Only the individual whose certitude is strong, and in whom the characteristics of the lower self are weak, can attain to the desired degree of patience. The person whose certitude is extremely weak, and in whom the characteristics of the lower self are dominant, is incapable of patience and will not persevere in it. He lowers his guard in a totally unrestrained fashion in response to the dictates of his natural disposition. As a result, such a person often verges on unbelief—may God be our refuge from that—by predicating injustice of God Most High.[1]

Just as people vary in countless ways in certitude, so do they range between these two extremes of patience. If a person's certitude is very strong he experiences no anguish when trials beset him, he may in fact take delight in them and consider them good. This is one of the highest stations of love and resignation. A story tells of how someone asked Sarī as-Saqaṭī, "Does the lover taste anguish?" "No," he replied. Then he was asked, "Even if he is struck with the sword?" "Even if he is struck seventy sword blows," he replied.[2] Let me explain further. A person may experience physical pain and yet delight in it in his heart, for it has been said, "Resignation means the delight of the heart at the enactment of the Divine Decree." Abū Ya'qūb an-Nahrajūrī said, "When the servant approaches the perfect realization of certitude, he considers tribulation a grace and ease a serious obstacle."[3] Going beyond that, such a person comes to regard the presence of tribulation as the same as its absence. If his certitude slackens he regresses, so that the core of his being contracts for lack of the expansive quality of the light of certitude. That regression in turn leads him to complaint and anguish.

When the servant is experiencing adversity, the words "There is no aid and no strength except in God" help to prevent the narrowing of the core of his being. For those who are still on the way, the truth of these words is a disadvantage; but for those who possess certitude it is something positive. Those words prevent even the groans of the sick person from degenerating into complaint, for they identify the illness as part of what is ordained for the servant. Even the peacock disdains groaning when he is sick. Tradition has it that Zacharia, peace be upon him, uttered a groan when the saw was put to his head. So God Most High inspired him, saying, "If one more of your groans arises to me, I will turn the heavens and earth topsy-turvy."[4]

65

When a person in affliction restrains his lower self from such words and outbursts, words that can lead one to take comfort in complaining, then he is practicing the most beautiful patience. As God Most High has said in His Book in reference to His prophet Jacob,[5] peace be upon him: "Patience is beautiful" (12:18). He was indicating that patience is that quality which shuns complaint and display. Now if such trials happen to a person and he manages to refrain from any great complaining and show of displeasure, and from exceeding the limits of knowledge, and from making a scene with his discontent and negative feelings, then that person has attained a station in patience even if it is not the station of the elect.[6] If, on the other hand, he responds negatively, then he has left the realm of patience altogether and has entered into its opposite, namely, restlessness. If one admits the evil of his action and exercises restraint on his lower self, and yet is forcing himself unnaturally in the process, then he is known as one who is attempting patience.[7] But it is an affected patience, just as forced asceticism is merely an affectation of asceticism. It does not lead to any station worth mentioning or to any state worth emulating.

My point is that the experience of anguish does not diminish patience because the servant does not experience it voluntarily. Only a free act which renders the experience of pain incompatible with the Revealed Law and the Mystic Truth can diminish patience. Actions of that kind occur in proportion to the degree of certitude; their frequency will vary as do the degrees of certitude. Those degrees are essentially the three categories mentioned in the Qur'ān (102:5, 7; 56:95): the knowledge of certitude, certitude itself, and ultimate certitude.[8] Within each of these categories there are innumerable gradations. One of the mystics has said, "The servant has not achieved complete certitude until he has cut off from himself everything between the earth and the Throne of God that separates him from God, so that God becomes his sole desire and he prefers God above all things."[9] Certitude has no upper limit. As one studies and comprehends the faith, certitude is added to certitude.

May God sustain us with His endless riches in His beneficence and generosity.

LETTER 8

To Yaḥyā as-Sarrāj. A letter concerning the actions and spiritual states required of the penitent if he is to be confirmed in the station of repentance. Other useful items are also included.

66

Praise to God alone.

I received your letter and have perused it thoroughly. Except for the matter of the penitent servant who has experienced conversion and is following the way of one who is dedicated to God, I see nothing in it that requires a fully developed response. I am delighted that you have concentrated on that issue, for we know that such a servant will receive ample recompense from our Lord in the next life. May our Lord mercifully grant the heavenly victory and the celestial fragrance that cannot be measured except by one who knows Him intimately.

Repentance is one of the principal requirements commanded in the famous Traditions of the Prophet. Among the crucial matters, the stations of faith are based on repentance: All of them begin, continue in existence, and end with repentance. No seeker can dispense with it in his spiritual progress, nor can he escape from it merely by turning away from it. It goes without saying that the servant must keep careful watch over the beginning, continuance, growth, and increase of his repentance. He must protect its essential nature through diligent works and strengthen it through increased resistance. For a full measure of surrender to and experience of conversion, he must be willing to go to great lengths in his devotions and generosity. That is the proper gratitude for the station in which God places the servant, and for the state that arises in connection with it. From the point of view of faith, knowledge and action on the basis of repentance are essential duties. The entire lives of the intelligent and spiritually insightful are immersed in penitence as one of their essential concerns. Once you have understood that clearly, I want you to know also that what I am referring to is divided into two categories, the general and the specific.

The general aspects of repentance are explained and exemplified in the revealed Book of our Lord, in the Traditions of His Prophet and Messenger, in the sayings of our forefathers in faith, and in the interpretations of the above sources handed on by the leaders of the religion. One who seeks to profit from this knowledge and travel this road must listen with the ear of his heart to the nonsensical refutations which the hypocrite and the disputatious person offer on these matters. He must put up with their twisted rationalizations until at some later time they are exposed for what they really are. Then all the seeker's doubts will be clarified.

67

As for the particular aspects, they include knowledge of the servant's stations and states, whether at rest or in action, in public dealings or in seclusion, in matters already ordained for him or in situations where he exercises personal freedom, in prosperous times or lean, in withdrawal or in involvement with others, in all his actions and words. The servant should not presume he possesses a full awareness, except through association with a truthful person who has already plunged into these seas and who has learned to discriminate between precious gems and rocks. He should accept the support that only a master can give as he passes on to the seeker what he will, and gives him a foundation in the Mystic Truth and in the renunciation of pretense. Let the master teach the seeker some of the secrets that are evident to him, point out the seeker's failings and obstacles, and give him appropriate instruction concerning his spiritual states. If the servant succeeds in finding this unique instructor, he should adhere tenaciously to him and travel along his clear path. Otherwise, he should follow the lead of caution and discretion unquestioningly. Thus will the way of the resolute and God-fearing lie open before him. This is the most helpful method for seeking and attaining the goal.

I have decided to mention here only a few of the qualities of the station of repentance that seem most appropriate in this context. An exhaustive treatment and exposition of the properties of each station could not so much as break the seal on the treasurehouse of their mysteries in our lifetime, and would be unhelpful in this instance.

You must understand that the station of repentance is the first of the stations and the foundation upon which the various other stations are built. Penitence is the exchanging of sinful ways for laudable behavior. This includes both exterior and interior movements, beliefs, words, and deeds. In his conversion, the servant must first of all trust firmly in the veracity of his master in order to be satisfied with him, be submissive to his tutelage, and seek out what the master desires as he associates with him. Then the servant must examine his interior behavior, abandoning foolish ways of acting and his predilection for worldly vanities. He scrutinizes his external conduct also, to bring it into conformity to the requirements of the law and purify it of the influences of habit and natural inclination. That prepares him for the various blessings and advantages of acceptable behavior as he hastens toward piety, fear of God, and preference for the next world over this world; and as he proceeds slowly in establishing a firm footing under the good supervision and oversight of the teacher.

In addition, the servant will reap the fruits of making the best use of his time: self-scrutiny, censuring his sinfulness and steadying his wayward tendencies; keeping watch over his lower self's every rebellious thought; verifying the soundness of his motivation and the sincerity of his intention; excellence in his inmost thoughts; promptness in redressing injustice and honoring agreements; making up for omitted duties and requirements; avoiding the evils of arrogance; staying away from the occasions of sin; diminishing the number of minor offenses; gentleness; keeping the core of his being safe from calamities and misfortunes; constancy and persistence in practicing the religion; and compassion and counsel for all Muslims in accord with the requirements of religion and the exemplary conduct of the Messengers of God. Thanks to these benefits the servant is freed from the tyranny of repression, serious sinfulness, and animosity. From those things we seek refuge in God.

68

Next you need to understand that in the initial stages the penitent is incessantly preoccupied with his own sadness and contrition. A sort of intoxication with his spiritual state takes possession of him, overpowers him, and threatens to exhaust him. He can see only his immediate condition and is powerless to change it. His spirit is subdued, his ability to pray diminished, and his human nature overcomes him. He continues that way until a host of inescapable anxious fantasies beset him. An army of fears, from which he had previously been free, encamps in his courtyard. Then he must trust in his faith and remain firm in his commitment. He must persevere thus in his original spiritual state and set about the task of vanquishing the army of inordinate affections.

A variety of people find themselves in this situation, and it tests the mettle of both the foolish and the shrewd. This is the "Greater Struggle," by comparison with which the struggle against infidels seems worthless and contemptible.[1] If the servant is victorious, he conquers the kingdom of the lower self and delights in gardens of holiness. If he is defeated, his human nature plunders him and he ends up with the opposite of what he desired. In the latter case he must again renew his repentance, put the central issue in perspective once more, and return to a more suitable and appropriate condition. And he must continue this process so long as he remains in this world. He must find in the total repudiation of his own power and ability a support for his exterior and interior actions, so that nothing can prevent him from throwing himself with abandon into the hands of his Lord forever. That is the foundation of this matter, and its solid mooring. The person who holds fast to it will persevere more surely.

Scores of devout ancestors in the faith have proceeded in this fashion in bygone generations and have hastened obediently toward this goal. Their religious attitude and habitual practice consist in all the qualities of faith and increased certitude, both those I have mentioned and those I have omitted. To them, that way of proceeding was like a way-station of refreshment for the seeker of eternal life. They experienced only delight in it; no exertion and no enemy plot to waylay them. They persevered in their purpose, for they possessed clear signs from their Lord and genuine certitude as a result of their religious practice.

People approach their matter in a great variety of ways and fall into several categories. Some pursue the method of examining the actions of body and heart, and use this as a means of reaching a thorough knowledge of their faults along with their external obligations. In that way they arrive at purity of mind, and confine their attention to what pertains exclusively to themselves. If someone asks them a legal question they refer the questioner to someone else, for they regard that as a way of protecting themselves. Other such things are reported about people in this category.

69

Others are quite concerned when they see innovation arising among people, or when love of this world wins others over. They believe they are duty-bound to respond to such people by delivering them from the ignorance that afflicts them in their belief and from the injustices that occur among them in their conduct of mundane affairs. These likewise fall into various subtypes.

LETTER 8

Some are consumed with a fear of any innovation beyond the limits of Islām as it was in its inception. They regard such change as a potential disaster for themselves; so they tread the path of caution, restricting themselves to practicing a faith that is rigidly traditional and avoiding intellectual discussions. Should anyone try to sway them or contest their opinion, these people dismiss them summarily and thoroughly despise them and their religious practice. They consider discussion with such people, and involvement in debate, a waste of time and an inconsequential occupation. As for their mundane activities, most of these people do not seek government office, either willingly or perforce, because they are terribly afraid of the danger inherent in holding office. Those whose religious practice and concern for the good of the Muslims does lead them to assume public responsibility are constantly on the alert, for they are incapable of being at ease in that situation.

Then there are those who are very much involved in debate and discussion, even totally immersed in it. When they perceive the torrent of controversy approaching and the flames of folly enkindled, they become expert in some chosen facet of the debate. Then they buckle down and prepare indefatigably for a defense against the adversary's point of view. They make laws that are binding on the people, and explain to them the paths of guidance so that the people may perchance be guided. They lie in wait for the enemies of the faith in every place of ambush, and barricade the bastions with the stoutest defenses. Then they accept governmental posts, such as I have just mentioned. They remain, nevertheless, frustrated in their hope that these positions will elicit the obedience and submissiveness necessary to help them fulfill their desires and prosper their designs and schemes. Ineluctable sufferings and trials assail them in those offices, and they are severely tested with struggles and adversity.

70

Each of the types I have described holds an acceptable point of view, each in accord with the lot granted by his Lord. But as time passes, these kinds of people become fewer in number and shorter-lived. The result is that the signs and traces of religion have been virtually effaced in our day. Zealous adherents of the religion are no more. People founder in the swell of this world; hearts languish; all sense of shame has departed. The intellects of the elite deviate from sound doctrine; masses are lost in the wastelands of ignorance and corruption; gone are the truly learned; and those possessed of certitude have vanished. The earth has gone dark with the extinguishing of its lights and the setting of its suns and moons; friends become enemies, religious scholars dilettantes, brothers disloyal, reciters of the Qur'ān dissolute and benighted. Truth is covered over with falsehood, while every mindless braggart and ignorant fool lays claim to learning and intimate knowledge of the Truth![2]

I could talk at length about people of this ilk, but few minds would comprehend. For your part, note how much better real insight is. Look to see whether in our time any solidly grounded person remains, in whose heart there is light and whose attitude is pure and clear. Find out whether there is anyone these days who is concerned with what is not strictly required and whose intention remains untainted even amid this welter of misfortunes.

Given the circumstances of this unique age, the seeker must seclude himself in protracted mourning, tears, and lamentation. He must seek advice from every authentically knowledgeable person, occupy himself entirely with personal matters, and be more unyielding than ever with his lower self. He must flee from people as he would flee from a lion, disregard small-minded interpretations, and refuse to be bound by their strictures except in clear cases. He must persevere in this work until death. Then security will be his portion and he will have gained double the reward promised to those who begin this work only at the last moment. But if the Devil turns the seeker aside from this clear path because he does not profit from the signs along the way, then God Most High does not care in which of this world's valleys he perishes.[3]

Every seeker must have a spiritual advisor with sound intellect and intuition if he is to weigh on the balance scales all that I have said and examine these matters with a mind that is free of tendentiousness and deviation. In that way the seeker can arrive at perfect understanding. With guidance and success from his Lord, he will keep to the high road of the Path, and practice his religion with sincerity and meticulous care. The accomplished Shaykh Abū 'l-Qāsim 'Abd ar-Raḥmān ibn Muḥammad ibn 'Abd Allāh al-Bakrī aṣ-Ṣaqallī has described the various types of servants and the species of corruption abounding on the earth, in his *The Book of Lights*.[4] I thought I would provide the reader a summary recounting of some of what he says there.

Aṣ-Ṣaqallī writes:

> The people of the first generation were the most astute in knowledge of the Book and in expounding on the intimate

knowledge of the Prophetic Example and the deeds of the Messenger, peace be upon him; for they were the most intelligent and broadly learned people. Then came the second generation. Next to the Companions, they were the most learned in the meaning of the verses of the Book and in imitating the deeds of Muḥammad, as well as in comprehending the commentary and explanations of the Companions. However, the altruism that especially characterized the Compansions diminished among the Followers. The same is true of asceticism in licit matters. And it was then that innovators arose, leading the ignorant astray covertly and winning over the masses surreptitiously.

71

Then came the third generation. Most of the learned, who had clung to sincerity and acted within the limits of the law, were gone. The knowledge of the Companions and the Followers was lost. Among the people of that time fear, hope, patience, and gratitude were scarce; but there was more than enough discussion, disputation, controversy, and hypocrisy. Dissension spread and propagandists took their positions along the paths of error. Knowledge of the Mystic Truth was rare, ignorance was commonplace.

Turmoil grew apace with the arrival of the fourth generation. There were no wayfarers on the road of guidance, and hypocrisy was rife. People were leaving the religion in droves,[5] trading the truth for lies and the next world for this. Deceit was the order of the day; evil triumphed; God's saints were vanquished; the wicked raised their voices; and the believer went into hiding. Perseverance disappeared and good advice was nowhere to be found. Familiarity was scarce; intentions in relation to God turned wicked; and people came to take swindling, debauchery, and unjustified bloodshed for granted. Forbidden matters became the stuff of life, and immoral people gained in prestige. Scarcely a person of conviction or one who sought to acknowledge the Mystic Truth remained on the face of the earth, but was dogged by tribulation and overtaken by strife. But still there were a few who gave witness to the power of God and stood firm in acknowledging the divine decrees.

With the fifth generation the Muslims' hardships intensified markedly even among their own ranks, so that they were entirely split into factions, the masters and the mastered. Some wrangled with others; some took revenge on others; for both their religious practice and their conduct of daily and mundane affairs had decayed. Those who kept faith in the Mystic Truth could find relief only when they kept themselves aloof from the crowds and hid themselves from the propagandists.

When the sixth generation came along, the just ones had disappeared and the wicked alone remained. Intellect had been robbed of insight and reduced to rational proof. Islām survived in name only. Study of the Qur'ān had vanished, leaving only a few traces. Then, most incredible of all, the people of the seventh generation were still more perverse. And so it will go on until the Day of Judgment.

That is aṣ-Ṣaqallī's view. His thoughts on the matter are excellent and unequaled by any of the religious scholars; but I have said quite enough on that subject.

72

I shall close now, for I have gotten carried away and have strayed into new topics. One could surely say more than this, for I have omitted many issues that require guidance, and have abbreviated my treatment of much that needs further explanation. I have done so in the interest of brevity and conciseness. I have attempted to respond to the essential items about which you asked in your letter, with spiritual counsel, advice, instruction, and sound recommendations. Aware as I am of my inability to address myself to your requests with the exhaustive treatment you deserve, I offer you a selective treatment and hope that I have explained the salient points, connections, and lines of argument whose soundness every intelligent person will grasp and whose usefulness will be patent to every penitent seeker.

As for myself, I acknowledge my shortcomings in the very actions I have been describing here. My own qualifications are diametrically opposed to the ones I have just mentioned and expounded. I am not swayed by my own line of argument and so I travel on aimlessly.

LETTER 8

> I point the way to the path of guidance, but I
> myself am not guided by the evidence;
> Even as I detail the disease's remedy, I myself
> continue to suffer from the illness.

I need to have the saints and beloved ones who read this letter make an effort to pray for me, that I might be enabled to repent and atone for my sins. May my hope be realized through obedience, and my deeds be sealed in goodness. That is easy for the One who initiates all things and teaches whom He will the way to live. Here I will end. Praise to our Lord, may He be exalted and glorified, and blessings upon His Prophet, the Messenger, who is our pride and the best of representatives.

LETTER 9

To Yaḥyā as-Sarrāj. A letter of counsel and advice to a man who suffers from a constriction of the core of his being as a result of spiritual states that he finds unacceptable, but which, try as he might, he cannot replace with states that are preferable and acceptable to him.[1]

73

Praise to God for the breadth of His grace.

I received your letter describing your present spiritual states. You expressed yourself well. The gist of your message is that you find some of the states you are experiencing despicable, not at all to your liking, and that you do not find them conducive to approaching your Lord. You wish that you could find your way to, and live in, certain new states which you fancy and regard intellectually as desirable and of positive value.

My brother, you are being too severe with yourself and are acting inappropriately. You have pointlessly and unprofitably wearied your mind by spending your time that way. Worse still, it is positively harmful for you to concern yourself with such matters, for they keep you from seeing the intent of the saintly mystics and keep you distant from the Lord of the Universe. I do nevertheless find your situation understandable, since it seems you share the lot of countless others, before you and still to come, who will have had the same experience. You subscribe to their opinion that they are self-sufficient and strong enough to do as they wish, whether in action or in repose, and that they can be entirely heedless of the First, the Designer, the Disposer, the Dispenser of Decrees. That opinion in turn leads them to the wrong questions and to spurious answers by which they are diverted unawares from the Straight Path (1:5).

These people fall into different categories. There are those who perform external works, such as ritual prayer, fasting, Pilgrimage, the lesser pilgrimage, invocations, voluntary almsgiving, military action, teaching, seeing to the needs of a Muslim, and other such deeds of devotion, be they occasional or frequent. Those who engage in these sorts of things without finding consolation in them or being aware of their merit in the eyes of their Lord, as you have described in your own case, find themselves in unacceptable spiritual states similar to yours.

Then there are those who are content with this level of involvement in external actions and do not want it to end. However, when they are remiss in their observances, being smitten with laziness or ennui or something in between these two, that for one reason or another weakens their resolve, then their life becomes quite confused. In their utter turmoil they believe they have been banished far from God.

74

There are also those who give no thought to acts of devotion and could not care less about them. They fancy themselves a match for whatever situation they might find themselves in. Still others assign a specific time and place for their deeds, as though the matter depended ultimately on them. When that time arrives, or they arrive in the appointed place, they realize they have made a habit of carelessness and procrastination. They look to themselves for the fulfillment of what has been promised, and for fidelity to the conditions that have been laid down. But they do not measure up and do not fulfill their promises. They postpone it until some other time, and so on indefinitely.

Then there are some who do not engage in religious practices and works, but who, upon hearing stories of their forefathers in the faith and their fidelity to the Prophetic Example and their pleasing deeds, consider themselves quite capable of such things should they but make their minds up to do them. They then say, "I will attend to that once I am free from such and such an occupation and when I am in the proper spiritual state." As I have already suggested, they spend their whole lives procrastinating.

Some people are convinced that their lives are in disarray and that they are capable of nothing. That may be quite true—that is, they may be so either in fact or metaphorically speaking; or perhaps they only imagine that to be the case. When these people hear of their exemplary ancestors in the faith or see a person who possesses their qualities, they say, "No one the likes of me is capable of that, or has either the desire or power to accomplish such things." So they let it go altogether and do not resolve to apply themselves to it. I have observed all of these false attitudes in myself and have noticed them in others, for the simple reason that they can conquer our hearts.

On the other hand, the mystics and those who are spiritually advanced concern themselves with interior actions and are free from such specious reasonings. They strive for the perfect realization of the Divine Unity from the very start, for they make a solemn pact and habitually pray in humility to their Lord so that their hearts are aware of Him at all times. They endeavor to make Him their companion in all their spiritual states, insofar as they are able. When God discerns that attitude in them, He is merciful to them by causing them to attend no longer to their own weakness or strength in whatever they undertake or leave aside. Instead He is their safeguard and protection. He guarantees their welfare and sustenance, for they are His servants and are dedicated to serving Him. God Most High has said, "Is God not sufficient for His servant?" (39:36). Again the Most High has said, "Behold, my Protecting Friend is God, who reveals the Book. He befriends the righteous" (7:196). And in the Sacred Tradition the Most High has said, "I am with my servant when he thinks of Me."[2]

75

The difficult becomes easy and the harsh bearable for these servants. God makes their every moment precious and most significant; He establishes them in comfort and in a great kingdom. In Him alone do they move or take their rest; on Him alone do they rely; to Him alone do they raise all their thoughts and aspirations. That is why this Community is preeminent among communities. In one of the Traditions of the Prophet, God Most High is said to have inspired Jesus, peace be upon him: "I will send forth a Community after you. If they love what befalls them, they will give praise and thanks for it. If they hate what befalls them, they will be mindful of their reward in the next life and bear it patiently, even though they possess no understanding and no knowledge." Jesus, upon whom be peace, replied, "O Lord, how will that be, if they possess no understanding and no knowledge?" God answered, "I will give them of My understanding and My knowledge."[3]

Muḥammad's faith community is therefore especially characterized by liberality and ease. The Community does not despise even troublesome burdens, because what they desire is so readily available. This facilitation of every situation is made possible only through the contemplative vision of which I have spoken. God has said, may He be exalted and glorified, "He has laid upon you no hardship in the religion;

yours is the faith community of your father Abraham. In this Scripture as well as from of old He has named you Muslims" (22:78). And the faith of that Community is none other than Islām and the acknowledgement of the Divine Unity.[4]

Our Prophet, may God bless him and give him peace, has said, "The tolerant party of the monotheists was sent forth, and it was the faith community of Abraham, upon whom be peace." A certain mystic commented on the words of the Prophet, may God bless him and give him peace, "They will find it easy and not difficult." The saying means that they are led to none other than God. Therefore anyone who leads you toward this world is deceiving you, and anyone who leads you toward external actions only wears you out; but the person who leads you toward God has given you good counsel. My point here is to let you know that people of this sort are subject to few of the errors such as I have mentioned, that is, errors relating to lack of genuine self-knowledge and an accurate assessment of their own ability and strength. If this were not so, they would possess neither spiritual state nor station.[5] But since they are seldom lacking in this regard, they are continually on guard and alert, and remain firm in their stations, finding solid footing in God's care for them. Lying and pretentious people, on the other hand, have severed their communication with God. You can understand from all this the cause of these people's error, as well as the means by which those who are secure remain secure. The latter state of affairs can come about only in that sublime state for which servants of God are singled out and in which they become saints of God.

Know, therefore, that that state functions in religion as the means to proximity to the Lord of the Universe. Look forward to ascending to this exalted station and to joining the wayfarers to whom God has bequeathed this great kingdom. Once you have begun to do this, you will perceive the truth of my contention that your only way to that state is by means of it, and your only help toward it is in the state itself. Someone has said in this connection, "I know my Lord intimately through my Lord, and were it not for my Lord I would not have known my Lord." A story tells how someone asked ʿAlī ibn Abī Ṭālib, "Did you come to know God intimately through Muḥammad or did you come to know Muḥammad through God?" ʿAlī replied, "Had I come to know God through Muḥammad, I would not have served God, and Muḥammad would have been more firmly fixed in my soul than God. God acquainted me with Himself through Himself."[6]

76

Once the identity of means toward God and means through God becomes evident to you—even though it may remain unintelligible from a purely rational point of view—so that you see no difference or disparity between the two, then you will have achieved the state that is the goal of seekers and the desired consummation of those who yearn. For the only available means is in the very being of the One who is Present and Near. If, therefore, what you seek is already found and present to you, why do you look beyond Him and why do you search for mediation from other than Him? I can only liken you in that respect to a man who holds in his hand a precious pearl whose value he does not appreciate. He considers it just another common stone and does not see it for what it is. He complains of injury and poverty, and begs from people. But look how his true condition becomes apparent even while he remains in that state. I mean that in that very state he is clearly capable of reaching the level of the kingdom, not to mention the ecstasy, delight, joy, and happiness that go with it. As the saying has it, "It is hardly surprising that a traveler looking for water finds a Joseph. What is amazing is that the sinner who seeks forgiveness finds God."[7] God Most High has said, "Yet whoever does evil or wrongs himself and then seeks God's forgiveness will find God merciful and forgiving"(4:110).

So now the significance of this matter is coming home to you; "Perhaps you will comprehend."[8] It is of course too subtle for words to capture or for mere allusions to contain. God's power is the ultimate cause of everything, quite apart from the strength and capability of the servant. My acquaintance with you and your reliance on me for the best guidance toward your goal, along with your letters to me and my responses to you on these questions, are merely the context within which you can achieve your desire without aid or power from either of us. Given this point of view, you will note that all of your spiritual states follow this same course. God declines to sustain his faithful servant except from sources unknown to the servant. So why all the toil and exertion and fatigue and searching? And what is the point of joy and regret and remorse and longing? "You desire other than God; and what thought do you give to the Lord of the Universe?" (37:86–87). You must understand that God more than substitutes for every transient thing, and stands in place of everything ephemeral. Indeed, the individual who finds God wants for nothing; but the one who loses Him possesses nothing.

LETTER 9

The mystics and those who are advanced in the spiritual life establish themselves on this foundation. Each and every temptation and misgiving that assails you and impedes your vision of the object of your desire and the attainment of your purpose will prevent you from realizing these truths. Once God has made available to you the understanding I am talking about and you have immersed yourself in it, yours will be endless devotion and everlasting proximity to God, from which neither exhaustion, nor the ennui that goes beyond fatigue, nor deception, can keep you—provided you live by that understanding in all your comings and goings. If you consider all things as having their being and source in God, you will give due gratitude to Him who has bestowed on you this easy conquest, this lucrative and burgeoning trade. Then you will have felicity and an excellent place in the next world (3:14, 13:29).

77

Therefore, my brother, accept with good grace what I have said to you. Learn to prefer it to rational and traditional learning. Understand that intellect cannot encompass it, nor can tradition express it clearly. It is a knowledge of divine origin that God entrusts to the secret recesses of hearts. It is related that one of prophets of the People of Israel received a revealed Book that says, "Do not say, 'Knowledge is in the heavens; who will bring it down?' or 'It is under the earth; who will bring it up?' or 'It is beyond the sea; who will bring it across?' The knowledge is in the core of your beings and placed in your hearts, so that even now you can conduct yourselves in my presence as people of the spirit and after the example of the holy prophets. This knowledge will spread from your hearts to your tongues until it surrounds you and fills you."[9] My sole purpose in writing to you about your spiritual states is so that you might have a firm principle to which you can return, and a foundation on which you can build.

Now about what you said regarding the sequence of your spiritual states in your nights and days. That progression is good and is a necessary help to you in giving thanks to God for guiding you to Him and for your attentiveness to Him. That involves a kind of proximity to God, may He be exalted and glorified, to which few people attain. However, you suffer from scruples in the ordering of your daily affairs. Your schedule of observances disturbs you to the point that you no longer experience consolation or find any beauty in it as you did before you lost your contemplative vision through neglect. If you would stop concentrating on yourself and considering your own ability and strength as your personal prerogatives, and would instead turn your gaze to the uniqueness of God Most High in His care for you, and set your thoughts right about Him, then you would become aware of God's kindnesses toward you and the many ways in which He shows his predilection for you. Then nothing could sidetrack you in your search, and you would give Him your undivided attention.

Here are some of the graces that are apparent to me, that will help you begin your consideration. He brought you out of the darkness of nonbeing into the light of existence. Then He nurtured you with His grace and reared you with His affection and tenderness until you were able to reason and understand. He then adorned you with the ornament of Islām and faith, and gave you an intimate knowledge and clear proof of it. He gave you access to His Book, through which He addressed His noble speech to you, making available to you the manifestation of His attributes and Names, and finding you worthy to receive His commandments and the trustworthy witness of His prophets. Then he provided you with expertise in learning and elevated you to the diginity of teaching.

His graces go beyond just these; many of them you and I cannot detect. And all of this has occurred without any intermediacy or merit on your part; it is His sheer munificence and bounty. Every one of these graces is beyond our reckoning, for "if you were to add up the bounties of God, you could not count them all" (14:34).

Anyone who experiences these graces and realizes that he is an uninvited guest in their midst will be overwhelmed with joy and gratitude for them. That prevents a person from pining for what God Most High has not given him. More often than not, the individual dies in the midst of such graces without ever noticing them. Nothing is dearer to God Most High than the servant's dealing with his actual situation, for that shows forth one's servanthood and is the touchstone of behavior. 'Amr ibn 'Uthmān al-Makkī, may God be pleased with him, has said, "Sufism means that the servant behaves at every moment as is most appropriate at that moment."[10] He means that the servant is present to His powerful and glorious Lord in each instant, carrying out the requirements of the Revealed Law ordained for that specific time.

78

I have spoken of the manner in which the servant is present to his Lord in relation to the deeds of those who acknowledge the Divine

Unity. That way of acting in accord with the Revealed Law proceeds from the jurists' elaboration of legal questions. If it is possible to perform a specific act on which the jurists are in agreement, without experiencing a lack of freedom or the constriction of the core of one's being, then the servant reaches the highest degree of fear of God and piety, and attains the rank of the God-fearing and devout. If that is not possible, then the servant should adhere to an alternate opinion, once he has apprised himself of the positions of the experts. In cases like this, a difference of opinion among the religious scholars is a mercy.[11] Otherwise many people would be lost. The reflective person who is content with a small portion of this world's goods and is not a slave to his appetites will understand this issue. However, it will be difficult for the person who makes himself at home on this earth and is hemmed in by mundane interests. Such an individual is not immune to incurring the wrath of God Most High at his ignorance and heedlessness. And when a person's thoughts and desires are tributary to every valley in this world, God does not care in which of those valleys he perishes.[12]

Your teaching of children is without a doubt one of the most excellent ways of being near to God. But your acceptance of compensation for that occupation is a matter of dispute among the religious scholars. Most of them either consider it simply permissible, or hold that, because the morality of it is unknown, it is permissible. Therefore what you accept is a justifiable wage. Of course it would be preferable for you to seek no material gain over and above that, and not to expect from your students what they do not have, and to think only of attending to their instruction as a way of being close to God Most High. Devout people before you have done work like yours. The story you have recounted about Ibn al-ʿArīf suggests just that.[13] In this instance, the touchstone of your sincerity is that you not prefer a student who gives gifts over one who gives you nothing or very little, and that you not prefer the company of one student over that of another.

This is the criterion in the question at hand. Try to hold yourself to it; for you know that you will inevitably find sustenance and that greed will not increase it, nor the absence of greed diminish it. What you must strive for is the sustenance of the next life. Spare no effort in seeking that, for "the provision of your Lord is better and more lasting" (20:131). Then you will be able to do your work well and will not be remiss in it. Whatever you accept in accord with this criterion will be such a blessing to you that a single dirham will be the equal of a thousand of them.

79

If you put into practice what I said at first about the contemplation of God's oneness, that will suffice you in the course of this search and in others. You will reap an insight into the governance and training of the children in spite of their diversity. They will range from intelligent to dull; they will include both local and foreign students, those of noble lineage and humble, the poor and the rich; and they will vary in many other ways as well. Every one of them deserves your best and fullest effort. You will be able to give them that so long as you possess four traits: firm faith, a sharp mind, solid learning, and a good disposition. If you have all four of these you will be able to meet every student at his own level and deal with him in a fitting manner. Unless you walk the path of care and flexibility, this undertaking will be impossible. Better to be excessively lenient than to be overly stern. This is all practical knowledge and there is no set procedure for mastering it.

You wrote also that you experience no sensible consolation when you chant the Qur'ān. You would very much like the gift of tears but are unable to cry. The reason for that is that when you recite the Qur'ān you do not keep in mind whose word it is, and to whom and under what circumstances it was revealed. How can tears come if you lack these essential prerequisites? God Most High described those who experience such consolation in chanting the Qur'ān as possessing exalted qualities, when He said, "Those who were given knowledge beforehand, when it is recited to them, fall down prostrate on their faces in adoration, and say, 'Glory to our Lord! Truly the promise of our Lord has been fulfilled!' They fall down on their faces in tears, and their humility increases" (17:107–109). God describes them, first of all, as receiving understanding and intimate knowledge of God Most High whenever they exalt and magnify Him with their words, "Glory to our Lord!" Secondly, He characterizes them as arriving at the goal of their servanthood when they fall prostrate on their faces in worship, for they are certain of a home hereafter with their due portions of reward and punishment there. Thirdly, God describes them as weeping and humbled. Elsewhere God Most High has said, "When they listen to what was revealed to the Messenger, you see their eyes overflow with tears because they recognize the truth" (5:83), and on down to the end of that text. In this way God portrays them as possessing intimate knowledge of the truth, as believing in it, as taking refuge in God Most High, as acknowledging their need for Him, as desiring to be near Him and to excel in

His works. The Messenger of God, may God bless him and give him peace, explained the term "to excel" or "to serve God constantly" in the trustworthy Tradition, "It means serving God as if you were seeing Him; and even if you were not seeing Him, knowing that He sees you."[14]

All of this brings us back to the contemplative vision I have mentioned before. Fix your attention on it, build your works of piety on it; then, as I have said, you will praise its results in all that you are and possess. Expansion of the core of your being will not always make chanting the Qur'ān easy for you, for that is a great grace and such graciousness may or may not accompany chanting.

80

You have remarked also that you fear death may come upon you before you are ready. That is a healthy fear, and it is one of God Most High's graces to you. You should thank God for it and ask for more, for it is among the most treasured stations of fear, and its net effect is security. As God Most High is reported to have said, "I do not join together in my servant two fears or two securities. Whoever fears Me in this world I will make secure in the next; and whoever finds security in Me in this world I will give cause for fear in the next."[15] Furthermore, these things are characteristic of those who know God and who are pleasing to Him. God Most High has said, "Among God's servants, those who possess knowledge fear Him" (35:28). He has also said, "God is pleased with them and they with Him. That is for the one who fears his Lord" (98:8). The best kind of fear is the fear that you will meet your Lord and discover that what you desired was not the same as the best He expected of you.

As for your qualms that this fear may lead you into despair, that is an idle fantasy, for hope rules that out. Fear and hope are among the stations of the learned mystics; but security is part of God's ruse, and despair of God's mercy is a mark of the foolish and negligent. The reason for their folly and heedlessness is that they focus on themselves, measuring the good or evil of their deeds. If only they would look instead to the Unique, the One, they would regard all their states as equal. Then they would possess the quality of that fear that is accompanied by hope and that hope that is the necessary concomitant of fear. Understand this and act upon it, and do not become fixated on your own deeds. What will happen will happen, and our refuge is in God alone.[16]

Another difficulty you mentioned is that when you undertake

works of devotion, you do not persevere in them. If I have understood you correctly, you become slothful in them and give your teaching and family concerns precedence over them. Your loss of the contemplative vision I have been talking about is the reason for that. If you were fully engaged in that vision, ennui and laziness and other concerns would rarely trouble you. Other daily business would not displace your devotional practices; on the contrary, you could actually give them more attention without becoming so easy a prey to deceit and illusion.

When things do not go just as you would like, you are more likely to lack faith. You need to have confidence in your Lord and set your mind straight about Him, for He knows best what is for your good. There is a story of how Ibrāhīm ibn Adham, may God be pleased with him, said, "One evening I omitted my night prayer. When I realized it, I repented. But for the next three days I was remiss in my religious duties. When I became aware of that, I heard a voice saying,

> All is forgiven you, for it is of little consequence to Us;
> What We have left up to you is passing, but
> what goes forth from Us endures.

Then I was told, 'O Ibrāhīm, become a servant.' So I became a servant and was at peace." In that spirit, therefore, whether your acts of worship are easy for you or few in number, give thanks to Him for them; for you are not lost in His eyes. My Master Abū 'l-'Abbās al-Mursī said, "A little action together with an acknowledgement of God Most High's bountifulness is preferable to a proliferation of deeds while one is enthralled with one's own stinginess."[17]

81

About your concern over the scruples that have plagued you incessantly, you must understand that this is one of the trials with which God tests some of His servants in order to single out those who are genuinely religious. The Enemy goes on casting scruples into the hearts of these individuals, until he has made them fall either into heretical innovation or apostasy or mental confusion. Under those circumstances, even the least significant problem that besets such a person can seriously disturb his life and rob him of his peace. This is all part of the divine providence and decree. So let us take refuge in God, from an adverse judgment, from being overcome by misfortune, and from the malice of enemies.

When people fall victim to the Enemy, it is because they have lost the contemplative vision I have been talking about. If they are truly contemplative, Satan has no way to get to them, for they are truly God's servants. God Most High said, "Behold, Satan is your enemy, so treat him as an enemy. He summons his minions only to take possession of the flaming fire" (35:6). He also said to Iblīs, "You have no power over my servants" (15:42). Should Satan trouble them with scruples, they return to their Lord and He turns Satan away from them. They seek refuge in Him and He gives them refuge. God Most High has said, "If even a legion of Satan's touches those who fear God, they bring God to mind and then they are given vision" (7:201), and, "If an insinuation from Satan comes forcefully upon you, seek refuge in God, for He is the Hearer, the Knower" (41:36).

Perhaps you will ask, "How can a suggestion be from Satan when it appears to encourage a stronger faith and when it seems to result in certitude? And how can one distinguish between reprehensible diabolical scruples and praiseworthy discernment, in a case where the two look alike?" You must understand that what originates from Satan is essentially credible. However, it conflicts with true religious knowledge and goes against the ease, facilitation, and liberality that have always characterized this religion. It is thus tantamount to excess and innovation. The distinction between diabolical suggestion and praiseworthy discernment is that the latter is conducive only to conformity to true religious learning. Furthermore, scruples ordinarily do not cease even after the servant has performed a good work and acted in accord with the Prophetic Example. True discernment, on the other hand, does cease when the servant has acted in accord with its promptings.

Scruples are a disease whose only remedy consists in a refusal to attend to them, adherence to legal requirements, and begging God Most High to put a stop to them. All of this rests on the foundation of the contemplative vision about which I have been talking since the beginning of this letter. It is the elixir that effects a radical transformation. It dispels darkness with dazzling light, and overcomes death with life. May God sustain us with this vision as He sustained His saints with His bounty and munificence!

82

A story relates how a certain saint came to know that someone was suffering from scruples. The saint's response was, "I am pledged to a group of Ṣūfīs who make fun of Satan; now Satan is making fun of them." My master Abū 'l-'Abbās al-Mursī, may God be pleased with him, violently abhorred scruples that arise in connection with ritual prayer and ablutions, so that he found it difficult to see someone who had the problem. One day he was told that So and So was a learned and devout person but very scrupulous. He responded, "O So and So, where is that knowledge and piety? Knowledge is that which makes an impression on the heart like that of whiteness on white and blackness on black."[18]

You have also mentioned that you spent time reading a very broad selection of books, but without a single focus or principle of discrimination. That is good, but it would be better to concentrate on the most important works. The critical books are the ones that provide you with some directly personalized application and supervision, such as Ibn 'Aṭā's book,[19] among others.

You said that on some days you spend your time reading the Qur'ān according to the prescribed rules. That, too, is good, provided you do not become inattentive as people often do. They become overly concerned with the exact pronunciation and exaggerated articulation of the letters, so that they pay little or no attention to the meaning of what they are reciting. That would make you the laughingstock of Satan. It would be better for you to seek out a man with spiritual insight in the knowledge of certitude, sit at his feet, and seek to get help from him. This would be much more valuable for you.

You tell me that my brother Muḥammad ibn Adībah,[20] may God have mercy on him and be pleased with him, had recommended that you read Abū Ḥāmid al-Ghazālī's *Revival*. That is an excellent suggestion, for Ghazālī's expositions there are as well done and refined as can be found anywhere. However I think you should read only the sections on worship and required observances. If you read his sections on esoteric knowledge or those that are not directly related to action, your attention will not be fully engaged and those parts will be of no practical use to you. Most of that is contained in the last quarter, "The Way to salvation." The first two quarters of the work deal with matters of legal science, on which Ghazālī is an acknowledged master. The third quarter is largely a refinement and selection of what is said in *The Book of Observance*,[21] along with many useful additions. That is my judgment of it.

Whenever you read one of these books, do so with the intention of elevating your thoughts to God Most High, so that He might make you comprehend, apart from your dependence on your intellect, that He is the Truth. In that way you will give priority to preferring what is best and more closely approximates a response to the truth and being victorious in it. As-Suhrawardī has already pointed out in his book *The Benefits of Intimate Knowledge* the importance of making the most judicious choice of reading material.

83

My first and last advice to you is this: Neglect nothing I have said to you, either explicitly or implicity, about various ways of contemplating God's oneness and about the degrees of certitude. I have emphasized these things in particular and have responded point by point on these fundamental issues so as not to leave any of them out of this letter. Put your trust in these things, rely on them, and seek them out in the most likely places, among those who put them into practice. For these things are, God be praised, the essence of understanding and the precious treasure which people of insight value highly. This world you live in will give you very little help in the way of response, given its injustice and turmoil, its contentment with an ease that entices people away from a sense of responsibility, its general approach to life, and its servitude to the lords of this earth. According to the Tradition handed down from the Messenger of God, may God bless him and give him peace, "Certitude is wealth enough."

But the masters of this world are so taken up with it that when care or grief assails them, they try to distract themselves through leisure or enjoyment. They search for relief in any way they can secure refreshment and delight. Look how they are addicted to wine, entertainments, gardens, musical competitions, listening to birdsong and musical instruments, and a host of other diversions. As one of the poets has said,

> Chase your sorrows away with wine; refresh the heart
> without keeping score.
> Say to anyone who criticizes what you do,
> "Forget about trying to convert me!"

And, of course, none of this is what people are really searching for. Such people are more than likely troubled in their mundane affairs with a variety of ordeals and anxieties that no intelligent person would find acceptable—to say nothing of the consequences that await those people in the next life!

If the seeker wants to work toward the next life in order to put an end to his sorrows and cares in this world, he must put his life in order here and now as a servant of his Lord, may He be exalted and glorified.

One must delight first and last in intimate conversation with Him. This is precisely the sort of genuine knowledge I have been talking about. A Tradition says, "Refresh your hearts hour by hour." And one of the mystics has said, "Improve your life by acquiescing in the course of the divine decrees, and do not be undone with restlessness and exhaustion when they are carried out." Another said, "Contentment is the widest door to God, the garden of this world, and the resting place for God's servants."[22]

This is how I decided to respond to your questions, and I believe it will provide you with what you are looking for. God Most High is the Master of Success for both you and me, according to His good pleasure. Peace to you and to all our friends, and God's mercy and blessings.

LETTER 10

To Yaḥyā as Sarrāj. A letter in response to a question raised by one who teaches children,[1] along with some suggestions he might find useful in his instruction, particularly as to how he might ward off scruples in that occupation.

84

Praise be to God.

And a warm greeting to you. I received the letter in which you asked for advice that might direct you toward freedom from the perplexity and scruples and lack of consolation you have been experiencing. You say they have gotten the better of you. You must understand that the states whose causes you have described are maladies of the heart. Rest assured that we can come to an awareness of their sources and find a way to remedy them.

First of all, the perplexity you say has beset you with regard to the children, and your lack of enthusiasm for that work, result from your failure to attend to, and inability to see, the material and spiritual graces that are yours. Keen awareness and mindfulness of those graces are the remedy. To be specific, an intimate knowledge of three things will suffice to put you in the requisite state of continual recollectedness. Fix these things in your mind: First, you need an intimate knowledge of God Most High's tremendous grace, in bestowing on you the task of instruction and in making you worthy of this high dignity without your meriting it and without your giving prior cause for it. Instruction is the office of none other than the prophets and the religious scholars! Strive to acquire this intimate knowledge by reading accounts of the excellence of the widespread practice of instruction in traditional religious studies. This intimate knowledge will increase your humility and reverence before your Lord, and will prompt you to seek His good pleasure in all of your circumstances.

Secondly, you must appreciate what an abundant grace teaching is, in making you resist successfully things that can overpower your lower self and in assisting you to act against selfish desires. Such are the prerequisites for immersing yourself entirely in teaching, giving up the leisure needed to satisfy your own whims, putting up with challenges to your authority and with the children's behavior, admonishing them, bearing with them, taking trouble to counsel them, and tutoring them—to name only a few duties of teachers. There are in those things marvelous benefits, the likes of which no traveler on the path to the next life can do without, if he is to mould his character and reform his lower self. Indeed your Lord has sent these things to you precisely according to your need in pursuing a praiseworthy course. Such an intimate knowledge will then bring you to a high degree of patience and to a fitting gratitude.

85

A third factor is the intimate knowledge of the surpassing grace by which He protects you in your work from this world's blandishments. He keeps you from having to engage in reprehensible ventures and defends you from all sorts of struggles and trials that preoccupy those who seek this world in their various achievements and accomplishments. Not the least of those ills is acquisitiveness. This realization will have the benefit of making you satisfied with your lot of life and content with what you are capable of doing.

Once you have attained an intimate knowledge of these three kinds of graces and go on keeping them continually in mind, you will begin to experience, by our powerful and glorious Lord's leave, joy and delight in your Lord's grace. You will thus be protected from developing a negative disposition, and from the narrowing of the core of your being. Be happy with your present condition. Then you will be able to share your Lord's truth with those you instruct, through your kindness, mercy, solicitude, counsel, gentleness, good governance, and in other ways that are beneficial to both teacher and pupil. Our powerful and glorious Lord is the Master of Guidance for you and for them, now and always.

You must be persuaded that the teacher's every thought must be oriented toward a longing for the Lord Most High as source of guidance and success. The teacher must be convinced that, whatever he says or does in the course of instructing the students, the Lord will provide for him and his students. If you understand this and act accordingly, you will discover His blessing, if our powerful and glorious Lord wills it.

Now about the scruples that have plagued you incessantly. Ignorance and distractedness are the cause of them, knowledge and recollection the cure. By knowledge and recollection I mean knowledge and recollection of God Most High. Seek to achieve these two things by associating with the upright and God-fearing, and by letting mindfulness of the Lord of the Universe rule over your heart and tongue. There is no other remedy.

You suffer from a lack of consolation during the ritual prayer and during the recitation of the Qur'ān. That is a type of hardness of heart caused by one, or both, of two things: either the commission of a sin or a worldly attachment. The magnitude or insignificance, strength or weakness of the hardness of heart and lack of consolation will be proportionate to these two causes. The remedy for them consists in sincere repentance, examination of conscience, and vigilance over one's thoughts, so that Satan cannot gain access to the heart.

Let your prayer under such circumstances be a request for forgiveness, both at dawn and at those other times when you experience a desire for the grace of the King, the Forgiver. That kind of prayer eradicates sins and polishes hearts and is pleasing to the Knower of Secrets. You should also make use of the method of invoking blessings upon the Messenger of God, may God bless him and give him peace, and similar prayers. That is one of the most excellent aids for those who seek help in attaining their desires.

Our powerful and glorious Lord is the Master of Success and Guidance. He is our portion and the summit of our expectations. This, then, is what I wanted to say in response to your request. Peace to you, and mercy and blessing.

LETTER 11

To Yaḥyā as-Sarrāj. A letter concerning the teacher's acceptance of stipends in the instruction of children, and how he might ward off scruples associated with that activity.

86

Praise to God alone.

Greetings. I received your letter concerning your displeasure over your relationship to the children. You mentioned, first, that you are fearful and anguished over the prospect of losing your eternal salvation as a result of your work; and second, that you are hesitant and doubtful about the propriety of the sources of stipends you accept from some of the students. You asked me in that letter to clarify the matter as I see it.

With regard to the first situation, you know best, because an eyewitness sees what one who is absent does not see. Therefore examine that situation with the eye of spiritual insight and reflect on your present state. If you are certain of the underlying causes and are sure that you can no longer discharge the responsibilities of your work, act upon that assessment and abandon teaching immediately, provided that your Lord gives you the strength to do so without anxiety and self-reproach. However, if you are capable of struggling through, so much the better; and your reward for that will be abundant. If what you are experiencing are unfounded scruples, reject them forcefully before they overwhelm you. Protracted scrupulosity and preoccupation with delusions are detrimental to faith, to reason, and to life itself. This is a proven fact. In short, your present circumstances need not cause you undue anxiety.

Secondly, your fear about the doubts that have intruded upon you and your attempt to work against them have led you to conclude that you must resolve the matter by separating yourself from your family. I have no doubt that this is a diabolic suggestion, and it may well be that your Enemy wishes to make you fall into a still greater peril. For that conclusion and the course of action you propose are not founded on the example of any of our ancestors in the faith or of the followers of those who are knowledgable and practice the religion. Such a lack of precedent is evidence that there is no good in what you propose. On the contrary, it is well established that exemplary people have sought counsel from their powerful and glorious Lord concerning themselves and others, and have acted accordingly, taking into consideration their own rights, needs, and desires, as well as those of others. They fulfilled the requirements of the Revealed Law and traveled the road of piety. So if you wish to emulate them and walk in their footsteps, accept what comes your way to the extent that it is generally agreed to be legally permissible, and regard it as in keeping with the Revealed Law.

87

If your work is sufficient for you and affords you a modest means of support, then be aware of what a grace it is for you and of how that is the full measure of what you deserve. On the other hand, if you should accept the kind of support that is legally debatable, that will still not be held against you so long as you follow the path of circumspection and caution, avoid excessive luxury, and accept your circumstances in the spirit of poverty and exigency. Once you have done that, your vexing doubts will depart and you will be subject to no legal action.

However, if your lower self rebelliously constrains you in set patterns of behavior, so that you readily succumb to your desires or quickly fall prey to doubts or become undisciplined, then you would be sinful and blameworthy—but not for the reasons you have mentioned. I mean that you would merit censure not because you failed to leave your family or because you acted in defiance of the religious scholars, but because you ceased to struggle with your baser instincts and failed to attend to the needs of your inner nature. What you should understand from all this is that it is only because of the lower self that any individual is destroyed. When a person is habitually strengthened by his Lord's bestowal of the help that empowers him to struggle against the lower self and turn down its invitations, then that person's actions and states advance in uprightness and freedom from corruption. This is the basis for vigilance over the lower self.

Therefore let that work be more important to you than your scruples over the dilemma of finding sources of support that are legally agreed upon. The legitimacy of what accrues to you in the course of your teaching is not under your control, either in general or in particular instances. You are therefore not responsible for becoming involved in debates over the opinions of those who are cautious. You have sufficient leeway above and beyond their opinions.

Thus my view concerning your question. Our powerful and glorious Lord is the Master of Success for both you and me, according to His good pleasure. There is no Lord beside Him and none other who is to be worshiped. Peace to you.

LETTER 12

To Yaḥyā as-Sarrāj. A letter containing some remarks on conditions for the recitation and transmission of the Traditions, along with some other useful comments.

88

Praise to God alone.

Greetings. I received your letter in which you focus on some questions concerning the recitation and transmission of the Qur'ān and the Traditions, specifically, whether an individual such as you have described may be permitted to recite and transmit them.

My brother, you must understand that this twofold question pertains to the domain of legal science. So do the other questions your letter posed for me; namely, what is required of a person who teaches youngsters, how he ought to behave toward them in view of their varying degrees of intelligence or ineptitude, and the opinion of Ibn al-ʿArīf you mentioned with regard to accepting a stipend for teaching them when such a thing was not originally intended. All of these are legal issues with which I do not involve myself, except when they arise in my reading and study. Then when the concerns of the religious scholars do come up. I acquaint myself with the necessary rulings. Besides, I do not at present possess the intellectual competence required to initiate a legal investigation of such matters and see it through to its completion. There are, in any case, people in your city[1] who are interested in and knowledgeable about those things. Some of these issues need not concern you in the least. In fact, I consider involvement in them as forbidden behavior and a distraction with things that are not important here and now. You ought to exercise caution in that regard.

I will, however, offer this much concerning the question of recitation. I believe that the work of the reciter and the one to whom he recites will be blessed, and their effort meritorious for them, and that their religious duty will have been duly fulfilled, on the following conditions: that the two do not seek an earthly goal in their labor, that the one who receives the transmission act as a regulator for that which is recited, and that the transmission be characterized by the integrity of which the Traditionists speak. Then the chains of transmission will be in keeping with the faith as the religious scholars have described it. If even one of these characteristics is lacking, then the work of the transmitter and the one who receives it is in vain, due to a lack of sincerity and failure to pursue the path of integrity. Such is the case with the majority of Qur'ān reciters these days, except for those whom God protects.

89

The other, nonjuridical, issues you mentioned fall into two categories. One relates to your request that I define for you such deadly vices as arrogance, hypocrisy, conceit, anger, rancor, envy, and the like. The other has to do with your becoming a more perfect believer, and with your request that I counsel you as to what will bring your faith to completion and that I instruct you, both in important matters of the faith, interior and exterior, which are incumbent upon the servant, and in the most excellent supererogatory works of devotion.[2] The religious scholars, al-Muḥāsibī in particular, have already answered the first question. Read and reflect on al-Muḥāsibī and you will find the remedy there.

To the second I can address myself only in a general way, but you are already familiar with the general issues and they are not adequate to your needs. More specific responses would presuppose that I have a familiarity with all of your interior and exterior states. I could arrive at that kind of familiarity only if you were to inform me directly, or after a long association with you. Since neither of those possibilities is available to me, how can I make an ample and useful response that would be more than generally applicable? The person who seeks advice ought rather to inquire about what he absolutely requires in order to become mindful of his relationship with his Lord both in faith and in action. He should examine the quality of his devotion in approaching the Blessed and Most High Lord. Then he should explain that clearly, so that the advisor may be apprised of the advisee's true condition and thus offer an overall response that will benefit both the advisee and the advisor. You did something like that in the first letter you wrote me, and that is how our brother Muḥammad ibn Adībah, may Our Lord be merciful to him and be pleased with him, used to write to me.[3]

You have asked which books on Sufism you ought to read. I suggest that the book you have by Ibn 'Aṭā', *The Book of Light [on the Elimination of Self-Direction]*,[4] is the epitome of all the books, long or short, on Sufism. And it combines completeness with conciseness. The way in which it leads the traveler is the road of the acknowledgement of God's Unity, a path that admits no one who denies the Oneness of God. To the person who sets out upon it unreservedly, the Path cannot but impart every praiseworthy quality, and will remove and purify from him every blameworthy quality. Once you have begun to grasp that and act accordingly, all that I have said will become clear, and the religious questions you have raised will be integrated with other beneficial and useful matters. If you add to that a study of the *Book of Wisdom*,[5] so famous and widely used, and strive to come to grips with it and assimilate it, you will have no need of any other renowned writings.

> Take hold of what is before your eyes and leave
>   aside that which you have only heard of:
> When the sun has risen, what need will you have
>   of Saturn?

That is all I wanted to say to you. Our powerful and glorious Lord is the Master of Success for both you and me, according to His good pleasure. Peace to you and to all our companions, and mercy and blessing.

LETTER 13

To Yaḥyā as-Sarrāj. A letter explaining a saying of my master Abū 'l-Ḥasan ash-Shādhilī describing the individual who recites his "Great Litany." And it is God who grants success.

90

Praise be to God.

I received the letter in which you spoke of your resolve to recite the "Great Litany." Act on that desire and realize that it is a confirmation for you from God. Do not be dissuaded by what you have understood to be the meaning of the saying attributed to the shaykh, may God be pleased with him: "Whoever recites this litany possesses what I possess and must do what I must do." You have taken the statement amiss. Actually Abū 'l-Ḥasan intended it as an encouragement, a way of turning the mind toward a resolute and determined undertaking of the litany. The conclusion of the saying indicates: "And the Messenger of God, may God bless him and give him peace, has made earnest intercession." In other words, it is as though the shaykh were saying, "If an individual recites the litany with upright intention and sincere hope, and is a lover following our path as embodied in the litany, and is careful to aspire to the qualities of the saints as mentioned in the litany, then that person has already reached the goal of hoping to attain his expectation. He has reached the rank of sainthood reserved for me; he has entered into my litany, and thus into my sponsorship. Hence, that person has what I have in the way of nearness to God and honor, and must do what I must do in the way of obedience and surrender."

Since the status and sainthood that come from God are prior to that which proceeds from the servant, that which precedes is the cause of that which follows. The effect follows upon its cause either as grace or as severity. Therefore, since the requisite grace and sincerity are present prior to the servant's initiative—that is the meaning of the words "He has what I have"—it follows that the servant's actions will conform to God's designs, as indicated by the words "He must do what I must do."

The statement is meant to facilitate and to smooth, rather than to induce anxiety and conflict in the servant.

This is the goal and ultimate recompense of obedience. Were that not so, the outcome would be quite the opposite. The point of all this is that the phrase "He has what I have" is a way of speaking about the final outcome of generosity and piety—namely, guidance, recompense, succour, and confirmation. All of these are, in turn, the necessary causes of all that must follow from them, according to the words "He must do what I must do." It comes down to acting in accord with what is enjoined on the servant, and being united with the desire of God Most High to expand the core of his being and ease his burden (94:1–2). My brother, there is nothing in this statement that ought to deter you or prevent you from doing what you propose to do. On the contrary, let it urge you on and incite you to it, if God Most High wills.

So much for my brief remarks. They are sufficient for an understanding of what the shaykh, may God be pleased with him, is reported to have said. As for the interpretation you said one of your companions suggested—"He has what I have in the way of holiness, and must do what I must do in the way of mercy"—it is a beautiful and elegant way of putting it, but far from the meaning as I have been discussing it. That interpretation lacks the depth of spiritual realization of the meaning as I have clarified it.

And in God is found success.

LETTER 14

To Yaḥyā as-Sarrāj. A response to the inquiry of a man whose anxiety over his means of livelihood is hindering him from achieving his ultimate goal.

91

Praise be to God.

I received the letter in which you describe the inner turmoil you are experiencing because of your means of making a living. But you are unable to abandon that means. You say you are waiting to see what will emerge from the Unseen World, believing that you would then understand the whole situation and be reassured about it.

What I propose to you is that you fix your eyes on the next life and turn your back on this world. Then, you need to choose an occupation that is consistent with that frame of mind. If you readily happen upon a means of livelihood that does not threaten your faith, support yourself that way; and if not, do not let the difficulty discourage you. Be utterly convinced that a person who renounces something for his Lord will be more than compensated with strong faith and the rewards of obedience to the Lord of the Universe. By way of illustration, here is a story told about a man who owned a field, some flour-meal, and a donkey.

The story tells how a certain devout man was asked, "What brought about your conversion?" He replied, "I was a man of wealth and status. One evening my work had piled up on me. I needed to water one of my fields, and I had taken some wheat to the mill, and my donkey had bolted and gone astray. So I said to myself, 'If I spend my time looking for the donkey, the field will go without water. If I water the field, the wheat and the donkey will be lost.' That was a Thursday night and the mosque was a good distance from my village. So I said to myself, 'I will leave all these matters and go to the congregational mosque, so that I can arrive for tomorrow's communal ritual prayer.' And I went and joined in the Friday prayer. On my return trip I passed by my field, and lo and behold, it had already been irrigated. I asked, 'Who watered this field?' I was told, 'Your neighbor wanted to water his field; but the border-dam burst while he was sleeping and the water flowed over into your field.' Then when I came to the door of my house, suddenly there was the donkey at the manger. So I asked, 'Who brought my donkey back?' Came the reply, 'A wolf attacked it and it ran home.' And when I entered the house, there was the milled flour! I asked how that had happened and I was told, 'The miller had ground this flour by mistake, and when he learned that it was yours he returned it to your house.' Then I said to myself, 'How true are the words, "Whoever is for God, God is for him. God looks after the affairs of one who acts out of devotion to God." ' So I rejected this world and was converted."

92

You must understand that the assorted trials, anxieties, and hardships that befall you in this world are paths to abundant benefits and the means to lofty goals. Only people of high ideals and clear, totally pure hearts know the value of these things. Therefore let your joy in the midst of things you hate surpass the delight you experience from things you love. A story tells how 'Aṭā'as-Sulamī tasted no food for seven days and had no strength at all, but his heart was happy as could be. He said, "O Lord, if you keep me hungry for three more days, I will offer a thousand ritual prostrations to you!"[1] It is also said that Fatḥ al-Mawṣilī returned to his house one night only to find no dinner, no lamp, and no firewood. So he began to praise his Lord and humble himself before Him, saying "My God, how is it possible that I deserve to have you treat me as you treated your saints?"[2]

There is a lesson in these stories for those who seek to learn, and a message for servants. May our Lord help us to live accordingly.

LETTER 15

To Yaḥyā as-Sarrāj. Advice that every seeker needs if he desires increase from the All-Sufficient and Most Praised One.

93

Praise to God alone.

Anyone who desires to walk the path of the truth in his practice of the faith, and be safe from his Enemy, and be free from the scrupulous suggestions of the lower self with its narrowness and inconstancy, and experience the expansion of the core of his being, must be firm in his exterior and interior behavior toward God in every circumstance. In a word, what is required for an increase from God is gratitude. The foundation of gratitude is twofold: first, the individual's recognition of his Lord's majesty and transcendence, and the knowledge of His sublime attributes and most holy Names; and second, one's awareness of his own pettiness, inferiority, deficiencies, and weaknesses. A person who has come to a full realization of these two fundamentals reflects upon himself and on the words and actions God Most High has brought to pass in him, and upon the stages through which God has brought him. From there he proceeds, thanks to God's graciousness, mercy, providence, and overflowing kindness toward him, to that which eludes the grasp of intelligence and understanding. And from there, love and awe move the person to gratitude to God Most High as he becomes fully sensitive to God's bounty and to the way he ought to act before God.

For example, if an individual sees himself as obedient, he rejoices in what his Lord has given him in spite of his unworthiness and lack of merit. How few people have received that gift! One ought then to act appropriately toward God by perfecting his obedience and removing defects from it, by deporting himself toward his powerful and glorious Lord with pure intention. The person who so regards himself and behaves will be far better off than one who does not do so and thus squanders his time with gestures of obedience and all kinds of devotional practices.

A similar situation will obtain if the individual sees himself as blessed with physical health or material wealth, however meager. Let him rejoice in that and give thanks to his Lord for it, knowing that he has neither merited it nor been worthy of it. In this case, the proper demeanor will involve making use of the two blessings, in obedience to his powerful and glorious Lord rather than in rebellion against Him. How many people suffer illness or poverty, who yearn for such gifts but never find them!

94

By the same token, if a person is afflicted with poverty or ill health or some of this world's trials, let him rejoice; for he is being led by that means along the path of the saints and the just ones. He should find joy in his powerful and glorious Lord's largesse, in that he has not been still more severely tested as so many people are. In his case proper demeanor will consist in patience and resignation, absence of grumbling and complaining, prayer to God Most High for abundant means of livelihood and the cessation of harm, and a request for prosperity in religious and mundane matters and in the next life. If such a person is able to avail himself of a means of material enrichment and a medical treatment for his illness, he should do so; for that, too, is consistent with proper demeanor. And he should be grateful that God Most High allowed him that opportunity.

Likewise, if someone is sinful or negligent or behaves inappropriately, he should not fail to be mindful of the grace and blessings of God that are hidden even in that condition. For that may prompt one to acquire the fear of God, act against his sense of self-importance, and have recourse to his Lord. As the Sacred Tradition says, "If you had not sinned, I fear you would have fallen into a state worse than that: arrogant conceit." How many people commit serious sin and consider it a source of delight! In this instance proper demeanor consists in a determination to repent, and an unremitting fear of God, along with deep contrition, prayers, and tears.

The same applies to the case of one who adheres to the legal opinion of a religious leader whose authority is widely accepted, or who finds someone from whom he can receive that teaching—that is, someone truly religious who has previously received instruction from his own spiritual guides, and they from theirs, and so on back to that first authority. Such a person should rejoice and give thanks to God. How many people have blindly followed some innovator, or have themselves become innovators and thus thrown themselves away and perished!

Proper demeanor here means revering one's teacher and following his every instruction. If a person should discover, in the legal opinion of yet another leader whose authority is widely accepted, a ruling that allows for some prudent action for which the individual has the capacity, or a ruling that grants permission for fulfilling some need, and if that action is not clearly forbidden by the legal school of his own leader, then the person may follow the alternate ruling without diminishing the propriety of his conduct.

Similarly, if someone encounters a Ṣūfī spiritual guide who travels the path of the Example of the Prophet, let him rejoice and thank God for that. How many people have been putty in the hands of erring innovators and have thus perished! In this case, proper demeanor consists in docility to the spiritual guide and his commands, in the rejection of contrariness, in not concealing any of one's inner secrets from the guide, and in not exchanging the one spiritual guide for another.

When a person has a friend or a brother—or a wife or husband, for that matter—in whose company his religious life is safe and with whom he experiences the amenities of this world, he should rejoice and thank God for that. How many people are saddled with friends whose company is detrimental to both religious and mundane concerns, and from whom they are unable to break away! In this case proper demeanor will take the form of loyalty to one's friends and the discharging of fraternal obligations.

Along the same lines, if a person possesses a means of support that provides him sufficient income, let him rejoice and thank God for it. How many people are unable to support themselves and must beg from others, and are neither content nor long-suffering! In this instance proper demeanor will consist in honesty with Muslims, avoidance of fraud and of all things prohibited by law, to which one's means of livelihood might expose him. When a person is engaged in a devotional activity, such as teaching the Qur'ān and the like, he ought to give thought to his ultimate reward and be as gentle in his teaching as possible, never treating a student harshly or unjustly. He must at all times focus his attention on his Lord.

95

Finally, when a person hears or reads such advice as this, he should give thanks to his Lord and rejoice in it. How many people are slaves of negligence and inattentiveness, who seek counsel but cannot find a counselor! Proper demeanor in this context involves heeding the advice, staying within its limits, and passing it along to those who are worthy of it.

The foundation of all of this is the sincere attitude of a person who is in need of God and who begs God to grant him that attitude in its fullness and help him to achieve it. Whoever receives this gift should rejoice and give thanks to God Most High for it. How many people are immersed in self-love and reliance on their own intelligence and cleverness! Proper demeanor here requires a suspicion of one's lower self, in recognition of one's total poverty, as I have suggested.

Everything I have said, from beginning to end, is implied in the authentic Tradition of the Prophet, peace be upon him: "Look at those who have less than you, rather than at those who have more than you; that way you will be less likely to belittle God's favor to you."[1] And our success is in God. There is no other Lord and none other to be adored.

LETTER 16

To Abū Isḥāq ash-Shāṭibī. A response to the question of whether a person can follow the Ṣūfī Path solely with the aid of books on the subject, or whether one requires a spiritual guide. It includes a discussion of the Path that leads to God.

96

In the Name of God, the Compassionate and Merciful. May God bless our Master, Muḥammad, and his Family. From Maḥammad[1] ibn 'Abbād, may God be kind to him, to my brother Ibrāhīm ash-Shāṭibī,[2] may God Most High protect him and give generously to him in this life and the next. I wish you peace and the mercy and blessings of God.

I received your letter and I understand what you are searching for. I have also read both of the letters you sent to my master Abū 'l-'Abbās al-Qabbāb,[3] and have familiarized myself with their contents. I am unable to address myself to all of the topics they include. They treat such diverse, wide-ranging issues at such length that I am far from capable of responding to the letters in their entirety, either with accuracy or in a superficial manner. In fact I should be able to say scarcely anything at all on the subject even if it were to become more encumbent on me to do so than your worthy inquiry has made it.

In the interest of conciseness and brevity I have decided to confine my remarks to my understanding of the role of the spiritual guide, and to as much as is clear to me concerning initiation on the Path. That is more likely to be generally applicable to those to whom God Most High grants a successful beginning in the spiritual life. If you find my proposal suitable, say so; if not, then tell me more about what you would like and kindly forgive the present abridgement. God Most High is the Master of Success for both of us, according to His good pleasure.

It is my view that, in general, one can scarcely deny the necessity of a spiritual guide in following the Path of Sufism. This is surely one of the crucial issues in actual practice. These spiritual guides, to whom followers of the Path have recourse, fall into two categories: those who both instruct and educate, and those who instruct without educating.[4]

Not all wayfarers require a spiritual guide who educates. Those who are of banal mind and rebellious lower self do need such a guide, but those who have an open mind and a docile lower self do not require the restraints of the first type of guidance. However, everyone who walks the Path needs an instructing spiritual guide.

97

A spiritual guide who educates is necessary for the sort of wayfarers I have mentioned above, for it is clear that a great coarseness shrouds their lower selves. Only the educating spiritual guide can raise and penetrate such a veil. Among individuals of this sort, there are many who need a spiritual guide because of the rivalries and enmities in which they are involved. Their situation is analogous to that of chronically ill persons whose physical cure remains a puzzle. There is no alternative but to seek out a competent physician who can heal their maladies with potent medication.

Individuals who have expansive minds, and who have their lower selves under control, are exempted from needing an educating spiritual guide by reason of their abundant intelligence and malleability. The instructing spiritual guide assigns tasks exactly suited to such individuals, but those tasks would be inappropriate for the other type of person. This type perseveres by the permission of God Most High, unafraid of what harm might befall him as he journeys along the Path. He remains intent on proceeding and approaching the Path in the proper fashion, such as I will describe, God Most High willing. Even this type, however, will not achieve perfection as will the person who entrusts himself to the educating spiritual guide. For the lower self is always heavily veiled and full of guile, so that it remains fickle. The lower self is never freed of such obstacles except through obedience to the first type of spiritual guide, and through docility to his judgment and tutelage. If one binds himself by the decisions which the educating spiritual guide lays down, he does not need the second type.

Reliance on the educating spiritual guide was the Path of the later Ṣūfī leaders, whereas adherence to the instructing spiritual guide was the Path of the earlier ones. It is evident that many of the earlier writings, such as those of al-Ḥārith al-Muḥāsibī, Abū Ṭālib al-Makkī, and others before them, did not stipulate recourse to the educating spiritual guide as did the books of later authorities. The earlier writers nevertheless spoke of the fundamentals of Ṣūfī learning and its branches, foundation, and implications. That is especially true of Shaykh Abū Ṭālib. Their failure to mention the educating spiritual guide therefore suggests that such a guide was not a condition or necessity for the following of the Path.

I am referring to the well-traveled Path pursued by the majority of wayfarers. It is similar to the way of life of our spiritual ancestors in ancient times, in that they are not reported to have sought out educating spiritual guides and become submissive to them and adhered to them in the way that is required of such a guide's disciples. On the contrary, the way of our forefathers was the acquisition of learning and the cultivation of the interior life, on the Path of companionship and brotherhood with one another. They achieved this by coming together and exchanging frequent and extended visits. Their interior and exterior demeanor gave evidence of the great benefit of this approach. They wandered freely over the countryside, seeking to encounter the saints and the religious scholars and the servants of God.

98

A consideration of the writings of the Ṣūfīs brings us back to the matter of the instructing spiritual guide. The use and study of these books is recommended only if their authors are people of learning and intimate knowledge, whose conduct is worthy of imitation. And only the person who seeks the company of a reliable spiritual guide whose spiritual genealogy is genuine can pass sound judgment on these writings. If the reader finds in them a helpful exposition that is totally consistent with the external demands of the Revealed Law, that may be sufficient for him. Otherwise he has no choice but to return to a spiritual guide who can elucidate the books for him; for, as I have already mentioned, the spiritual guide is indispensable in that instance.

The spiritual guide who educates is hard to find these days and "more precious than red sulphur." So also is the instructing spiritual guide, for many who are associated with this Path and who are both recommended and trusted do not in fact render an accurate account of the meaning of Sufism, nor do they acquaint people with the Mystic Truth, let alone with what is beyond that. I do not know which of the two calamities is the greater: the disappearance of the spiritual guide with profound understanding, or the lack of sincere disciples. But we belong to God and to Him we return.

Now the question arises: How does a person who wishes to pursue the Ṣūfī Path make do under these circumstances? Does he occupy himself with the quest of the spiritual guide? Or does he abandon the search and simply wait? And in either case, does he engage in the activities of the wayfarers, or not, in the meantime?

I say there is no point in searching for the spiritual guide, whether or not one is actively practicing Sufism. The spiritual guide is a gift of God Most High. It is His way of directing the aspiring servant who has turned his attention entirely to following the way and is sparing no effort and using all of his capabilities, however humble or grand. It is in this context that God Most High leads the individual to a more excellent state, safe from innovation and error, in which the seeker is secure from the pitfalls that await everyone who relies on the spiritual guide's solicitude and supervision as a buffer against past and future tribulations.

It is equally pointless merely to wait for the spiritual guide while postponing the active practice of Sufism. That is a fruitless waste and an inappropriate mode of behavior. Only the fourth option remains: involvement in spiritual activity while one waits for the spiritual guide. The seeker can attain that goal by purifying his intention through vigilance over the sincerity of his relationship with God Most High. Anyone who desires the presence of God needs complete truthfulness, for God is present to those who are veracious. Sincerity[5] consists in making demands of the lower self and disciplining it for the state of piety required in Sufism. That includes personal prayer, a heart intent on the door of the Master, a positive frame of mind, genuine hope, and an entering into the presence of God Most High with awe, reverence, and humility. As one disciplines himself and brings his lower self into line in these matters, he should ask God Most High to fulfill His promises, and he will arrive at his desired goal.

99

One who seeks guidance must understand that the Ṣūfī way of life is a gift God Most High bestows because of His solicitous predilection for certain of His servants. He opens the door to Sufism and lifts its veil only to one who is authentically convinced of his need for God and who is in an advanced stage of relying on God. Ṣūfīs are therefore set apart from their fellow human beings, and have no desire for others to share their life and lodgings. As the spiritual masters have said, "The Ṣūfīs dwell in a single house and no one else moves in with them." That is so because when God wants some of his creatures to belong to Him—that is, to exist essentially and absolutely for Him—He casts faith into their hearts and inscribes it there, and supports them with His Spirit. All of that happens without any initiative or merit on their part. Therefore, when God bestows the gift on them and makes them aware of it, He opens for them the door of refuge and of utter need of Him. His creatures in turn see themselves as powerless, capable of almost nothing, and existing at the limit of weakness and indigence.

When God opens this door to them, He sends them all manner of gifts, blessings, graces, and kindnesses, true to His promise that He will be enough for His servants who dedicate themselves to Him and take refuge in Him. At that very moment the lights of faith are increased and intensified. God Most High arranges their spiritual states and actions in such a way that the lights become visible to them and secrets are manifested to their hearts. They continue to dwell unceasingly at the door of God Most High until they arrive at the station of serving God constantly.[6] There they experience the ultimate vision of God's Oneness and realize fully His Uniqueness. At that moment, the vestiges of their fleshly humanity are effaced; their most mature judgments seem foolish; and in the presence of Existence itself, appearances fade away. "Say: The Truth has come and falsehood has vanished. Indeed falsehood is a vanishing thing" (17:81).

This is the consummation wayfarers long to experience. Their faithful service of their Lord is brought to completion and they are freed from constant vigilance over their sincerity. That is their sole desire. At that point, "wayfaring" and "being drawn" come together.[7] The difference is that God brings to this station those who have been "drawn" in a shorter time than He does those who are "wayfaring." In addition, He leads the former type to this station without any exertion or effort on their part. In neither case does God Most High leave them without His protection and custody at any level of the ascent, from beginning to end. They are acted upon and are not the agents, according to the saying, "The Ṣūfīs are children in God's lap."[8]

So you can see how God, to whom be glory, chooses to look after the person He has singled out, so that he is not reduced to searching and pursuing while relying solely on himself. The traveler on the Path must strike out in this direction. For example, he should consider his own state in the light of his understanding of the Ṣūfī Path, taking the eminent status of one who is known to be a Ṣūfī as a paradigm by which he might arrive at a full realization of the Path and its levels. There is no doubt that a thorough comprehension and understanding of that is crucial. Without it no one would seek out the Path or take care to arrive at it, for a quest for something totally unknown is inconceivable.

100

Now the individual's thorough grasp of the nature of the Path does not arise in him spontaneously. It is brought about by means of the predisposition of his intellect. A close investigation of this situation reveals that God Most High gives three graces in relation to this conceiving and understanding: the very life of the intellectual faculty; the predisposition of the intellect toward perceiving this precious thing; and the act itself of conceiving and grasping it. And all of this occurs in an individual apart from his assistance, power, or enduring worthiness. How few people are endowed with even one of these three graces, let alone all three!

Once the individual has encompassed a knowledge of the things I have been talking about, God Most High has a fourth grace in store for him, greater and more splendid than the others. It is the intimate knowledge that he cannot effect these things by his own conduct. This is the fourth grace. So long as the servant is mindful of this, attentive to it, and intent on arriving at the goal he has conceived in his mind, then what is most obvious to him is his own powerlessness, poverty, lack of ability and cleverness. He is convinced that it is his powerful and glorious Master who is filled with those things and who is in control of him. The servant sees that only proper conduct in the presence of God, flight from his lower self toward Him, and reliance on God as his sole concern can gain him victory in this arena. Under those circumstances God will supply all of his provisions, ease every difficulty for him, and smooth for him all that is rough.

As a result of his experience of this knowledge and the perspective it gives him, the servant will have the freedom of movement to be transported where God carries him, without having to search anxiously or having to choose where he will go. If he persists in this awareness, he will already have arrived at the station to which all other stations are connected. He will have achieved the object of his desire, by contrast with which every other desideratum is despicable.

If, on the other hand, this realization does not come over him and he is incited to seek out things that cause him to be inattentive to the One who bestows these graces I have been describing—this condition begins with a lack of full understanding and mindfulness—then his misfortune will be greater than the disaster of merely failing to reach his goal. The servant will, in addition, suffer from weariness in searching, and his exertion will lead to the constriction of the core of his being. He must then return to the healing condition in which he was at the outset. This is the conversion that is the prelude to guidance. Achievement can never dispense with first principles. In the course of his journey the seeker must appropriate to himself all these works of the heart and must make them the foundation of his entire life.

101

In addition the seeker must flee from every occasion of strife and evil, withdraw from public gatherings and crowds, and sever those external associations that entice him into sinfulness and iniquity. The latter include all situations essential to holding political office or positions of authority and leadership, or to the study of a science, and so forth. All of those things are major distractions and are opposed to traveling the Path. The seeker should eschew speculative study beyond the minimal requirements, for it tends to agitate people and becomes a great veil between the individual and his set purpose. Few people who are concerned with studying the law and who are skilled in it and strict in practicing it are in any way touched by Ṣūfī learning, with the exception of the individual who travels the Path of "being drawn." Quite the contrary. The approach of the jurists is such that they become so convinced about their own path that many of them imagine there is a rift between the outward and the inward, and a quarrel between the Revealed Law and the Mystic Truth! Their suspicion causes them to despise Sufism on the grounds that it departs from the procedures and prescriptions of their legal science. They have brought many spiritual guides to trial, accusing them of unbelief, free-thinking, and a variety of errors and innovations.

It is most important that the wayfarer flee such people as he would flee a lion. He should avoid getting involved in their studies altogether, except insofar as they pertain directly to his worship and devotional practice.[9]

On the more positive side, the seeker must get down to the specific actions encumbent upon wayfarers. He will already have arrived at some knowledge of these things, if only in the form of turning away from rebelliousness, refraining from legal error, keeping his thoughts from becoming dissipated, or other internal or external works of that sort. Now he must embark upon overcoming his fear of failure and not give it another thought, for he is bound to experience more than enough of failure, especially in his initial exercises. He must then devote his spare time, outside of his spiritual exercises, to investigating the conduct of our ancestors in faith, the nature of their relationship to God Most High as evidenced by their worship, and the sincerity of their aspirations toward Him.

One must also read assiduously the Ṣūfī writings, in order to gain a thorough and intimate acquaintance with them and assimilate their profound learning and grasp their implications. The seeker must set aside the aversion most people experience toward studying some of the writings of the Ṣūfīs. As I have said, this applies especially to those who are deeply involved in legal, intellectual, and doctrinal studies. Receptivity to these writings can occur once the individual comes to prefer the way of Sufism and takes refuge in God Most High in hopes that God will open the door of understanding to him in these matters. One must also seek help by associating with someone who is genuinely learned and has a sincere love for the Ṣūfī Path.

The seeker must occupy himself with the things I have been describing and be in no way deterred by his failure to find the spiritual guide to whom he can return at every juncture of his journey. He must also realize that he need not depreciate the very considerable benefits that accrue to him in this beginning stage. On the contrary, he should consider himself fortunate, and grasp those positive results tightly with a miserly hand. That is the kind of gratitude for the grace of his vocation that is required if one desires an increase.

Once the servant has begun these requirements, seeking the aid of God Most High, trusting Him, exhibiting an appropriate fear of Him, and obeying His commands, then he has arrived at that greatest of hopes: that God Most High will teach him what he needs to know for his journey, as He promised when He said, "Fear God and God will be your teacher" (2:282) and "O you who believe, fear God and He will give you a criterion" (8:29). God Most High has also said, "Surely We will guide in Our ways those who struggle in Our cause" (29:69); and again, may His Name be glorified, "God will provide a way out for those who fear Him" (65:2). As a result, the seeker will have every kind of superabundance heaped upon him and will make rapid and direct progress on his journey.

102

God Most High will send him the kind of right guidance that will quiet his lower self and soothe his heart. As part of this process, God

Most High will lead him to a saintly spiritual guide who will help him advance more quickly in understanding. In time he will have need neither of the guide nor of anyone else. The seeker need only purify his intention toward God Most High and refine his way of thinking about Him. And he will already have begun to achieve that. Strictly speaking, however, there is no formal introduction for him in these things.

To sum up, then, the person who sets out to travel the Path, acting purposefully through deeds of heart and body such as I have described, whether by commission or avoidance, will be among those who are unfailingly led along the Path, if they are worthy of it. And anyone who has been successful in these matters is worthy. The mystics generally agree that one can come to God only by God's help and that only the lower self stands as a barrier between the servant and God. The lower self that does not go against itself struggles against God. If the lower self struggles against God, it is inconceivable that a person could travel the Path while fending off and thwarting the protection, watchfulness, and support that God wishes to give the seeker in the way He wishes to give it. God refuses to sustain the faithful servant except in ways of which the servant has no knowledge. The lower self's veil between darkness and light does not simply vanish; it is lifted and dissolved little by little until certitude comes.

This is the beginning of the Wayfarer's Path toward the multileveled states of Sufism. Its culmination is none other than the total realization of the Divine Unity, "And that is the gift of God which He gives to whom He will" (62:4). So long as one remains preoccupied with "being on the way" and with "getting there," the goal is unattainable. One must abandon himself at all times. Only then will he experience a freedom and an exaltation commensurate with his stage of advancement, and that is to experience the joy of homecoming.

Contrary to the speculations of some people, there is no desert or wasteland on the Path of God Most High. Wherever the wayfarer makes camp he is provided a dwelling and a place of comfort. Every situation is easy for him; servants and helpers facilitate all his comings and goings. But if the servant of God should fall back on the familiar, on things he feels sure of, then indeed he experiences a desert and a wasteland in the hunger of the lower self and in reliance on his intellect and conjecture. When at last the veil is lifted, that will become abundantly clear to him. And we seek refuge in God from an unfavorable judgment.

Once the seeker has grasped the full truth of all that I have been talking about, the journey along this Path will hold no terrors for him and he will not deem it difficult. He will undertake his travels with delight and expansion of the core of his being, and he will not tax his soul or his intellect with the kind of superfluous investigation the speculative thinkers talk about. Such concerns only confuse, baffle, and restrain one, making him reticent to embark on this Path and effectively blocking for him the door to the journey. Even if a servant were compelled to hold most of these speculative concepts as authentic, and were able to fulfill his duties by acting in accord with their essential requirements, in conformity to the Revealed Law and the legal procedures of the religious scholars, he would probably not achieve fulfillment that way. And how could he? Thank God, the matter is much more accessible than all this!

103

Let me explain. God Most High has sent us His Messenger Muḥammad, may God bless him and give him peace, with the true and tolerant religion. He imposed no constraint upon us in the religion. Any requirement above and beyond that of wayfaring which is not in line with the means of the people is divisive, produces controversy, and leads to the absence of proper guidance and of the one essential thing required of the servant—namely, sincerity in worshiping God, may He be exalted and glorified. The only thing that might prevent the servant from progressing through the stations of servanthood is a yielding to his passions.[10] Every passion is manifest to him, for they are undeniably part of his constitution and creatureliness. How could a person be unaware of his interior state so long as he demands an account of his lower self, acts in good faith toward his Lord, and strives for purity of heart?

The seeker must therefore apply himself to resisting his lower self in all temptations as long as his resistance does not threaten him with mental or bodily harm. He must persist in refusing to cling to whatever comes along that could cause him to fall back on his own devices and understanding, in whatever difficulty he experiences. In fact, the difficulty itself will be of greater benefit to him. The net result of calamities that befall the seeker, and which he discerns in the course of going against his lower self, is that they invite him to a variety of acts of obedience. However, the seeker may be unaware of this purpose and fight off the trials, thus losing the opportunity for obedience. The same is true of one who refuses to adhere to what his mind grasps when some rational truth becomes apparent to it: He ignores it and pretends not to notice it. But trials pose no danger to him. On the contrary, they are the clearest course to follow. The servant is ever the one whose lot is weakness and insufficiency, even if he is totally successful in both knowledge and action.

For the seeker, reliance on this self-discipline I have been describing will become an occupation that will protect him from distraction and deviation from the highway of full spiritual realization, and from exposure to dangers and susceptibility to all sorts of injuries. The person who pampers his lower self, either by failing to fast or by fasting too strictly and for too long, without several days' respite, has already gone far astray. The same is true of the person who likes to give away all that he possesses without keeping some for himself; or the one who delights in seclusion in mountain recesses or sequestering himself in deserts without ever taking a break and resting awhile at home. Hidden tendencies of the passions[11] cause all these things. Treatment is difficult; it requires religious and secular testing suited to the illness.

It is better to remain within the limits of the Revealed Law and travel the road of piety and fear of God, for there is no passional tendency in that whatsoever. One can then intensify his vigilance in moderating the lower self and its proclivity for the extremes of negligence and excess. If the servant remains sincere in all his states, God Most High will keep and support and protect him from destruction. He will lead him, and send him to an insightful spiritual guide who will delight him. The servant's task is to make a beginning; that of God Most High is to perfect and bring to completion. And from first to last, the matter is in God's hand.

This is what has occured to me as a response to your inquiry. I am fully aware that by getting involved in what does not concern me I have overstepped my bounds and am guilty of inappropriate behavior. From God Most High I seek forgiveness, indulgence, and pardon; for that is His proper domain. He gives me enough of those things and is the best of patrons. Let us ask Him, may He be exalted and glorified, to show us the truth as true and give us the ability to follow it; to show us the false as false and destine us to abandon it.[12] And may God bless our Master Muḥammad and his Family and Companions, and give them perfect peace.

Notes

Abbreviations in Notes

AS:	Arberry, *Sufism*
BW:	Danner, Translation of *The Book of Wisdom* of Ibn ʿAṭāʾ Allāh
DS:	Arberry's translation of Kalabādhī, *The Doctrine of the Sufis*
EC:	Nwiya, *Exegèse Coranique et langage mystique*
FH:	McKane's translation of al-Ghazālī's *Book of Fear and Hope*
IAA:	Nwiya, Arabic text and French translation of the *Hikam* of Ibn ʿAṭāʾ Allāh, *Ibn ʿAṭāʾ Allāh et la naissance de la confrérie šāḏilite*
IAR:	Nwiya, *Ibn ʿAbbād de Ronda*
IN:	Dodge's translation, *The Fihrist of Ibn al-Nadīm*
JCI:	Saint John of the Cross and Islam, Douglas and Yoder translation of Asin-Palacios' *Un Precursor . . .*
KL:	Nicholson's Arabic text, *Kitab al-Lumaʿ Fī 'l-Taṣawwuf of Abū Naṣr al-Sarrāj* (Gibb Series XXII)
LJ:	Abdel-Kader, *The Life, Personality, and Writings of Al-Junayd*
MDI:	Schimmel, *Mystical Dimensions of Islam*
MM:	Robson's translation, *Mishkāt al-Maṣābīḥ*

IBN ʻABBĀD OF RONDA

MP:	Asin-Palacios' Arabic text and French translation of *Maḥāsin al-Majālis* of Ibn al-ʻArīf
MS:	Smith, *Al-Muḥāsibī, 781–857, Mystic of Baghdad*
QR:	Arabic text of Qushayri's *Risālah* (various editions as noted in parentheses)
RK:	Ibn ʻAbbād's *ar-Rasāil al-Kubrā*
RS^1 and RS^2:	Nwiya's Arabic text editions of Ibn ʻAbbād's *ar-Rasāil aṣ-Ṣughrā* (1958 and 1974); marginal numbers in translation correspond to same in both RS^1 and RS^2
SB:	M. M. Khan's Nine Volume Arabic-English edition of *Ṣaḥīḥ al-Bukhārī* (Kazi)
SM:	A. H. Siddiqi's translation of *Saḥīḥ Muslim* (four vols., Ashraf)
ST:	G. Böwering, *The Mystical Vision of Existence in Classical Islam: The Qur'ānic Hermeneutics of the Ṣūfī Sahl At-Tustarī*

Introduction

1. Edward Kinerk, S.J., "Toward a Method for the Study of Spirituality," *Review for Religious*, January 1981, 40:1, pp. 3–19, quoting page 6.

2. Matthias Neuman, O.S.B., "Am I Growing Spiritually? Elements for a Theology of Growth," *Review for Religious* 42, no. 1 (January/February 1983): 38–49, quoting from pages 39–40.

3. See MDI 98–99.

4. IAR 239.

5. My paraphrase of L. Puhl's translation, *The Spiritual Exercises of St. Ignatius* (Loyola University Press, 1951), p. 12.

6. See JCI for a collection of material from Ibn ʻAbbād's commentary on Ibn ʻAṭā' Allāh's *Book of Wisdom*, esp. on this "renunciation of charisms."

7. Hans Urs von Balthasar, *Prayer* (New York: Paulist Press, 1961), pp. 81–82.

8. Abdallah Laroui, *The History of the Maghrib: An Interpretive Essay* (Princeton, N.J.: Princeton University Press, 1977), p. 89.

9. Translated from French of IAR 149.

10. M. Mahdi, *Ibn Khaldūn's Philosophy of History* (Chicago: University of Chicago Press, 1964), p. 140.

11. JCI 51.

12. JCI 70–71.

13. RS^2 205–6.

14. IAR 167, citing RK XXXIV, entirely on this topic.

15. JCI 52.

16. IAR xlvii–xlviii.

17. IAR 98–99, 232.

18. IAR 233–37.

19. IAR 227–29, translated from Nwiya's French.

20. IAA 4–18.

21. MDI 23ff.

22. See P. Nwiya, *Exégèse coranique et langage mystique* (Beirut, 1970).

23. MDI 77ff.

24. JCI 48.

25. See MDI 259–86 for an excellent survey of "Theosophical Sufism."

26. *Sufi Orders in Islam* (Oxford University Press, 1973), p. 20.

27. G. Parrinder, *Africa's Three Religions* (London: Sheldon Press, 1976), p. 209.

28. For more on the Ṣūfī orders, see MDI 228–58.

29. *Op.cit.*, 4.

30. Cited in A. M. M. Mackeen, "The Early History of Sufism in the Maghrib Prior to Al-Shādhilī," *Journal of the American Oriental Society* 91, no.3 (1971): 402.

31. MDI 264.

32. See the two items on Ibn al-'Arīf by Asin-Palacios in Bibliography.

33. For a sample of Abū Madyan's prayer, see R. W. Austin, "I Seek God's Pardon . . . ," in *Studies in Comparative Religion* 7, no.2 (Spring 1973): 92–94.

34. "The Rise of al-Shādhilī," *JAOS* 91, no.4 (1971): 477–83.

35. "The Prayer of Ibn Mashīsh," *The Islamic Quarterly* nos.1 and 2 (1978): 68–75.

36. Mackeen, art. cit., 484–86; Trimingham, op. cit., 46–49.

37. According to MDI 200, "One may assume a close structural relationship between the concept of the *quṭb* as the highest spiritual guide of the faithful and that of the hidden *imām* of Shia Islam."

38. IAR 27–34; MDI 57, 80.

39. *The Travels of Ibn Baṭṭūṭa*, trans. H. A. R. Gibb (Cambridge, 1958), vol. 1, pp. 25–27. Italics indicate quotations from the Qur'ān.

40. *Muslim Devotions* (London, 1960), pp. 23–24. See also M. S. Seale, "The Mysterious Letters of the Qur'ān," in his *Qur'ān and Bible* (London, 1978), pp. 29–46, on various theories about the letters that are uttered frequently in Shādhilī's Litany of the Sea.

41. Padwick, op. cit., 135. For more samples of Shādhilī's prayers, see E. H. Douglas, "Prayers of Al-Shādhilī," in *Medieval and Middle Eastern Studies in Honor of A. S. Atiyah*, ed. S. A. Hanna (Leiden, 1972), pp. 106–21. The term *shirk* here rendered as "association" refers to the sin of behaving toward something other than God as though it were God.

42. MDI 249–50.

43. Mackeen, art. cit., p. 486.

44. Op. cit., 205–6.

45. MDI 254.

46. Cited in Trimingham, op. cit., 188–89. I have taken the liberty of omitting some of the Arabic terms the translator has included in the text.

47. IAA 34.

48. More information on the Mālikite law school will be provided further on, in the section on Ibn 'Abbād's life.

49. For the following information on Ibn 'Aṭā' I have relied on IAA 19–79; IAR 95–99; BW 13–43.

50. Quoting from IAA 43.

51. IAR 95, note.

52. IAR 115.

53. For more on the *Tanbīh*, see IAR 100–19.

54. IAA 27–35.

55. Mackeen, art. cit., pp. 403–4.

56. Under the leadership of Yūsuf ibn Tāshfīn (ruled 1061–1106), the western Maghrib became for the first time a single political entity. The Almoravid dynasty (from al-murābiṭūn, "those who dwell in ribāṭs" [fortified monastery-like buildings]) thrust itself upon Spain as well, and from its capitals at Marrakesh and Seville, Yūsuf's followers set about enforcing a strict and rather puritanical reform. Striving to return to a pristine vision and practice of Islam, the Almoravids modeled their polity on that of Medinah as they believed it was in the time of Muḥammad. To this nostalgic reconstruction they added the Shi'ite concept of the Mahdī ("The Guided One," a kind of messianic figure) and the asceticism of the Kharijites. The Mālikite school became the repository of religious authority.

According to A. Laroui, Almoravid religious policy inculcated three features: the preaching of a moral reform along with asceticism; a theological dogmatism that opposed overexclusive ideologies and aimed at a communitarian consensus; and a juridico-political role in structuring public life that involved a return to ancient Medinan practice (Abdallah Laroui, *The History of the Maghrib* [Princeton, N.J.: Princeton University Press, 1977], pp. 160–172). Yūsuf ibn Tāshfīn's son 'Alī (ruled 1106–1143) ordered all of al-Ghazālī's works burned in 1109. He alleged that Ghazālī (d. 1111) had accused the Mālikite school of being too rigid and narrow, even though Ghazālī had, in Hitti's words, "headed the list of Eastern divines who expressed unreservedly their approval of the Andalusian *faqīhs'* (i.e., jurists) legal opinion that Yūsuf ibn Tāshfīn was absolved from any pledges he had made to the party kings of Moslem Spain and that it was not only his right but his duty to dethrone them" (P. Hitti, *History of the Arabs* [London, 1963], p. 542).

Almoravid theology had a tendency toward anthropomorphism that some critics interpreted as weakening the Islamic teaching of God's unity. Ibn Tūmart (d. 1130), born in the last quarter of the eleventh century, was one of the Almoravids' severest critics. Of Berber stock, Ibn Tūmart studied in Spain and Baghdad. When he returned to Morocco full of insights from his schooling in

Ash'arite theology, he confronted the Almoravid religious establishment, taking exception especially to their literalistic exegesis of the Qur'ān. His views proved unpopular at first and he fled. Not much later, Ibn Tūmart returned with the support of a religio-political machine potent enough to topple the moribund Almoravid dynasty. By then the new reformer had accepted for himself the title of Mahdī, thus enhancing the resolve of his followers to reform Moroccan Islam once again.

Ibn Tūmart's followers came to be known as the Almohads (al-muwaḥḥidūn, "those who proclaim God's unity"). His "native Moroccan synthesis," as Laroui calls it, was to be forged of several elements. He built his system on the earlier synthetic labors of al-Bāqillānī (d. 1013), an Ash'arite thinker who had combined theology with jurisprudence; Ibn Ḥazm (d. 1064), a Spanish jurist, whom Ibn 'Abbād mentions with approval in one of his letters, and who joined Tradition study with jurisprudence; and al-Ghazālī.

57. IAR xxviii–xiiii, xiii–xvi. Abū Ya'qūb Yūsuf (reigned 1286–1306) promoted the remembrance of the Prophet's birthday by instituting in 1292 the annual celebration of the *mawlid* ("birthday feast"). The later Abū 'l-Ḥasan (1331–1348) is reported to have lived a pious and austere life. He read al-Bukhārī's (d. 870) collection of sayings of the Prophet; Abū Nu'aym al-Iṣfahānī's (d. 1037) *Ornament of the Saints* (Ḥilyat al-Awliyā'), a hagiographical work; and other religious classics. Abū 'l-Ḥasan also retained jurists of the Mālikite school in his entourage. He enjoyed visiting the tomb of the Ṣūfī saint Abū Madyan (d. 1126) in Tlemcen and, as an act of devotion, had the tomb beautifully restored. (Some have seen in his restoration of the tomb but one more way for the sulṭān to win over the adherents of the popular cults.)

Abū 'l-Ḥasan's son and successor, Abū 'Inān Fāris (1348–1357), also favored Sufism, and even traveled to Salé to visit Ibn 'Āshir, one of Ibn 'Abbād's teachers. The Ṣūfī refused to grant the sulṭān an audience. Nwiya is of the opinion that there is little reason to doubt the sulṭān's sincerity or suspect that he was merely currying favor with the influential Ṣūfīs for the purpose of exploiting their appeal to the masses.

Ibn Baṭṭūṭa, an older contemporary of Ibn 'Abbād and one of Islam's most famous world travelers, visited Fez in 1349–1350. He describes the religious and cultural scene at the court of his patron, the Sulṭān Abū 'Inān Fāris: "Our master holds scholarly assemblies every day after the dawn prayer in the mosque of his illustrious palace; the princes and the juris-consults and the most distinguished of their disciples attend. Before the sovereign is read the commentary of the noble Koran, the tradition of the Prophet chosen by God . . . works relative to the doctrine of Malik and books of the mystics. In all these phases of learning, our master holds first rank. . . . Among all the other kings of the earth, I have never known a one whose solicitude for learning attained such a high degree" (quoted in Roger Le Tourneau, *Fez in the Age of the Marinides* [Norman, Okla.: University of Oklahoma Press, 1961], p. 78).

58. IAR xxi–xxviii.

59. *Muqaddimah*, vol. 3, p. 15; trans. F. Rosenthal (New York: Pantheon, 1958).

60. *Ibn Khaldūn's Philosophy of History* (Chicago, 1964), p. 30.

61. In an extensive five-part article entitled "The Spanish Arabs and Islam," Ignaz Goldziher proposes some conclusions about the Mālikite school that may be considered applicable in many ways to the situation in Morocco in the fourteenth century. Goldziher's purpose is, first, to survey some fundamental spiritual inclinations of a regional group of Muslims (in this case those of Spain); and, second, to estimate the effects of those factors on the regional mentality, noting how that mentality differs from that of Muslims further to the east. Goldziher builds his theory on the basis of his studies of the major Islamic law schools, and their respective approaches to the four "roots of law," namely, the Qur'ān, the Prophetic Example (*Sunnah*) as enshrined in Tradition and living practice, Consensus (*ijmāʿ*) and Analogical reasoning (*qiyās*). In theory, the first two roots are unchangeable; the second two allow considerable leeway and give some authority to human judgment.

Goldziher's theory amounts to this: The more a law school restricts or rules out the use of the third and fourth roots of law, the more will that school tend to be conservative, relying only on already accepted tradition, and allowing no scope at all for adaptation. Goldziher surveys the schools, studies their attitudes toward Consensus and Analogy, notes the region in which each school is predominant, describes how it arrived there, and cites numerous specific case-decisions as illustrations of how the liberal-conservative scales dip. He then concludes that "it was the tendency of Eastern Islam in its religious and social institutions, to allow freedom of mind to prevail beside Tradition, whereas with the Spanish and Maghribī Arabs the system of religious and social life excluded at least theoretically, free-thinking, and allowed no constructive element beside tradition to prevail or to exert effective influence."

The principal reasons for the differences between Eastern and Western Islam, according to Goldziher, are four. The first agrees with Ibn Khaldūn's analysis: Traditionalist and pietistic Medinan elements that migrated to the West appealed to the "patriarchal simplicity" of the Berbers, with their moral and religious rigorism. Second, the more liberal style developed in the East because in Syria and Persia, Islam met with cultures superior to itself. Cultural patterns and political institutions had to be able to coexist with the lively and assertive forces of the conquered cultures. Berber culture Goldziher judges to have been inferior to that of the invading Arabs. Third, the now-defunct Ẓāhirite school of law may have paved the way for the eventual takeover of the Mālikite school. The "Literalist" school was even stricter than the Mālikite, and the multiplication of international contacts in both Spain and the Maghrib may have necessitated some softening of the Ẓāhirite approach. The Mālikite school was in place and ready to fill the need. Meanwhile in the East, the Hanafite school's more pliable attitude to traditional values had a theological parallel in Ashʿarite concessions to foreign religious concepts, for the followers of al-Ashʻarī did battle with both the pure spiritualism of the Muʻtazilites and the rigid anthropomorphism of the strict traditionalists. The more liberal mentality endeavored to steer a middle course, by means of Consensus and Analogy, between changing political and social conditions and the defensive posture of traditionalist orthodoxy. Finally, both the Spanish Umayyad dynasty and many of the politico-religious movements in North Africa were in some ways protests against Baghdad's central authority. Goldziher suggests that part of the language of protest in the West was the adoption as patron of a man who had been a bitter enemy of Baghdad, namely, Mālik ibn Anas (d. 795), founder of the Mālikite school. In *Gesammelte Schriften*, ed. J. de Somogyi (Hildesheim, 1973), vol. I, pp. 370–423.

62. IAR 16–21.
63. MDI 115; KL 163.
64. IAR 165 (RK XXXI).
65. I have summarized IAR 43–80 and 87–90 on IA's life and sermons.
66. KL 233–41.
67. LJ also contains excellent introductory essays on themes in Junayd's letters.
68. Abdul Qayyum's translation, *Letters of Al-Ghazzali* (Lahore, 1976), p. viii.
69. See A. Schimmel, *The Triumphal Sun* (London, 1978), esp. chap. 1.
70. Paulist Press, 1980. B. Lawrence's Foreword has more on Ṣūfī letters.
71. IAR 1–2, 121–25.
72. IAR 127–38.
73. IAR 145–48.
74. IAR 241–42.
75. IAR 169.
76. IAR 170–75.

Letter 1

1. *The Food of Hearts* is a major systematic treatise on Sufism by Abū Ṭālib al-Makkī (d. 996), the first comprehensive work on the subject. Along with the writings of al-Ghazāli (d. 1111) and al-Muḥāsibī (d. 857), this author's work was influential in shaping the thought of Ibn ʻAbbād and other members of the Shādhiliyyah order.

2. The often-used technical term *murīd* is translated throughout as "seeker." It could as well have been rendered as "novice" or "aspirant", but Ibn ʻAbbād uses the term in a way that does not always refer specifically to a member of a Ṣūfī religious order. Rather, the term applies more generally to anyone who is truly in search of God, whether formally under the tutelage of a spiritual guide or not. IA often used the word as a kind of synonym for "servant" (*ʻabd*), a term applicable to any devout Muslim.

3. “Traces of a campsite” is evidently an allusion to a theme commonly found in the opening sections of pre-Islamic Arabic odes. The traveler is arrested by the sight of the vestiges of a campfire and is brought to a halt with reminiscences of past relationships. Cf. Ilse Lichtenstaedter. “Das Nasīb der altarabischen Qaṣīde,” *Islamica*, vol. V, pp. 17ff. (Leipzig, 1931).

4. “Pretensions” here translates the plural of *da‘wa*, one of IA’s favorite terms to designate a fundamental psycho-spiritual disorder. See Introduction.

5. “Jurists” translates *ahl aẓ-ẓāhir* (people who recognize only the external meaning), a term that IA juxtaposes to *ahl al-bāṭin* (people who acknowledge a spiritual meaning). IA frequently warns of the danger of associating with the “exotericist” jurists and of the need to seek the company of Ṣūfīs, the “esotericists.” IA never counsels disregard for the religious law itself, but he thinks very little of the counterproductive rationalistic speculations of professional legal scholars.

6. “Transcendence and anthropomorphism” translate *tanzīh* and *tashbīh* respectively, standard technical terms. The affirmation of the former and the denial of the latter are a fundamental principle in Ash‘arite theology. Cf. Richard McCarthy, S.J., *The Theology of al-Ash*‘arī (Beirut, 1953), p. 188 and *passim*.

7. “Proper demeanor” translates *ḥush al-adab*, a phrase IA uses often to characterize all that is required of a creature in the presence of the Creator; here also rendered as “proper, fitting, appropriate conduct or behavior.”

8. Al-Junayd, a prominent mystic of Baghdad (d. 910), appears several times in IA’s letters. He was a chief proponent of “sober” mysticism and was therefore quite appealing to IA and the generally more sober Shādhiliyyah. Cf. MDI 58–59 and *passim*. Also R. Zaehner’s *Hindu and Muslim Mysticism* (London, 1960), pp. 135–53, 218–24. “Believing” translates *taṣdīq*.

9. “Mystic Truth” translates *ḥaqīqah*, a technical term variously defined by different Ṣūfī authors, but generally referring to the ultimate goal of the journey along the Path. It could as well have been translated as “The Real,” “The Ultimate Reality,” “The Reality,” etc.

10. Abū Ṭālib (in *The Food of Hearts*, i.e., *Qūt al-Qulūb* [Cairo ed., 1932], vol. 1 pp. 139–40) and al-Ghazālī (*The Revival of the Religious Sciences*, FH 57ff.) both treat of a concept often mentioned in the Qur’ān (3:47, 8:30, 13:42, 27:51, etc.): the *makr* of God. IA spends several pages discussing their approach to this fascinating aspect of God’s transcendence: His “ruse, wiles, machinations, strategems.” This is a metaphorical expression meant to remind the servant that the Master always has the last word, and that a human being is in no position to “hold God to His word.” God is not required to do even what He has said He will do. The servant must be wary of becoming too comfortable even in the midst of consolation that seems to come authentically from God Himself.

11. “Intimate knowledge” translates the technical term *ma‘rifah*. Often translated as “gnosis,” the term refers to God-given, intuitional, nondiscursive insight into the creature’s relationship with the Creator. MDI 130 gives Junayd’s

definition: "Gnosis . . . is the hovering of the heart between declaring God too great to be comprehended, and declaring Him too mighty to be perceived. It consists in knowing that, whatever may be imagined in the heart, God is the opposite of it."

12. Discerning the "disparity between the recent and the eternally ancient" is IA's paraphrase of Junayd's definition of *tawḥīd*, the acknowledgement or mystical experience of God's unity: "The separation of the Eternal from that which has been originated in time by the Covenant" (MDI 58).

13. "Expansion of the core of his being" translates *inshirāḥ aṣ-ṣadr*. *Ṣadr* is often rendered, in translations of the Qur'ān and other works, as "mind, heart, breast." The phrase evidently alludes to Surah 94:1, "Have we not expanded your *ṣadr* for you. . . . " The term clearly refers in Ṣūfī writings not to the actual heart, but to a spiritual faculty both "deeper" and "wider" than the heart (cf. MDI 192). "Purification of the heart" translates "snow of the heart," one of IA's favorite formulae. It may be an allusion to Ibn Hishām's account of how angels opened the chest of the very young Muḥammad, removed a dark substance, and cleansed his heart with snow from a golden basin (A. Guillaume, *The Life of Muḥammad* [Oxford, 1955], p. 72).

14. IA seems to be paraphrasing Ibn 'Aṭā. Compare with IAA pp. 91–92, #15, trans. in BW 50.

15. "To die," literally to experience *fanā'* or mystical union through loss of self.

16. *Lisān al-ḥāl*, a Ṣūfī expression meaning that one's whole being speaks for itself—i.e., one's state, and that of every created thing, utters by its very nature what cannot be put into words.

17. Quoting al-Ḥallāj (d. 922), famous martyr-mystic of Baghdad who was executed for claiming union with God in a way that Muslim authorities deemed blasphemous. IA seems to suggest that the verse is well known to his addressee. The verse continues, "but they all came together once my eye had seen You" (IAR 177, citing L. Massignon's translation of the poem in *Journal Asiatique*, Jan.-Mar. 1931, p. 39).

18. "Mother of the Book" is the name given to the Qur'ān before it was revealed, i.e., when the revelation still existed only in the mind of God.

19. For more on the "two paths" see Introduction: *sālik* and *majdhūb*.

20. "Analogical reasoning" translates *qiyās*, a term derived from legal science and widely known as one of the "four roots" of the law. Here used to refer to human intelligence in a wider sense, conceptual knowledge as opposed to the "pre-conceptual" knowledge suggested by the other path.

21. Ghazālī's version of the story: "It is related that the Prophet and Gabriel were weeping for fear of God, and God revealed to both of them: Why do you weep, since I have made you both secure? So they said: And who is secure from your strategems? And it was as if both of them, since they knew that God Himself is the Knower of hidden things, and that He does not acquaint them

with the ultimate goal of affairs, did not think themselves secured against His saying 'I have made both of you secure' being a way of trying and testing them and plotting against them, so that, if their fear had been quietened, it would have been clear that they thought themselves secure from the strategems and had not fulfilled their saying." Immediately above this account, Ghazālī alludes to Qur'ān 7:97, to which IA will also refer a few lines below (trans. from FH 58). Abū Ṭālib explains that Muḥammad and Gabriel seemed to know that "there is no end to God's wiles and no limit to His decree."

22. Two Mss. identify the "someone else" as ash-Shādhilī.

23. "The story of Abraham" here refers to the time the prophet prayed when he was in trouble: "Bear me in mind, O God." Gabriel came to help Abraham and asked, "Are you in need?" Abraham replied, "Not of you." In that way God altered the state of his chosen one so that he relied only on God Himself and not on an intermediary (FH 58).

24. "Abrogation" generally applies to the theory that, although some verses in the Qur'ān appear to contradict each other, they actually represent God's freedom to replace an earlier revelation with a later one or to substitute a more binding injunction for a lesser one, etc. Here IA refers to the wider implications of the theory of *naskh*.

25. Both Abū Ṭālib and Ghazālī cite the Tradition (given in Note 21) without including its *isnād* (chain of transmission). "Prophetic Example" translates *Sunnah*. Ibn Ḥanbal (d. 855) was the founder of one of the four chief Sunnī law schools. He was noted for his staunch adherence to Qur'ān and Tradition (Hadīth, Saying of the Prophet) as the principal sources of guidance for Muslims. His *Musnad* was one of the most important collections of Tradition. 'Abd ar-Raḥmān ibn Mahdī (d. 813) was a teacher of the science of Tradition. Several of the major collections of Ḥadīth contain chapters on "Knowledge"; cf. F. Rosenthal, *Knowledge Triumphant* (Brill, 1970) pp. 70–96, re: "Books and Chapters on Knowledge."

26. Ghazālī goes on to include Abū Bakr's response to the Prophet's prayer, and then explains the meaning of this Tradition and its relation to the one about Muḥammad and Gabriel: "And Abū Bakr said: Leave off badgering your Lord. Surely He will fulfill for you according as He has promised you. For he [Abū Bakr] was at the station of the *Sincere*, the station of reliance on the promise of God. And the station of the Messenger of God was that of fearing the strategems of God and it is the more complete, because it can derive only from perfection of 'knowledge' concerning the secrets of God and the concealed aspects of His actions and the meanings of His attributes which He expresses by such actions as derive from them by way of plotting" (FH 59; the Tradition is also in MM 1273 and KL 122).

27. The "story of Moses" refers here to the prophet's fear as he confronted Pharaoh and his magicians. Ghazālī's version says, ". . . it is reported concerning Moses that, when he said: Truly we [Moses and Aaron] are afraid that He

may neglect us or be remiss, He [God] said: Do not be afraid, surely I shall be with both of you, hearing and seeing (20:48). And, in spite of this, when the magicians cast their spells (20:66f), Moses quaked with fear within himself, because he did not feel secure from the strategems of God, and was confused over the affair until security was renewed to him, and it was said to him [what IA refers to as the "second address"]: Fear not, surely you are the uppermost (20:71)" (FH 59).

28. IA's grammatical exegesis of the "second address" (20:71) cannot be understood without explicit reference to the Qur'ānic text: *innaka anta 'l-a'lā*. The "emphatic or intensified subject" is *innaka anta*—"Indeed you yourself . . ." evidently meant to make it clear that God was specifying Moses beyond any doubt. The "predicate in the superlative [literally *af'al*] form" with the definite article [literally "*alif* and *lam*"] prefixed to it, is *al-a*'lā, "the uppermost." Cf. Wright, *A Grammar of the Arabic Language*, ii, pp. 54C, 282B, and 283B. On Ja'far aṣ-Ṣādiq's exegesis of Moses' two encounters with God, see EC 178–83.

29. "The story of Jesus" refers here to his conversation with God in Qur'ān 5:116–18. God asks Jesus whether he has instructed people to consider him and his mother as gods. Jesus replies that he has told the people only to worship God, for the people are God's servants. Ghazālī explains that Jesus "transferred the affair to the will and disassociated himself entirely from pronouncing as to his knowledge of it; because he had nothing to do with the affair, and because affairs are tied to the will [of God] with a connection which issues beyond the boundary of things intelligible and familiar, so that it is not possible to give a ruling on them by use of analogy or conjecture or opinion, *a fortiori* by verification and proof, and this is what the hearts of the Gnostics have grasped" (FH 59). In other words, Jesus predicated all knowledge of God and admitted that it is unfathomable.

30. Evidently Abū Bakr al-Khaṭīb al-Baghdādī (d. 1071), who wrote a history of the eminent Muslims of Baghdad, of whom Abū Ṭālib was one. IA refers to "The Preacher" also in the context of a discussion of how to interpret utterances of spiritual sages concerning the divine attributes, in RK XVI (cf. IAR 158).

31. Shiblī (859–945) was a mystic of Baghdad, a friend of al-Ḥallāj, and was famous for his rather bizarre behavior and enigmatic utterances. IA will introduce him again in later letters.

32. Both RS^1 and RS^2 read *fāza bi-quwwati 'l-'ayn*, but I believe it makes better sense to read *qurrah* for *quwwah*—a minor change—and translate "be joyful" or "attain delight" rather than the more forced "Succeed by virtue of the essential power"; for *qurratu 'l-'ayn* is so common an idiom.

Letter 2

1. "A man with a highly developed spiritual life" translates *rajul[un] min arbāb al-qulūb*; literally, "a man among those endowed with (or who are masters of) hearts."

2. "Spiritual states" translates *aḥwāl*. IA develops certain aspects of the doctrine of "states" and "stations" (*maqāmāt*) in this letter. They are the principal elements in the Ṣūfī psycho-spiritual development typology. A state is a fleeting condition, given by God, unmerited by the seeker. A station perdures and is the result of human striving, at least in part. While a seeker remains in a given station, he may experience a variety of states. Hence, even though a seeker may remain in one station for a considerable time, he experiences it as something dynamic, for the experience is continually modified by the states God bestows on him. Ṣūfī authors differ in the sequences, number, and names they assign to the elements in this typology. Cf. MDI 99–100.

3. Nwiya notes (RS² 30) that Sha'rānī attributed the verses to al-Junayd (*Ṭabaqāt al-Kubrā* [Cairo, 1355 A.H.], vol. 1, p. 74).

4. This is evidently a reference to the notion of *iktisāb*. According to the theologian al-Ash'arī (d. 935), God creates all acts and those acts are in turn acquired or appropriated by the morally responsible individual. DS 30–32 sums up the Ṣūfī understanding of the concept: "They are agreed that every breath they draw, every glance they make, and every motion they perform, is by virtue of a faculty which God originates in them, and a capacity which He creates for them at the same time as their actions. . . . They are agreed that they are accredited with acts and merit (*iktisāb*) in a true sense, for which they are rewarded and punished . . . the meaning of the term 'merit' being, that a man acts through a faculty (divinely) originated."

5. A variation on this story appears in MSM 208. For more background and anecdotes about Junayd, cf. MSM 199–213.

6. Literally, "Give me without a thing"—that is, give to me unconditionally. JCI 51 has the text almost verbatim, but translates "Give me, Lord, nonbeing."

7. The first of many citations of Ibn 'Aṭā' Allāh of Alexandria (d. 1309); see Introduction. IAA 120–21, #77.

8. IAA 124–25, #86.

9. "Contemplations" translates the plural of *mushāhadah*, a term IA uses most frequently in the singular. Contemplation, contemplative vision, or inner vision is the underlying theme of this letter. It is the foundation of the seeker's spiritual development along the Path as he progresses through the various stations and states. See Introduction.

10. Abū Hurayrah (d. 676/7 at Medina) was one of the Companions of the Prophet (i.e., a "first-generation" Muslim), and was a trusted and often-cited source of Traditions (IN 1007). This Tradition is found in MM 494, SM 1622.

11. Ibrāhīm ibn Adham (d. 776 or 790) is said to have first described the practice of asceticism as tripartite: renouncing the world, renouncing delight in one's renunciation, utter lack of interest in this world (MDI 37). IA tells a slightly different version of this anecdote in Letter 6. IA's versions both differ slightly from Ghazālī's (FH 19). The story is very similar to a tale told about Nūrī (d. 907) in MSM 228.

12. Here Iblīs (the Devil) is addressing God. The full text reads, "Iblīs said, 'Now because you have sent me astray, I shall indeed . . . Path. Then I shall come upon them before them and behind them, from right and left, and . . . ' " (7:16–17).

13. IA quotes this Tradition again later, in Letter 15. MM 1087.

14. In KL 118, Sahl at-Tustarī (d. 896) comments on this Tradition: "One's good deeds are God's grace; one's evil deeds are under control of his lower self."

15. IA does not name the shaykh in this story, but MSM 131 recounts a tale very similar to this one, about Sufyān ath-Thawrī (715–778).

16. Ḥudhayfah (d. 656/7 at Medina) was a Companion of the Prophet, held military and government posts, and was a specialist on hypocrisy. He is the source of many Traditions (IN 1006; SM 82–83, Note 251). This anecdote occurs in FH 64, where Ghazālī makes special mention of Ḥudhayfah's expertise in the ways of hypocrites.

17. IAA 124–25, #88. According to BW 138–39. Ibn Abījah (d. 1809) quoted this same Tradition as a commentary on these same verses of Ibn ʿAṭā'.

18. IA is evidently alluding here to a Tradition, "Your worst enemy is between your two sides" (MDI 112; KL 12).

19. IAA 110–11, #51.

20. A similar saying on repentance is attributed in KL 142 to Ibn al-Mubārak. See following note.

21. Ibn al-Mubārak (736–797) was a noted ascetic and Traditionist from Merv. He was also known as a poet and jurist. This anecdote appears in FH 89. (Cf. IN 936; MSM 124–28.)

22. IAA 92–95, #16. On the crucial importance of being a "son of the moment" (*ibn al-waqt*), DS 80 quotes Junayd: "Sufism is the preservation of the moments: that is, that a man does not consider what is outside his limits, . . . and only associates with his proper moment." "Moment" here refers to one's actual condition, in which one deals with whatever stations and states he finds himself in. "Moment" is also translated "time."

23. Jonah (Yūnus) is the biblical figure whose story is told in the Qur'ān (esp. 37:139–48). He is also called Dhū 'n-Nūn ("He of the Fish"). This supplication also became part of a Tradition (MM 484) in which it is used as an example of an unfailingly efficacious prayer.

24. IAA 126–127, #92.

25. IAA 154–155, #162; JCI 60–61.

26. Abū 'Uthmān al-Ḥīrī (d. 910) was one of the leaders of the Ṣūfī movement in Nīshāpūr. He was born in Rayy, but later visited Junayd in Baghdad and became a pupil of Abū Ḥafṣ al-Ḥaddād in Nīshāpūr (MDI 52–53; MSM 231–35). Abū Ḥafṣ (d. 879) lived most of his life in Nīshāpūr, but traveled to Baghdad and met Junayd and Shiblī there (MSM 192–98). IN 991 says he was "a Persian associated with the Mu'tazilah, but with original ideas." This anecdote also occurs in DS 150.

27. Ibrāhīm al-Khawāṣṣ (d. 904) was noted for his desert wanderings. He was born in Samarra and died at Rayy. He was a friend of Junayd. This anecdote is similar to one recounted in MSM 273. (Cf. MDI 119; MSM 272–76).

28. Sahl ibn 'Abd Allāh at-Tustarī (c. 815–896) is a very important figure in the history of Sufism. ST 7–42 gives a detailed history of the "Tustarī Tradition," a chronological study of how Sahl's thought was utilized and preserved in the major Ṣūfī writings other than Sahl's own. Sahl was a student of Sufyān ath-Thawrī, and died in Baṣrah, where Ḥallāj (d. 922) had traveled with him (MSM 153–60).

29. KL 396 attributes a similar statement to Shiblī, in which he says that, if his vileness were compared to that of the Jews and Christians, his would be greater.

30. JCI 63 attributes this to ash-Shādhilī and uses it to comment on the following quote from Ibn Aṭā' (see Note 31).

31. IAA 156–57, #165, here quoting only lines 1 and 4 of the saying. RS^2 p. 41, Note 3, indicates that four Mss. include also lines 2 and 3: "Come to know your lowliness and He will lead you to [Nwiya has "help you with"] His magnificence; Come to know your deficiency and He will lead you to His power." JCI p. 62–63.

32. Abū 'r-Rabī' Sulaymān al-Yāzighī, for whom no dates are available, was probably one of the shaykhs who initiated IA into Sufism at Fez (IAR 53).

33. The recommendation of the mystics is quite likely based on the strong endorsement of the practice given in the Traditions, e.g. MM 188–91.

Letter 3

1. For more on "unquestioning acceptance of authority" (*taqlīd*) and "innovation" (*bid'ah*), see Introduction. IA's interest in these things is not that of a systematic theologian, but of a spiritual director or pastoral theologian. He therefore concerns himself with how the deviations affect the individual's spiritual growth, rather than with their theoretical aspects.

2. The personalities whose names appear in this paragraph and the next are as follows: al-Walīd was the leader of the Meccan group known as the Makhzūm; he was by no means the Prophet's worst enemy. Mas'ūd, also a tribal leader, was from nearby aṭ-Ṭā'if, where the Quraysh tribe's opposition to Mu-

ḥammad evidently first became very active. There was a shrine there to the goddess al-Lāt. Abū Ṭālib was the Prophet's uncle and the father of Muḥammad's cousin ʻAlī. The young Muḥammad became "Abū Ṭālib's orphan" after the Prophet's grandfather, ʻAbd al-Muṭṭalib, died, leaving the boy to his uncle's care. Muḥammad's own father had died shortly after he was born. Quṣayy, long dead by the Prophet's time, had been a very prominent member of the Quraysh. It was probably he who founded Mecca as a city, developing it out of what had previously been merely a camp around the sanctuary of the Kaʻba. Abū Jahl, "Father of Ignorance," was one of the Prophet's bitterest enemies. Slight variations on the story IA relates here are found in SB 5:141 and SM 18. On the identity of the personalities, cf. W. M. Watt, *Muhammad at Mecca* (Oxford, 1953).

3. Ṣāliḥ was an Arabian prophet, according to tradition. The main elements of his story appear in Qur'ān 7:71–77; 11:64–71; 26:141–58.

4. The Qur'ānic accounts of Moses' conflict with Pharaoh may be found in 7:101–32; 10:76–89; 14:5–17; 20:41–78; 26:9–51; 40:24–53; 44:16–32; 51:38–40; 79:16–25, to name the principal texts. The story of Noah and his unbelieving people occurs in 11:27–36; 23:23–31; 26:105–20; 37:73–80; 71:1–29.

5. "One who aspires to be a Ṣūfī is a *mutaṣawwif*." Cf. MDI 20 on Ṣūfī caveats for those who would keep the company of the holy.

6. Traditions such as these may be found in the major collections, in their sections on "Faith"; e.g., MM 5–49; SM 1–146; SB 1:15–49.

7. ʻAbd Allāh ibn (al-)ʻAbbās (c. 619–87), an important Traditionist, was influential in laying the foundations of Meccan legal science (SM 12).

8. Abū ʻAbd ar-Raḥmān ibn Masʻūd (d. c. 653), a Companion of the Prophet, was a major authority in the legal tradition of Kufah. (Cf. J. Schacht, *The Origins of Muhammadan Jurisprudence* [Oxford, 1950], pp. 231ff.)

9. Shurayḥ is presumably the semi-legendary Judge of Kufah who died around 700. (Cf. Schacht, op. cit., pp. 228–29; and *An Introduction to Islamic Law* [Oxford, 1964], p. 24.)

10. Shaʻbī (d. c. 728) was a leading Traditionist of his time in Kufah (Schacht, *Origins*, 230–31).

11. Mālik ibn Anas (715–795), a Traditionist of Medinah, was the founder of the Mālikite law school, to which IA adhered (IN 493–98).

12. Sufyān ath-Thawrī (715–775) was a Traditionist who was born at Kufah and died at Baṣrah. A very frequently cited source of Traditions (IN 443–44, 545–46).

13. "Pre-Islamic age" translates *jāhilīyyah*, the age of paganism or "ignorance."

14. "All things else" is an attempt to translate a very enigmatic and apparently idiomatic phrase, *as-sabad wa 'l-labad*. It seems to mean, literally, something like "goathair and felt-padding"; I assume it is an idiom for "anything at all" or "everything else."

15. "Death of a pagan" translates what is literally "jāhilīyyah death." MM 781; SM 1030; SB 9:145–46.

16. "Making the emigration" translates *hijrah*, and "fighting in the way of God" translates *jihād*. MM 785. On the former, see Note 24 below.

17. I.e., the four caliphs (successors of the Prophet) who ruled between 632 and 661: Abū Bakr, ʻUmar, ʻUthmān, and ʻAlī.

18. SM 1344.

19. The following "Traditions of Discord" and others like them may be found in sections of several of the major collections, entitled *Fitan* ("dissensions, discords"). Cf. MM 1120–1386; SM 1393–1528; SB 9:143–88.

20. MM 1125–26.

21. MM 1066–67 gives a variation on this commentary-Tradition.

22. MM 1121–22, with a variant on 1126.

23. Ḥasan al-Baṣrī (642–728) is one of the most famous early ascetics, noted for his tendency to discern dire consequences in almost everything. He was born in Medinah, and later became secretary to the governor of Khurāsān and then secretary to Anas ibn Mālik (see note below). His mother was a servant of one of the Prophet's wives (IN 998; MSM 19–25).

24. MM 1123. "Making a Hijrah" (emigrating) to the Prophet is the pinnacle of religious practice, in the sense that the Emigrants of 622 may be regarded as the truest of Muslims. But during the time of discord, any expression of faith—even the most obvious and least demanding—will be like making the Hijrah; for the simplest act of worship will stand out against the backdrop of that time as the Hijrah stood out in its time.

25. Ibn ʻAdī was evidently a student of Anas ibn Mālik, but I can find no further information about him. Anas (d. 711/712) was a servant of the Prophet, a soldier, and an important source of Tradition.

26. SM 82–84 gives a variation on this Tradition of Ḥudhayfah; SB 9:161–63.

27. MM 1120–21.

28. Better to adhere to the root of a tree than to maintain membership in a Community that is no longer worthy of the name (MM 1121, with variant on 1124); SM 1028 translates the last sentence, "Separate yourself from all these factions, though you may have to eat the roots of trees [in a jungle] until death comes to you and you are in that state" (SB 9:159–60).

29. Usāmah ibn Zayd (c. 614–668) was one of the Prophet's freedmen and an important transmitter of Traditions (SM 56). Tradition in MM 1123, SM 1495, SB 9:148–49.

30. MM 1122; SM 1495; SB 9:157–58.

31. MM 1122; SB 9:163–64.

32. I can find no information on Ṣamād ibn Sulmah. "Foul-smelling" here translates a rather peculiar word, *al-anṭān*, for which I could find no other plausible meaning in this context.

33. ʿAlī (d. 661) was the Prophet's cousin and the fourth caliph. I am unable to identify Kamīl, evidently to be regarded as the transmitter of this saying.

34. On how difference of opinion among both jurists and mystics is a "mercy" from God, cf. KL 107, and DS 71–72.

35. ʿAwn was a Traditionist who passed on many of the Traditions that have come down from Ibn Masʿūd.

36. See LJ 3–5 for the second of these sayings of Junayd, and others like these.

37. According to RS[2] Index, this is Ibn ʿAṭā' al-Ādamī (d. 922), friend of Junayd until they parted over the question of whether God would accept the wealthy, or only the poor. Junayd considered the poor superior (LJ 41–42). Ibn ʿAṭā' was Hallāj's most faithful friend (MDI 77).

38. Abū Ḥamzah al-Baghdādī, also known as "The Ṣūfī," was a mystic of Junayd's generation (d. 883 or 902) (MDI 473).

39. Abū Bakr aṭ-Ṭamastānī (d. 951) was "an eminent Muslim thinker and a preacher of Islam," who lived his last years in Nīshāpūr (G. Allana, *A Rosary of Islamic Readings* [Karachi, 1973], p. 153).

40. Abū 'l-Qāsim an-Naṣrābādhī (d. 977) was a disciple of Sulamī (d. 1021) and an influence on Abū Saʿīd ibn Abī 'l-Khayr (d. 1046), noted for his "fervent passion" (MDI 88, 298).

41. Abū Yazīd (Bayezid) al-Bisṭāmī (d. 874) was the original "intoxicated" Ṣūfī and was known for his enigmatic sayings (*shaṭḥīyyāt*) (MDI 47–51; MSM 100–23). This anecdote appears in KL 103, and is related to several Traditions that discourage the practice of spitting toward the *qiblah* (the wall of the mosque that indicates the direction of Mecca, in which wall there is always a niche), e.g., MM 150.

42. This second anecdote about Bayezid occurs in KL 104 and DS 120.

43. Jaʿfar ibn Nuṣayr (d. 959), also known as al-Khuldī, was a pupil of Junayd and is mentioned frequently in KL. A dirham is a coin whose name derives from the Greek *drachma*. Both anecdotes appear in KL 210, but the discrepancies between IA's text and the wording in KL suggest that the story was miscopied somewhere between KL and the form in which IA received it. The anecdote about the servant Bakrān combing Shiblī's beard as the latter was on his deathbed also occurs in KL 104. The combing of the beard was a part of the ablution, before ritual prayer, that the Prophet had recommended.

Letter 4

1. This letter is called a "chapter," and was meant to be part of the preceding letter. It has been separated from Letter 3, according to Nwiya, "either because IA wrote it as a supplement, or because the compiler found the entire composition too long." IA continues here his critique of the jurists, and all who engage in "speculative" sciences. IA has no quarrel with the studies in them-

selves, for study and learning are encumbent on Muslims both as individuals and as a community. He is concerned with people who engage in these studies out of improper motives. Any "intention" in action or thought that looks more to the aggrandizement of the human being involved vitiates the deed (IAR 185). IA therefore is not criticizing the "religious scholars" or "the learned" (*'ulamā'*). He often quotes individuals whom he calls by that name, in such a way as to make it clear that he respects their views and considers them truly wise. When he refers to the "religious scholars" in a negative fashion, he is thinking of those among them who have contributed to the decay of religious learning.

2. Al-Ghazālī quotes this hadīth in the *Iḥyā*, Book VIII, trans. M. A. Quasem as *The Recitation and Interpretation of the Qur'ān* (Kuala Lumpur: University of Malaya Press, 1979), p. 31.

3. This is from Ḥasan al-Baṣrī again. Like the previous lengthy quotation in Letter 3, this is evidently from one of Ḥasan's sermons. L. Massignon gives some information on the collections of his sermons in *Essai sur les du lexique technique de la mystique musulmane* (Paris, 1928), p. 155.

4. 'Abd ar-Raḥmān ibn Hurmuz (d. 735) was a Qur'ān reciter and an authority on Tradition in Medinah (IN 941).

5. Rabī'ah ibn Abī 'Abd ar-Raḥmān (d. 753) was a Medinese jurist of the generation before Mālik. He was the most prominent jurist of his time in Medina. As a Traditionist, he was an important source for Mālik, who was one of Rabī'ah's students (Schacht, *Origins*, pp. 247f., indicates that Rabī'ah was not *actually* a Traditionist, but that his name was inserted into chains of transmission in order to add his authority).

6. The Prophet is quoting the poet Labīd (born late sixth century, d. c. 661), youngest of the seven composers of the *Mu'allaqāt*. The pre-Islamic poets seldom speak of God; but Labīd became a Muslim, and is reported to have forsaken his poetry, saying, "God has given me the Koran in exchange for it." Even before his conversion, however, he and his fellow poet, Zuhayr, had both evidenced religious interests in their poetry (R. A. Nicholson, *A Literary History of the Arabs* [Cambridge, 1969], p. 119). This Tradition appears in MM 1000, and is cited in KL 110 and 387.

Letter 5

1. "Zayd or 'Amr" is an Arabic way of saying "Every Tom, Dick, and Harry," or "So and So."

2. Ash-Shāfi'ī (767–820) was one of the most influential jurists in the formation of Islamic religious law. One of the four extant law schools bears his name, and Schacht considers him the very pinnacle of Islamic legal achievement (*Origins*, 315ff., 324ff., and *passim*).

NOTES

Letter 6

1. LeTourneau's description of Pilgrimage in the Fez of IA's time is worth quoting here: "Each year took place the departure for the Pilgrimage . . . unless circumstances were extremely unfavorable, as for example, when war prevented the movement of caravans. There were individual departures, notably those of the rich, bold men who did not hesitate to confront the risks of a sea voyage. Some pilgrims went to embark at Ceuta, at Badis, or at one of the ports which served Tlemcen, and in general took a Christian boat, Venetian, Genoese, Provencal, or Aragonese, for Egyptian or Syrian ships rarely called at these ports, and Maghrebian boats were few in number. Other pilgrims, the poorest ones, set out toward the east on foot; these spent several years in accomplishing the round trip, and without fail there were some who never returned. Still others set forth in private caravans. But the greatest number joined the official caravan which was organized each year, unless overcome by an insurmountable obstacle. This was a caravan all the more official in character since it often included one or more members, and at times even women, of the royal family. The preparations began several months in advance; the day of departure was a day of merrymaking throughout the city; people came to bid the fortunate travelers farewell, and many accompanied them during one stage, or even several stages, of their long journey toward the east. According to the political and climatic circumstances, the official caravan took different routes; either it proceeded not far from the coast, passing through Taza, Ouijda, Tlemcen, Constantine, and Tunis, or else it skirted the foot of the Saharan Atlas, by way of Tafilalet, Figuig, Laghouat, Biskra, Tozeur, and Gabes. Frequently the return trips were individual, for some went on a pilgrimage to Jerusalem before returning to Fez. But, individual or collective, the returns were always celebrated with a flourish: people went out to meet the pilgrims, who had their arrival made known in advance, and accompanied them to the threshold of their dwellings. For several days after their return, they entertained relatives and friends who came to congratulate them and to receive their share of the divine grace which the pilgrims brought back. . . . Naturally no statistics are available on the pilgrimage in the fourteenth century; it may be assumed, however, that the pilgrims were not numerous: the risks and the length of the trip and the magnitude of the expenses to be undertaken made of this a veritable ordeal, reserved for a small number of wealthy and courageous men. Nevertheless, we have proof that several notables of Fez accomplished the pilgrimage at least twice in their lives, and we have mentioned that the number of pilgrims was sufficient to create a far from negligible stream of trade between Fez and the countries of the Moslem East. This indicates that it was a flourishing institution and furnishes an appreciable means for measuring the piety of the city" (*Fez in the Age of the Marinides*, 137–38).

2. *Ibn Khallikān's Biographical Dictionary* (trans. M. DeSlane [London, 1843–1871]), vol. I, pp. 147, 151, lists two *possible* identities for this "al-Lakhmī";

of the two, the more likely says he was a holy man of Fez who died around 1085 (p. 151). The rather enigmatic verse that ends the anecdote seems to mean something like, "If you really have no intention of making Pilgrimage, and are worried only about the duty and not the devotional aspects of it, why talk about it so much?"

3. The term for "one who has not yet made Pilgrimage" (*ṣarūrah*) also has the meaning "one who has not married," "bachelor." IA's treatment on Pilgrimage matters reveals his extraordinary common sense. He counsels fulfillment of religious duties at all times, but never if the duty is to be performed solely out of a sense of formalistic compulsion or if the duty will cause the individual to neglect more important concerns.

4. Abū Naṣr Bishr ibn al-Ḥārith al-Ḥāfī ("The Barefoot") (767–841) was a mystic from Merw, who studied Tradition in Baghdad and died there. "Absolute sincerity" (*ikhlāṣ*) was his hallmark (MDI 37–38; MSM 80–86; IN 974). Bishr himself is the Abū Naṣr addressed later in the anecdote. I have been unable to identify precisely the Abū Naṣr at-Tamār who transmitted the story.

5. 'Alī ibn Ḥazm (994–1064) was a prolific author, born in Cordova, and a member of the strict Ẓāhirite law school. According to Majid Fakhry, "he dismisses all forms of scholastic theology as vain and pernicious. The speculation of the theologians, whether Mu'tazilites, Ash'arites, or others, on such questions as the essence of God . . . etc., is entirely futile. Man must resign himself to the impossibility of plumbing such mysteries and, in particular, the mystery of God's essence and the rationality of His ways. Only what lies within the grasp of our senses or is an object of direct intellectual apprehension, on the one hand, or is laid down explicitly in Scripture, on the other, is a genuine object of knowledge" (cf. *A History of Islamic Philosophy* [New York: Columbia University Press, 1970], pp. 348–50).

6. This Tradition occurs in MM 1123.

7. "Original monotheists" here translates the plural of *ḥanīf*. Abraham is said to have been the first of them.

8. "Therefore," i.e., because one's trials occur as a result of his commitment to his faith, and not because of some trials the individual has contrived to secure some merit for suffering in this life.

9. For more on IA's thought on servanthood (*'ubūdīyyah*), see Nwiya's summaries of RK in IAR 156–57, 160. "Doing good" translates *iḥsān;* "surrender" translates *islām* (cf. KL 5–6; MM 5; and MDI 29 on the distinction between *īmān*, *islām*, and *iḥsān*).

10. KL 12; MDI 112.

11. For the Qur'ānic accounts of the prophet David, see 21:79–81; 27:15–6; 34:10–12; 38:16–29.

12. QR 71 (Cairo 1948 edition).

13. Job appears in Qur'ān 21:83–84; 38:40–44. Zacharia was the prophet

who was sawn in two. His story is told in Qur'ān 3:32–36; 19:1–12; 21:89–90; but the story of his martyrdom is a folkloristic detail (KL 51).

14. ʿAbd Allāh ibn Abī Awfā (d. 705) was a Companion of the Prophet. He moved to Kufah after the Prophet's death and spent the rest of his life there (SM 252). This Tradition appears in MM 833–34.

15. MM 533–34; SM 1413–14.

16. MM 530.

17. MM 524.

18. Al-Maʿāfirī could be any of ash-Shāfiʿī's correspondents who belonged to Maʿāfir, a tribe in Egypt originating from the Hamdān group of Yemenī tribes (MM 859, Note 2).

19. IAR 189 indicates, on the authority of L. Massignon, that al-Ḥallāj wrote this verse. MP 40 also quotes the verse, but there the author, Ibn al-ʿArīf, says, "They say it was Abū Yazīd (al-Bisṭāmī) who said it."

20. Sumnūn al-Muḥibb ("The Lover") ibn Ḥamzah (d. c. 900) was a mystic of Baghdad and a friend of Sarī as-Saqaṭī. Numerous Ṣūfī writings, including Ghazālī's *Revival*, quote this verse of utter abandonment to God (MDI 62; MSM 239–42, with verse quoted on 240).

21. Muʿādh ibn Jabal (d. c. 639) was a Companion of the Prophet who helped collect the revelations of the Qur'ān and transmitted many Traditions (IN 1045). The citation appears also in KL 134.

22. Part of this story of Sumnūn is told in MSM 241.

23. "Red Sulphur" translates *kibrīt al-aḥmar*. Nicholson translates the words as "The Philosopher's stone," in *The Kashf al-Maḥjūb* (London, 1959 [reprint]), p. 7. A. Schimmel notes in *As Through a Veil: Mystical Poetry in Islam* (New York: Columbia University Press, 1983) that red sulphur was a critical ingredient in alchemy, and that the phrase IA uses in Letter 16, "more precious than red sulphur" (also in reference to a spiritual guide), is an Arabic proverb (pp. 64 and 231, Note 53).

24. Al-Ḥārith al-Muḥāsibī (781–857) was a prominent mystic of Baghdad. Of his many works, *The Book of Observance (Kitāb ar-Riʿāyah)* has probably been the most influential, especially among the religious order to which IA belonged. MS 266–67 indicates that IA's predecessor, Ibn ʿAṭā' Allāh, is said to have been reading the work to his teacher al-Mursī. The shaykh then said the book could be summed up in two phrases, "Serve God according to knowledge, and never be satisfied with yourself." IAR says the work was known in the West before 1067 and was preferred by IA's stern teacher in Salé, Ibn ʿĀshir (IAR Iv). Cf. also MS, the fullest single treatment of this author; also MSM 143–45.

25. Abū ʿAbd ar-Raḥman as-Sulamī (d. 1021) is most famous for his biographical work *The Classes of the Ṣūfīs*, a source of lore on the Ṣūfī saints (MDI 85–88).

26. Abū 'l-Qāsim al-Qushayrī (d. 1074) wrote one of the Ṣūfī works that was most influential on IA, the *Risālah* (QR, *Treatise on the Science of Sufism*). Writ-

ten in 1046, the *Treatise* "describes Sufi teachings and practices from the viewpoint of a full-fledged Ash'arite theologian" (MDI 88; cf. also AS 71, and esp. 74–79 for a partial summary of the work).

27. Shihāb ad-Dīn Abū Ḥafṣ 'Umar as-Suhrawardī (1144–1234), part of a family of influential Ṣūfīs, led a very active life as head shaykh in Baghdad. His *'Awārif al-Ma'ārif* (*Benefits* . . .) became a standard text on the mystical life and on daily practices in a Ṣūfī order. A portion of that work has been translated (from a Persian translation of the Arabic original) into English: H. Wilberforce Clarke, *The 'Awarif-u'l-Ma'arif*, (Lahore: Ashraf reprint, 1979). (Cf. MDI 245.)

28. "Speculative theologians" translates *ahl 'ilm al-kalām*.

29. Ghazālī's *Revival* (*Iḥyā*) is in four "quarters" with ten books (chapters) each.

30. IA refers here to the *Food of Hearts* (*Qūt al-Qulūb*) discussed in Letter 1.

31. *Mudawwanah* means "Code of Law" or "Body of Written Legal Material." IA is referring to a six-volume (in modern print) compendium of Mālikite law, written by a Tunisian jurist named Saḥnūn (d. 845). Selections of a commentary on the work, by Ibn Rushd (d. 1126) (the grandfather of the famed philosopher by the same name [d. 1198]), may be found in *Islam from Within*, ed. K. Cragg and M. Speight (Wadsworth, 1980), pp. 100–3.

32. QR (1948) 19. On the first saying, see MS 28.

33. KL 156 contains a variant of this anecdote.

34. MSM 201.

35. Ruwaym ibn Aḥmad (d. 915) was a mystic of Baghdad, a friend of Junayd, but somewhat less strict than the latter. For example, Junayd said that conversion meant repenting of one's sins; but Ruwaym said conversion meant repenting of repentance (MDI 59, 110). This saying is from one of Ruwaym's letters to the Shīrāzī mystic ibn Khafīf (MDI 15).

36. The last sentence of this citation from Ruwaym appears in MDI 235.

37. Yūsuf ibn al-Ḥusayn ar-Rāzī (d. 916), from Rayy in Persia, seems to have been influenced by Dhū 'n-Nūn of Egypt (d. 859), from whom he imbibed a strong belief in utter trust in God. He evidently passed that along to one of his disciples who has already appeared in IA's letters, Ibrāhīm al-Khawāṣṣ (MDI 53; MSM 185–91).

38. Ibn Khafīf (882–982) was a Baghdad-educated Shāfi'ite legal scholar who had also studied under al-Ash'arī the theologian in Baṣrah. In Baghdad he knew Ruwaym, Ḥallāj, and Shiblī (ST 93). MDI 112 indicates that the present saying appears in Sulamī's *Classes of the Ṣūfīs*. After spending much of his life away from his hometown of Shīrāz, ibn Khafīf returned there to die. (Cf. also MSM 257–63.)

39. Abū 'l-Ḥusayn al-Ḥuṣri (d. 981) was a contemporary of Sarrāj, who in KL 28 suggests that Ḥuṣri passed along some material to Sarrāj. Nicholson also suggests (*Kashf* ix) that Ḥuṣri taught the teacher of Hujwīrī (d. c. 1071), Abū 'l-'Abbās ibn Muḥammad al-Shaqānī.

40. Abū 'l-Ḥusayn an-Nūrī (d. 907) was a mystic of Baghdad, a pupil of Sarī as-Saqaṭī and a friend of Junayd and Ḥallāj. He was noted for his emphasis on love's "tearing the veils"— i.e; uncovering the secrets of his mystical longing, thus leaving himself open to the censure of the authorities (MDI 60–61; EC 316–48; MSM 221–30).

41. Abū 'Alī ar-Rūdhbārī (d. 934) was a member of the Shāfi'ite law school (MDI 54) and studied in Baghdad under Aḥmad ibn Masrūq (d. 910), a disciple of Muḥāsibī. Abū 'Alī thus fell heir to a strongly ascetical tradition (MS 34–35). He is often cited in KL.

42. Abū Bakr az-Zaqqāq appears often in KL, where this anecdote also occurs (173). Beyond that, I am unable to identify him.

43. Ismā'īl ibn Nujayd is cited three times in KL, but I can make no further identification.

44. Abū 'l-'Abbās ad-Dīnawarī died in 951.

45. MSM 234 gives a variant of this story, and identifies the shaykh as Abū 'Uthmān al-Hīrī.

46. Abū Bakr Muḥammad al-Wāsiṭī (d. after 932) was a mystic from Khurāsān who spent some years in Baghdad, where he mixed with Junayd and Nūrī (MDI 80).

47. Both RS[1] and RS[2] give this man's name as ibn Munāzil, with no critical note calling for a correction. It appears to me, however, that the text should read 'Abd Allāh ibn Mubārak, for the following three reasons: (1) MDI 156 indicates that QR (1912) 144 attributes the saying to ibn Mubārak; (2) I can find no information at all on anyone named ibn Munāzil; (3) the names Munāzil and Mubārak are so similar to each other in Arabic script that a scibal error could easily account for the discrepancies.

48. A variation on this story appears in Wilberforce Clarke's translation of the *'Awārif*, p. 178.

49. Ḥabīb al-'Ajamī was a Traditionist who transmitted from Ḥasan al-Baṣrī (MSM 32–38).

50. Abū 'd-Dardā' (d. 652) was one of the "People of the Bench" (poor devotees known for their asceticism). He believed that one hour of reflection was better than forty nights of prayer (MS 63).

51. One Ms. identified that spiritual guide as 'Abd as-Salām ibn Mashīsh, the successor to ash-Shādhilī (cf. Introduction).

52. This entire text, from the mention of Abū 'l-Qāsim (al-Qushayrī) on, is quoted verbatim from QR (1940) 46. Abū 'Alī ad-Daqqāq (d. 1015 and 1021) was the teacher and father-in-law of Qushayrī (MDI 88). The verse attributed to him occurs also in KL 292, with one minor difference in wording. Cf. also EC 318–9.

53. See Letter 1 above.

Letter 7

1. Certitude (*yaqīn*) is not conceptual; it is affective. It is an experiental conviction in a person "whose heart has rested in the beauty of the Lord Most High's sovereignty and who remains patient in the throes of servitude . . . " (EC 277–78, quoting the mystic Kharrāz).

2. Sarī as-Saqaṭī (769–867) was, according to biographers, the first to elaborate on the idea of diverse mystical states (*aḥwāl*). A prominent Baghdad mystic, he was the teacher and uncle of Junayd (MDI 53–54; also MSM 166–72).

3. Abū Ya'qūb an-Nahrajūrī (d. 941) was a disciple of Junayd. He spent some years in Mecca (where he died); and when Ḥallāj came to Mecca, Nahrajūrī denounced him as a magician (MSM 266).

4. The wording of this story about Zacharia is almost identical to that of KL 51.

5. The story of Jacob, father of Joseph, is told in Qur'ān 12. Jacob became the paradigm of patience because of the way he suffered through separation from his beloved Joseph.

6. Within the station of patience, as in others, three levels are distinguished: that of the faithful, that of the elect (*ahl al-khuṣūṣ*), and that of the elect of the elect (*khuṣūṣ al-khuṣūṣ*). See KL 52, 337.

7. "One who is attempting (or even feigning) patience" is a *mutaṣabbir*. For definitions of the three types of patience, see KL 50.

8. On the three types of certitude, see MDI 141–42, KL 70–71.

9. KL 71 attributes this saying to Nahrajūrī. The wordings of KL and IA are identical.

Letter 8

1. "Greater Struggle" (*al-jihād al-akbar*) is the more crucial of the two *jihāds*, with all external combat relegated to the class of "Lesser Struggle" (*al-jihād al-asghar*).

2. In the final sentence of this paragraph, IA is alluding to Qur'ān 17:81 (and a number of similar texts, e.g., 2:42, 3:71, etc.): "Truth has come and falsehood has vanished." It is a reverse-allusion, however, and one gets the feeling IA is using the vocabulary of the Scripture in a way directly opposite to that of the Qur'ānic text precisely to heighten the irony and tragedy of the situation. DS 3 expresses a view very similar to IA's. Written in second half of the tenth century, the text is worth quoting for comparison: "Finally, the meaning departed, and the name remained, the substance vanished and the shadow took its place: realisation became an ornament, and verification a decoration. He who knew not [the truth] pretended to possess it, he who had never so much as described it adorned himself with it: he who had it much upon his tongue denied

it with his acts, and he who displayed it in his exposition concealed it by his true conduct. That which was not of it was introduced into it, that which was not in it was ascribed to it: its truth was made false, and he who knew it was called ignorant. But he who had experienced [the truth] drew apart, being jealous for it. So the hearts [of men] fled from it, and the souls departed; science [i.e., knowledge] and its people, exposition and its practice, vanished; the ignorant became the scientists, and the scientists became the guides."

3. As Ghazālī does in FH 79, IA here quotes the last part of a Tradition without mentioning that it is a Tradition. MM 61 gives this translation: "If anyone makes the care of his eternal welfare the sum total of his cares God will protect him from worldly care, but if he has a variety of cares consisting of matters related to this world God will not be concerned in which of its *wādīs* he perishes." Later, in Letter 9, IA will use the same Tradition, quoting the second half of it as it appears in MM 61. DS 114 gives a slightly different translation.

4. ST 13–16 gives information identifying this Ṣaqallī ("Man from Sicily," spelled Ṣaqalī in ST) as the final compiler, transmitter, and commentator for a work whose source was Sahl at-Tustarī. "This Ṣaqalī was known as a traditionist, a jurist and a Ṣūfī who wrote a Ṣūfī treatise, known as *Anwār aṣ-Ṣaqalī* ["Lights on the Knowledge of Secrets and the Stations of the Upright" is the full title]. . . . We are told that Ṣaqalī rebukes the jurists (*al-fuqahā'*) for their refusal to recognize the *karamāt*, God's charismatic gifts to the Ṣūfīs." He was a student of some of the most eminent teachers of Qayrawān, and died before 996 but not earlier than 990.

5. "Leaving the religion in droves" is another "reverse allusion" to scripture. In Qur'ān 110:2, the Prophet is told to praise God when he sees "people entering the religion of God in droves." Ṣaqallī uses the Qur'ānic term meaning "in droves," *afwāj^an^*. This allusion is followed immediately by another one, similar to IA's mention of truth replacing falsehood earlier in this letter.

Letter 9

1. Nwiya regards this letter as undoubtedly the most interesting of the RS, for here IA "displays in a remarkable way his qualities as spiritual director and his gifts of psychological analysis" (IAR 197).

2. This *Hadith Qudsī* appears in MM 476, SM 1408, SB 9:369. W. Graham has translated it, "I fulfill My servant's expectation of Me." (Cf. *Divine Word and Prophetic Word in Early Islam* [The Hague: Mouton, 1977], pp. 127–30.)

3. Another of the "Sacred Traditions," this one appears in MM 368. See also Graham, op. cit., p. 210, #87.

4. "Faith-community" translates *millah;* "community" translates *ummah.* Abraham's story appears in Qur'ān 6:74–82; 19:42–49; 21:52–70; 26:69–104; 29:15–24; 37:81–96; 11:71–78; 37:100–12; 51:24–34.

5. I have adopted the variant reading of *maqām* for *maqāl. Maqāl*, rhyming

here with *ḥāl*, would mean something like "point of argument, contention." If that reading were kept, then *ḥāl* could be taken to mean "case." Then the phrase would mean something like "they would have not a leg to stand on." Opting for *maqām* allows the sentence to speak directly about the spiritual life, using the technical terms IA uses throughout the letters.

6. KL 104 puts the following saying in the mouth of Dhū 'n-Nūn of Egypt: "I came to know God intimately through God; I came to know everything beside God through the Messenger of God."

7. The story of Joseph is found in Qur'ān 12. IA's point is that, as great a wonder as it would be to find Joseph in a well, that is nothing compared to God's forgiveness of sinners.

8. "Perhaps . . . " (*la'al*) followed by some verb of understanding, praising, thanking, etc., is a construction frequently used in the Qur'ān.

9. This is a near-quote of Deuteronomy 30:11–14, a text also cited by Ghazālī in the *Revival*, the first quarter, first chapter ("Knowledge").

10. 'Amr ibn 'Uthmān al-Makkī (d. 909), "probably the first to compose a systematic treatise on the degrees of love, intimacy, and proximity" (MDI 57), was one of Ḥallāj's mentors in Baghdad (MDI 66). KL 25 also includes this definition of Sufism, a statement of the idea that the servant of God must be first and foremost a "son of the instant."

11. See DS 71–72 for a similar explanation. See also KL 107 on the "mercy" of difference of opinion.

12. This is the same Tradition IA quoted in Letter 8, without mentioning that it is part of a Tradition (MM 61; DS 114; FH 79).

13. Ibn al-'Arīf (1088–1141) was born in Spain and received his education in Tradition, law, and Sufism in Almeria, then the center of Sufism in the Iberian peninsula. Here, and again at the beginning of Letter 12, IA mentions Ibn al-'Arīf in the context of a discussion of the teaching vocation. RS[2] includes an Appendix (E) with excerpts of four of his letters, of which especially the fourth describes his views on teaching young children (pp. 217ff.). For more on Ibn al-'Arīf's life, see MP 1–8.

14. The Tradition of *iḥsān* occurs in MM 5 and KL 6, 117.

15. FH 40 also cites this Sacred Tradition.

16. For more on the subject of fear and hope, see Letter 1.

17. Mursī (d. 1287), "The Man from Murcia," was the spiritual heir of ash-Shādhilī and the spiritual father of Ibn 'Aṭā' Allāh. See Introduction. "My master" is used here, as elsewhere in IA's letters, as a term of respect rather than as an indication that the individual named was actually IA's teacher in person.

18. Mursī's comment is a pithy restatement of what IA has been saying about the incongruity of scruples and genuine knowledge: i.e., if one possesses authentic knowledge, diabolical suggestions will not constitute a harassment, for they can gain no entry. Mursī's gentle rebuke to the person who was reputed to be learned and devout is his way of saying that, if that person were truly learned,

he would know the devil's lies from the truth. His image suggests that genuine knowledge is never disturbing: "Praiseworthy discernment" (*al-khāṭir al-maḥmūd*) does not continue to exercise the individual's mind and heart, whereas scruples do not cease to badger the person. In his *Spiritual Exercises*, a classic of Christian spirituality, St. Ignatius Loyola (d. 1556) gives some "Rules for the Discernment of Spirits" that will help to clarify the matter. Assuming that an individual is striving to advance in the spiritual life, the good spirit will encourage, strengthen, console, inspire, and bring the individual peace. The mark of the evil spirit in such a person is that it brings anxiety, sadness, and doubts, and proposes fallacious arguments, including scruples, to the soul. The individual is thus stymied. Ignatius compares the action of the good spirit in such a person to a drop of water penetrating a sponge. The action of the evil spirit, on the other hand, is likened to a drop of water falling on a stone. (See any translation of the *Exercises* that uses the standard numbering system, ##313–336.) For an analogous use of "black-on-black" imagery, see *The Hundred Letters*, pp. 169–70, and DS 70–71.

19. IA is evidently referring to the *Kitāb al-Ḥikam* (IAA, BW; see Introduction).

20. Muḥammad ibn Adībah is the man to whom IA's first six letters are addressed. The words "May God have mercy on him" (the equivalent of "May he rest in peace") indicate that he is now deceased.

21. *The Book of Observance (of what is due to God and Abiding Therein)* is al-Muḥāsibī's most famous work. It also came to be known as *The Observance of the Principles of Sufism*. According to MS 44–45, "This is al-Muḥāsibī's great treatise on the interior life, which reveals a profound knowledge of human nature and its weaknesses, while in the means which he suggests for combating these weaknesses and for attaining to the single-hearted service of God, he shows also the discerning wisdom and inspired insight of a true spiritual director and shepherd of souls." The key topics contained in it are: the need to listen for the voice of God; a method for self-examination; hypocrisy and how to deal with it; the formation of proper intention toward God; the need to prefer contempt of others over their esteem; the need for humility; the dangers of delusion. The work concludes with a description of a way of living by which the servant can be always mindful of God. The ten chapters of the Third Book (quarter) of Ghazālī's *Revival* contain much detailed discussion, along with copious illustrations from Traditions and stories of the saints, of virtually every kind of sinfulness.

22. KL 53 contains a variation on this last saying, giving the first two-thirds of it exactly as IA cites it. KL 54 goes on to say that contentment (*riḍā*)is the last of the stations.

Letter 10

1. Since several of IA's letters deal with difficulties arising in connection with his correspondent's work as a teacher of children, it might be useful to have

some sketchy notion of what that occupation involved. Children of five or six and older would come to a one-room school, often next to a mosque, where a single teacher instructed all ages. The classroom was available without charge to all. The teacher received no regular salary, but each week he received some stipends from his pupils, and on feast days he might receive gifts of money or food. The teacher's own formal education often consisted only in his memorization of the Qur'ān. He would in turn teach the children how to memorize the scripture; and when a student was successful in committing the whole text to memory, the teacher might hold a party in the school. The student had no books, only a board for writing texts with his quill pen. Once a text had been memorized, the board was washed and a new text copied. Class began in early morning, broke for lunch, and resumed until mid-afternoon (LeTourneau, *Fez*, 116–18). Given the teacher's financial circumstances, it is not difficult to see why IA cautions against playing favorites with the students who are able to give more generous gifts to the teacher.

Ibn Khaldūn, a contemporary of IA, gives this description of school curriculum in North Africa: "The Maghribī method is to restrict the education of children to instruction in the Qur'ān and to practice, during the course [of instruction], in Qur'ān orthography and its problems and the differences among experts on this score. The [Maghribīs] do not bring up any other subjects in their classes, such as traditions, jurisprudence, poetry, or Arabic philology, until the pupil is skilled in [the Qur'ān], or drops out before becoming skilled in it. In the latter case, it means, as a rule, that he will not learn anything. This is the method the urban population in the Maghrib and the native Berber Qur'ān teachers who follow their [urban compatriots], use in educating their children up to the age of manhood. They use it also with old people who study the Qur'ān after part of their life has passed" (*The Muqaddimah*, trans. F. Rosenthal [Bollingen Series XLIII], vol. III, p. 301).

Letter 12

1. Yaḥyā lived in Fez.

2. In this and the previous sentence, the requests that I have translated in the form of indirect statements could as well have been construed as direct statements and put in quotations, for the text has them in the second person singular, as though addressed directly to IA. For example: "Will you define for me . . ."; "I want you to counsel me . . . "; and "Will you instruct me. . . . "

3. As IAR 204–5 notes, we have here an indication of how IA regards the relationship of spiritual director to directee. He does not know his addressee well enough at this point to make specific recommendations; and he feels that Yaḥyā already knew what he needed to know in the way of more general guidance. The advisor ("the one questioned" in this instance) needs to have the full confidence of the "questioner" in order to get to the heart of the individual's needs in the spiritual life.

4. The *Kitāb at-Tanwīr fī Isqāṭ at-Tadbir* was, according to BW 30, written around 1300–1309, and is a companion piece to the *Ḥikam*. The "elimination of self-direction" is the one overarching virtue, subsuming all other virtues. It alone makes the servant open to God's direction. Self-direction arises out of that psycho-spiritual disorder, pretentiousness or ego-centrism (*da'wā*), which IA regards as the major obstacle on the journey to God.

5. Literally, *al-kalimāt al-ḥikmiyyah*, the "wisdom sayings," or "aphoristic utterances," i.e., the *Ḥikam*.

Letter 14

1. 'Aṭā' as-Sulamī (d. 739) was one of the Followers (KL 322), came from Baṣrah, and was reputed for his piety and asceticism (IN 965).

2. Fatḥ al-Mawṣilī (d. 835) was a slave who became an ascetic (IN 986). IA spells his name Fatḥā; he was apparently from Mosul in 'Irāq.

Letter 15

1. See Letter 2, Note 13.

Letter 16

1. IAR 43 notes that IA insisted his name should be spelled Maḥammad and not Muḥammad, according to common Maghribī practice.

2. Abū Isḥāq Ibrāhīm ash-Shāṭibī (d. 1388) was a famous Mālikite jurist of Granada. He was very much involved in a debate over the legitimacy of Sufism in Spain and North Africa. IAR xxxii cites a communication, indirectly, in which someone asked ash-Shāṭibī "about the situation of a group of people who claim to be Ṣūfīs, professing poverty, and who congregate often at night in one of their homes. The gathering begins with some communally recited recollection (*dhikr*). Then they move into singing, clapping their hands, and making ecstatic utterances until dawn . . . . Some of the jurists participate in their gatherings, so that if anyone questions them about their behavior and the permissibility of their meetings, they merely respond that the jurists would not attend if they were illicit."

3. Abū 'l-'Abbās al-Qabbāb (d. 1375) was a celebrated Moroccan jurist and the mentor of ash-Shāṭibī. He had spent some time in Salé with IA's teacher, Ibn'Āshir. Ash-Shāṭibī had written to both al-Qabbāb and IA in Fez. Al-Qabbāb was of the opinion that the Ṣūfīs in his time were neglecting works they ought to read in favor of some sections of Ghazālī's *Revival* that he judged to be of questionable value for people in earlier stages of the Path (IAR 174, 1–1i; see Introduction).

4. "Instructing" translates *tarbiyah;* "educating" translates *ta'līm*.

5. "Truthfulness," "veracious," and "sincerity" are all from the root *ṣdq*.

6. "The station of serving God constantly" translates *maqām al-Iḥsān*.

7. Literally, "The *majdhūb* (the one drawn, attracted) among them and the *sālik* (wayfarer) among them are equal in this respect." See Introduction on these two types of mystical experience.

8. DS 81 attributes the saying to Abū Yazīd al-Bisṭāmī.

9. IA's advice against engaging in legal studies is reminiscent of Ghazālī's remarks on the same topic in the *Revival*. Here is a sample of what he says there (FH 69): ". . . the safety of the populace consists in their occupying themselves with sound actions and not becoming entangled with what is outside the limit of their capacity. But at the moment the rein is loose and rubbish is being disseminated and every ignoramus comes down on the side of what suits his nature, armed with supposition and conjecture, and believes it is science and proof and unadulterated faith; and supposes that whatever he alights on by the use of hypothesis and appraisal is established science and certainty itself."

10. "Passions" here translates *hawā*.

11. "Passions" here translates *shahwa*.

12. IA may be alluding to a Tradition that was popular among Ṣūfīs, but not contained in any of the standard collections: "Show me things as they truly are," or, in another version, "Let the false appear as false, and the true as true." See LJ 94.

Erratum

On page 60, the beginning of the second paragraph should read: This is a serious matter that is part of the science of acknowledging the unity of God. It is thus a matter of great moment to those who are convinced of God's uniqueness.

Bibliography

Abdel-Kader, A. H. *The Life, Personality and Writings of Al-Junayd*. London: Luzac, 1976.

Aberry, A. J. *Sufism: An Account of the Mystics of Islam*. London, 1950; New York: Harper Torchbooks, 1970.

Asin Palacios, Miguel. "Un precursor hispanomusulman de San Juan de la Cruz." *Al-Andalus* 1 (1933): 7–79. Also in his *Obras Escogidas*. Madrid, 1946, pp. 243–336. Translated as *St. John of the Cross and Islam* by E. Douglas and E. Yoder. New York: Vantage Press, 1981.

——— "Šâḏiles y alumbrados." *Al-Andalus* 9 (1944): 321–45; 16 (1951): 1–51

——— "Caracteres de la Escuela Šâḏili y de su método espiritual." *Al-Andalus* 1945 fasc. 1, 34ff.; fasc. 2, 255–84.

——— "Abenmasarra y su escuela." *Obras Escogidas*. Madrid, 1946.

——— "Biografia de Ibn al-ʻArīf, (1088–1141)." *Obras Escogidas*, 219ff.

——— French trans., text edition, commentary to *Ibn al-ʻArīf: Mahāsin al-Majālis*. Paris, 1933.

ʻAṭṭār, Farīd ad-Dīn. *Tadhkirat al-awliyā'*. Ed. R. A. Nicholson. 2 vols. London, 1905–1907. Selections translated by A. J. Arberry in *Muslim Saints and Mystics*. London: Routledge and Kegan Paul, 1979.

IBN 'ABBĀD OF RONDA

Austin, R. W. "I Seek God's Pardon" (Translation of a Prayer of Abū Madyan) in *Studies in Comparative Religion* 7 no. 2 (Spring 1973): 91–94.

Bannerth, E. "Dhikr et Khalwa d'apres Ibn 'Aṭā' Allāh." *MIDEO*, 1974, pp. 65–90.

Bel, A. "Sidi Bou Medyan et son maître Ed-Daqqaq a Fez." *Melanges R. Basset*, I. Paris, 1923.

Böwering, Gerhard. *The Mystical Vision of Existence in Classical Islam: The Qur'ānic Hermeneutics of the Ṣūfī Sahl At-Tustarī*. New York: de Gruyter, 1980.

Bukhārī. *Ṣaḥiḥ al-Bukhārī*. Trans. M. M. Kahn. 9 vols., Arabic-English. Kazi Publications, 1979.

Douglas, E. H. "Al-Shādhilī, a North African Ṣūfī, according to Ibn Ṣabbāgh." *MW* 38 (1948): 257–79.

——— "Prayers of Al-Shādhilī." *Medieval and Middle Eastern Studies in Honor of A. S. Atiyah*. Leiden: Brill, 1972, pp. 106–21.

Dunlop, D. M. "Abū 'l-'Abbās al-Mursī, A Spanish Muslim Saint." *The Muslim World* 35 (1945): 181–96.

Faure, A. "Le Tasawwuf et l'école ascetique marocaine des XIe—XIIe—XIIIe siècles de l'ère chrétienne." *Melanges Louis Massignon*. Damascus, 1957. II, 119–32.

Ibn 'Aṭā' Allāh. *The Book of Wisdom*. Trans. Victor Danner, with Introduction and Notes. Classics of Western Spirituality. New York: Paulist Press, 1978. See under Nwiya, P., also.

Ibn Khallikān. *Ibn Khallikān's Biographical Dictionary*. Trans. MacGuckin de Slane. 4 vols. (1843–1871) New York: Johnson Reprint Corp., 1961.

Ibn an-Nadīm. *The Fibrist of al-Nadīm*. Trans. Bayard Dodge. 2 vols. New York: Columbia University Press, 1970.

Kalabādhī, al-. *The Doctrine of the Sufis*. Trans. A. J. Arberry. Cambridge: Cambridge University Press, 1977.

Le Tourneau, Roger. *Fez in the Age of the Marinides*. Norman, Okla.: University of Oklahoma Press, 1961.

Mackeen, A. M. Mohamed. "The Early History of Sufism in the Maghrib prior to al-Shādhilī." *JAOS* 91 no. 3 (1971): 398–408.

——— "The Rise of al-Shādhilī." *JAOS* 91 no. 4 (1971): 477–86.

——— "The Sufi-Qawm Movement." *MW* 53 (1963): 212–25.

Mahdi, Muhsin. *Ibn Khaldūn's Philosophy of History*. Chicago: University of Chicago Press, 1964.

Massignon, Louis. *Essai sur les origines du lexique technique de la mystique musulmane*. 2nd ed. Paris, 1954.

——— "Note bibliographique sur la direction spirituelle en Islam." *Etudes Carmelitaines*, 1951, pp. 168–70.

McKane, William. *Al-Ghazālī's Book of Hope and Fear*. Leiden: Brill, 1962.

Moubarac, Youakim. *La Pensée Chrétienne et l'Islam*. Beirut, 1977. (Sections on

Asin-Palacios's studies, "Saint Jean de la Croix et Ibn 'Abbād de Ronda," and "Shādhiles et Illumines," pp. 310–21).
Muslim. *Saḥīḥ Muslim*. Trans. A. H. Siddiqi. 4 vols. Lahore: Ashraf, 1976.
Nwiya, Paul. *Ibn 'Abbād de Ronda*. Beirut: Imprimerie Catholique, 1956.
——— *Lettres de Direction Spirituelle* (The *Rasāil aṣ-Sughrā* of Ibn 'Abbād of Ronda). Beirut, 1958 (RS[1]) and 1974 (RS[2]—revised, with new appendices).
——— *Exégèse coranique et langage mystique*. Beirut: Dar el-Machreq, 1970.
——— "Ibn 'Abbād de Ronda et Jean de la Croix, à propos d'une hypothese d'Asin Palacios." *Al-Andalus* 22, Fasc. 1, 1957.
——— "Notes sur quelques fragments inédits de la correspondence d'Ibn al-'Arīf avec Ibn Barragān." *Hesperis* 1er-2e trimestre, 1956.
——— *Ibn 'Aṭā' Allāh et la naissance de la confrérie Šâdilite*. (Critical edition with French translation and introduction.) Beirut: Dar el-Machreq, 1972.
Schimmel, Annemarie. *Mystical Dimensions of Islam*. Chapel Hill, N.C., 1975.
Smith, Margaret. *Al-Muḥāsibī: An Early Mystic of Baghdad*. Amsterdam: Philo Press, 1974 (reprint).
——— *Al-Ghazālī the Mystic*. London, 1944.
Sulamī, Abū 'Abd ar-Raḥmān as-. *Ṭabaqāt aṣ-Ṣufiyya*. Ed. J. Pedersen. Leiden: Brill, 1960.

Index of Qur'ān References in Introduction and Translation

Index to Introduction

INDEX

INDEX

INDEX

INDEX

Index to Texts

INDEX

INDEX

INDEX

INDEX